W9-DII-758

Yellow Journalism

Puncturing the Myths, Defining the Legacies

W. Joseph Campbell

Westport, Connecticut
London

Library of Congress Cataloging-in-Publication Data

Campbell, W. Joseph.
Yellow journalism : puncturing the myths, defining the legacies / W. Joseph Campbell.
p. cm.
Includes bibliographical references and index.
ISBN 0–275–96686–0 (alk. paper)
1. Sensationalism in journalism—United States—History—20th century. 2. Journalism—United States—History—20th century. I. Title.
PN4784.S4 C36 2001
071′.3′0904—dc21 00–058024

British Library Cataloguing in Publication Data is available.

Library of Congress Catalog Card Number: 00–058024
ISBN: 0–275–96686–0

First published in 2001

Praeger Publishers, 88 Post Road West, Westport, CT 06881
An imprint of Greenwood Publishing Group, Inc.
www.praeger.com

Printed in the United States of America

The paper used in this book complies with the Permanent Paper Standard issued by the National Information Standards Organization (Z39.48–1984).

10 9 8 7 6 5 4 3 2 1

For Ann-Marie

Contents

Preface and Acknowledgments

This study of yellow journalism in the United States has its beginnings in West Africa, specifically in a comment attributed in 1995 to a Ghanaian university lecturer, Audrey Gadzekpo. In an article about West Africa's fledgling independent news media, Gadzekpo was quoted as saying that the antics and sensationalism of newspapers in Ghana were evocative of what she had read about the days of the yellow press in the United States. "When I read about the history of the private media in the U.S., in the time of yellow journalism," she said, "I think, 'They're talking about us!'"[1]

I was at the time immersed in a study about the emergent independent press in French-speaking West Africa and found Gadzekpo's characterization intriguing. Its implication was that emergent news media may follow recognizably similar patterns of development. I fashioned a modest content analysis designed to test whether West Africa's newspapers were indeed mirroring the classic features of America's yellow press. The content analysis was drawn from Frank Luther Mott's interpretation of yellow journalism's defining elements[2] and I presented the results of my study to the American Journalism Historians Association in 1996.[3] I concluded, however, that the emergent independent press in West Africa only remotely and unevenly resembled the American yellow journals of 100 years ago.

But in pursuing that line of research, I was struck to find that yellow journalism had been considered almost entirely through the biographic treatment of its leading practitioners—notably, William Randolph Hearst and Joseph Pulitzer—or in the studies of the New York press and the Spanish-American War. The literature revealed no detailed attempt to assess the genre, and its legacies, topically or systematically.

The mythology of the yellow press was also quite striking. The tale about the supposed exchange of telegrams between Hearst and Frederic Remington—in which Hearst famously vowed to "furnish the war"[4] with Spain—was described by several media historians as probably apocryphal but instructive nonetheless.[5] Even so, the literature revealed no sustained effort to examine and assess the evidence surrounding the purported Remington-Hearst exchange. The tale, to me, simply sounded suspect: It seemed altogether too tidy, too succinct, and almost too good to be true.

A detailed assessment of the purported Remington-Hearst telegrams appears in Chapter Three.[6]

A central objective of this study is to confront the spiraling mythology of the yellow press and, in so doing, encourage a fuller, more accurate understanding of an invariably maligned genre of American journalism. A related objective is to assess whether, or to what extent, the characteristic features of yellow journalism live on in the mainstream press of the United States, as Mott and others have suggested.[7] This study finds that the genre's most reprehensible elements and excesses have been cast aside and some of its more imaginative contributions live on, notably in bold and colorful typography. If nothing else, yellow journalism was lively and irresistible—attributes that American newspapers seem so desperate to recapture today.

This study by no means is a descriptive account of the yellow press, nor is it another biographic treatment of William Randolph Hearst. Inevitably however, Hearst and his *New York Journal* are focal points, given that they figure inescapably in the mythology of yellow journalism. They are, for example, central to the legend of the Remington-Hearst telegrams. They contributed, if indirectly, to the popularization of the term "yellow journalism."

But Hearst and the *Journal* are not the sole focal points of this study, which draws on the content of many other titles, including the *New York World*, the *New York Press*, the *New York Sun*, the *New York Times*, the *New York Evening Post*, and the *New York Tribune*. Also important to this study were the *Boston Post*, the *Cincinnati Enquirer*, the *Cincinnati Times-Star*, the *Denver Post*, the *St. Louis Post-Dispatch*, the *St. Louis Chronicle*, and the *San Francisco Examiner*. The trade journal *Fourth Estate* also was a vital resource.

This study was inherently intricate, requiring the scrutiny of countless reels of microfilm and the review of thousands of pages of documents in manuscript collections across the country. Throughout my research I was the beneficiary of unstinting support and assistance, notably from graduate students at American University who helped immensely as research assistants. I owe a debt to gratitude to Laura J. Bailey and

Kathy Utan for their unflagging energy and for their discerning eye for detail.

Faculty colleagues at American University's School of Communication, including Glenn Harnden, Barbara Diggs-Brown, Rodger Streitmatter, Marianne Szegedy-Mazsak, John Doolittle, and Pat Aufderheide, merit special thanks for their interest, collegiality, and encouragement. I am very grateful to Ivy Broder, the university's dean of academic affairs, and Sanford J. Ungar, formerly dean of the School of Communication, for the research grant that permitted me to consult important, far-flung archives.

I benefited enormously from the insights and suggestions offered by Robert L. Stevenson, Donald L. Shaw, and Margaret Blanchard at the University of North Carolina at Chapel Hill. J. Mark Sweeney and his staff at the Newspaper and Current Periodicals Reading Room—an extraordinary resource at the Library of Congress—deserve special thanks. They were invariably helpful, especially in allowing Greg Staley to photograph pages from bound volumes of the *New York Journal* at the newspaper reading room. The staff at the Library of Congress manuscripts division was also very helpful, and always highly professional.

The American University interlibrary loan staff was earnest and exceptionally patient in responding to my steady succession of requests for obscure articles and long out-of-date publications. I also enjoyed the friendly support of the library staff at the Freedom Forum in Arlington, Virginia. The library houses bound volumes of *Fourth Estate,* a rich and revealing resource that few scholars appear to have tapped. Jerrie Bethel, Nancy Stewart, Max Brown, Priscilla Trujillo, and Kurt Carroll at the Freedom Forum library all were generous in their help and their courtesy. I am grateful, too, for the encouragement given this project by Charles Overby, chairman and chief executive of the Freedom Forum, and Chris Wells, the foundation's senior vice president/international.

Don Ross of the Newseum proofread the manuscript and offered valuable suggestions. Elva Griffith of the rare books and manuscripts division of the Ohio State University library was very generous in sharing her time and expertise. I also benefited from knowledgeable library staffs at Columbia University, the University of Virginia, the University of California at Berkeley, and the University of North Carolina.

Pamela St. Clair, formerly an acquisitions editor at Greenwood Publishing Group, deserves special thanks for her support of this project, and for her patience. Megan Peckman, a production editor at Greenwood Publishing, was extremely helpful and encouraging, and her attention to detail was remarkable.

My wife, Ann-Marie Regan, put up with the many Saturdays I spent at the Library of Congress, and never seemed to tire of hearing about the project's twists and turns. She was there to hear about the breakthroughs of this research, and it is to Ann-Marie whom the study is dedicated.

NOTES

1. Daniel J. Sharfstein, "Ghana: Radio Free Ghana," *Africa Report* 40, 3 (May–June 1995): 48.

2. Frank Luther Mott, *American Journalism: A History: 1690–1960,* 3d ed. (New York: Macmillan, 1962), 539.

3. W. Joseph Campbell, "'They're Talking About Us': Yellow Journalism and the Press of West Africa," paper presented to the annual conference of the American Journalism Historians Association, London, Ontario, October 1996. The paper concluded that resurgent yellow journalism was not rampant in West African newspapers, even though the Ghanaian nonofficial press exhibited an activist role that was reminiscent of the crusading spirit of the American yellow press.

4. James Creelman, *On the Great Highway: The Wanderings and Adventures of a Special Correspondent* (Boston: Lothrop Publishing, 1901), 177–178.

5. See, for example, Phillip Knightley, *The First Casualty: From the Crimea to Vietnam: The War Correspondent as Hero, Propagandist, and Myth Maker* (New York: Harcourt Brace Jovanovich, 1975), 55.

6. An earlier version of Chapter Three won the Best Faculty Paper Award in 1999 of the history division of the Association for Education in Journalism and Mass Communication. See W. Joseph Campbell, "Not Likely Sent: The Remington-Hearst 'Telegrams,'" paper presented to the annual conference of the Association for Education in Journalism and Mass Communication, New Orleans, August 1999. An earlier version of Chapter Two received the Top Faculty Paper and Best Convention Paper awards in 1999 from the American Journalism Historians Association. See W. Joseph Campbell, "The Yellow Press and Urban America, 1900: What Explains the Contagion?" paper presented to the annual conference of the American Journalism Historians Association, Portland, OR, October 1999.

7. See Mott, *American Journalism,* 539.

Introduction

Twentieth-century American journalism was born in a little-remembered burst of inspired self-promotion. It was born in a paroxysm of yellow journalism.

Ten seconds into the century, the first issue of the *New York Journal* of 1 January 1901 fell from the newspaper's complex of fourteen high-speed presses. The first issue was rushed by automobile across pavements slippery with mud and rain to a waiting express train, reserved especially for the occasion. The newspaper was folded into an engraved silver case and carried aboard by Langdon Smith, a young reporter known for his vivid prose style. At speeds that reached eighty miles an hour, the special train raced through the darkness to Washington, D.C., and Smith's rendezvous with the president, William McKinley.

The president's personal secretary made no mention in his diary of the special delivery of the *Journal* that day, noting instead that the New Year's reception at the executive mansion had attracted 5,500 well-wishers and was said to have been "the most successful for many years."[1] But the *Journal* exulted: A banner headline spilled across the front page of the 2 January 1901 issue, asserting the *Journal*'s distinction of having published "the first Twentieth Century newspaper . . . in this country," and that the first issue had been delivered at considerable expense and effort directly to McKinley.[2]

There was a lot of yellow journalism in Smith's turn-of-the-century run to Washington. The occasion illuminated the qualities that made the genre—of which the *New York Journal* was an archetype—both so irritating and so irresistible: Yellow journalism could be imaginative yet frivolous, aggressive yet self-indulgent. It advocated an ethos of activist journalism, yet did so in bursts of unabashed self-adulation.

For all its flaws and virtues, yellow journalism exerted a powerful influence in American journalism at the turn of the twentieth century. Yellow journalism was much decried but its salient features often were emulated. The genre was appealing and distinctive in its typography, in its lavish use of illustrations, in its aggressive newsgathering techniques. To a striking degree, features characteristic of the yellow press live on in American journalism, notably in the colorful layouts that characterize the formerly staid titles that used to disparage the yellow press—titles such as the *New York Times* and *Washington Post.* Indeed, it may even be appropriate to think of leading mainstream U.S. newspapers at the turn of the twenty-first century as embodying a kind of tempered or "reformed" yellow journalism.[3]

But in the decades since the twentieth century's first American newspaper rolled from the presses, the swagger and excesses of yellow journalism—and, to be sure, the arrogance, wealth, and ambitions of its leading practitioner, William Randolph Hearst—have managed to obscure the genre and its contributions. Myth, the blight of serious history, has overrun yellow journalism, distorting popular and scholarly understanding of the genre. The stuff of American journalism's best-known legends comes from the time of the yellow journalism, a period bracketed by Hearst's arrival in New York in 1895—a seismic event in the city's journalism[4]—and the undeniable fading of the genre's most flamboyant signature features by 1910. In that time, newspapers embracing the salient elements of yellow journalism appeared in Boston, Chicago, Denver, and San Francisco, among other American cities.

Perhaps the myth told most often about yellow journalism is that of the purported exchange of telegrams between Hearst and the artist Frederic Remington, in which Hearst is said to have vowed, "I'll furnish the war," [5] between the United States and Spain.[6] That Hearst made good on the supposed vow—that the yellow press succeeded in bringing about the Spanish-American War in 1898, that it was "Mr. Hearst's War"[7]—is another undying myth, one that tidily, if mistakenly, serves to illustrate the power and the lurking malevolence of America's news media. Indeed, all of American journalism suffers indirectly from such mythology.[8]

Yet another durable, widely held myth is that the yellow press was primarily an entertainment medium,[9] that it frivolously discounted and even corrupted,[10] fact-based journalism in order merely to titillate and distract its readers.[11] Hearst's best-known biographers have tended to support this impression.[12] In reality, a defining characteristic of the yellow press—and, notably, of Hearst's *Journal*—was abundant spending on newsgathering, especially on news from afar.[13] "Its conquests," a Boston editor said of the *Journal*, "are costly."[14] The *Journal* figured that its expenses related to covering the Spanish-American War exceeded $750,000,[15] or the equivalent 100 years later of $15 million.

The *Journal* gloated about its extravagant spending on newsgathering. Not atypical was this claim, in which the *Journal* disparaged its rivals, notably the *New York Sun*: "The reason the old journalism doesn't like the Journal is that the Journal gets the news, no matter what it costs. The Sun and its kind cannot afford to spend money since the Journal has taken their readers away from them, and the probability is they would not do so if they could afford it. They are still living in the Silurian age."[16]

AN ENTERPRISING GENRE

In reading the issues of the yellow journals, it is difficult to remain unimpressed by their zeal and their enterprise in obtaining confidential reports and documents. The *Journal*'s scoops in this regard were notable. They included obtaining and publishing in 1896 the text of an ill-fated arbitration treaty[17] between the United States and Britain; disclosing in 1898 the contents of an indiscreet but exceedingly revealing private letter written by Spain's minister to the United States, in which he disparaged McKinley during the unfolding crisis over Cuba; and divulging in 1899 the text of the peace treaty[18] that ended the war between the United States and Spain. Contemporaneous observers were known to congratulate the *Journal* for its "extraordinary" enterprise.[19]

Some of the *Journal*'s most notable exclusives came close to home, in its frequent crusades against graft, incompetence,[20] and municipal corruption in New York. The Ice Trust exposés in 1900 offer a revealing example of ferocity, and even the nonpartisan nature, of the newspaper's investigative enterprise.

The *Journal* in the spring that year disclosed the equity holding of Robert Van Wyck,[21] the first mayor of the consolidated boroughs of New York City, in a company that controlled much of the sale and distribution of ice. At the turn of the twentieth century, ice was essential to the health and comfort of New Yorkers, especially to the tens of thousands of people crowded into tenements. The *Journal*'s revelations about the corrupt mayor came shortly after the company had doubled the price of ice to sixty cents per 100 pounds,[22] and after the *Journal* had pursued Van Wyck on a mysterious trip to Maine, where he joined the Ice Trust's president[23] in inspecting the company's plants.[24]

Although the *Journal* had vigorously supported Van Wyck's candidacy for mayor in the 1897 election,[25] the newspaper turned on him relentlessly in the Ice Trust scandal, referring to him as a criminal official who should be prosecuted and removed from office. In the end, the price of ice was rolled back but Van Wyck escaped trial. The disclosures had, however, destroyed his political career and Van Wyck left office in disgrace in 1901.

Commentators in the early twentieth century were not in error in noting that the yellow press "had proved a fearless and efficient instrument for the exposure of public wrongdoing."[26] The Ice Trust scandal was one of several anticorruption crusades.[27]

ACCOUNTING FOR THE MYTHS

So why, then, did such an intriguing and aggressive genre become the object of such abundant distortion, of such towering mythology? Why is "yellow journalism" little more than a sneering epithet for sensationalism and other failings of the news media? The reasons are several.

Its hearty indulgence in self-congratulation was no doubt a factor. Self-promotion was a signal feature of yellow journalism and the *Journal* and its principal rival, the *New York World*, boasted ceaselessly about their reporting accomplishments, modest though they sometimes were. Their self-indulgence invited the loathing of rival newspapers, the editors of which were ever eager to malign the yellow press. Indeed, as we shall see, the term "yellow journalism" emerged and spread from New York City amid an ill-fated campaign to ban the *Journal* and the *World*. For those editors, "yellow journalism" was an evocative term of reproach, a colorful way of excoriating—and marginalizing—the *Journal* and the *World*.

But the unabashed self-congratulation that characterized the genre accounts only partly for the extravagant growth of myth and misunderstanding. Another part of the explanation is that the genre's leading practitioners—Hearst, notably, and, to a lesser extent, Joseph Pulitzer of the *World*, as well as regional figures such as Frederick G. Bonfils and Harry H. Tannem of the *Denver Post*—seemed to invite censure and scorn. They were ambitious and controversial figures, and their foes recognized they were vulnerable to personal attack by impugning their journalism. After all, what better way to impugn and discredit Hearst than to blame him and his newspapers for fomenting an "unnecessary" war?

Hearst was a ready target for such scorn, especially after his political ambitions became clear at the end of the nineteenth century.[28] His politics and the self-indulgence of his newspapers invited attacks such as this one in *Harper's Weekly* in 1906:

> The man, therefore, who as the owner of newspapers, would corrupt public opinion is the most dangerous enemy of the State. We may talk about the perils incident to the concentration of wealth, about the perils flowing from a disregard of fiduciary responsibility, about abuses of privilege, about exploiting the government for private advantage; but all of these menaces, great as they are, are nothing compared with a deliberate, persistent, artful, purchased endeavor to

pervert and vitiate the public judgment. Why? Because upon that judgment we must all of us rely in a self-governing community for the conservation of everything we prize and for all the progress for which we hope.[29]

The searing portrayal of Hearst in the 1941 motion picture *Citizen Kane* undoubtedly sealed his reputation as a cynical, ruthless manipulator.[30] *Citizen Kane* also helped popularize the purported Hearstian vow to "furnish the war" with Spain.[31]

Perhaps a more important explanation for the myth that has obscured yellow journalism is that the genre proved so elusive to definition. Yellow journalism has been equated to lurid and sensational treatment of the news;[32] to egregious journalistic misconduct of almost any kind, and to Hearst, himself. None of those shorthand characterizations is adequate, revealing, or even very accurate. None captures the genre's complexity and vigor.

The term "yellow journalism," as we shall see in Chapter One, emerged in early 1897, popularized by the *New York Press* and its stern and fastidious editor, Ervin Wardman. But the editor who pressed the phrase into the vernacular never explicitly defined it. For Wardman, "yellow journalism" was an evocative and dismissive epithet applied interchangeably to the *Journal* and the *World*. (While they shared many features and elements, the *Journal* and *World* were fierce competitors and resisted being so linked. But they were certainly not conservative newspapers in appearance or content.)

SHADES OF YELLOW JOURNALISM

The phrase "yellow journalism" and the salient features of the practice were quickly diffused in the late nineteenth century. The *New York Tribune* adopted the term in February 1897, with a bow to Wardman's *Press*,[33] and within weeks, newspapers beyond New York were also referring to "yellow journalism." Meanwhile, the elements characteristic of yellow journalism were said to have spread "like a prairie fire,"[34] taking hold to varying degrees in newspapers in several U.S. cities.

It was a highly idiosyncratic genre: Not every exemplar of yellow journalism was a facsimile of the *New York Journal*. The *Denver Post* and *San Francisco Examiner* were, for example, noticeably less inclined to indulge in self-promotion than either the *Journal* or the *World*. The *Boston Post* opened its flamboyant front pages to display advertising, a practice not uncommon in Boston at the turn of the twentieth century.[35] The *Journal* was more inclined to use banner headlines than the *World*.

Such differences notwithstanding, those newspapers that can be classified as "yellow journals" were, at a minimum, typographically bold in their use of headlines and illustrations. They certainly *looked* different from their gray, conservative counterparts, and their use of design elements was more conspicuous and imaginative. They were, moreover, inclined to campaign against powerful interests and municipal abuses, ostensibly on behalf of "the people." And they usually were not shy about doing so.

That there were shades of yellow journalism is hardly surprising, given the genre's dimensions and inherent complexity. But that variance contributed to difficulties in defining the genre (difficulties that evoke the definitional imprecision associated with "public" or "civic" journalism, a practice that emerged in the United States during the 1990s). Practitioners of yellow journalism recognized the definitional vagueness,[36] but offered little clarification. Hearst, who came to embrace the term, unhelpfully described yellow journalism as "truthful journalism of an aggressive, not a negative, character. "[37] Arthur Brisbane, one of Hearst's top editors, said: "Anything in journalism that is new and successful is yellow journalism, no matter what you or I see fit to call it."[38] Not surprisingly, foes of the yellow press were more eager to disparage than define. Thus were the yellow journals accused of such malevolent effects as "corrupting the young and debauching the old, championing vice and lewdness, and defying respectability and decency."[39] The practice of yellow journalism was likened, moreover, to a "contest of madmen for the primacy of the sewer."[40]

The Search for Definition

The definitional elusiveness of yellow journalism was underscored in a study published in 1900 (and often cited since) that said yellow journals had emerged in many metropolitan areas of the United States.[41] The study was drawn from a very limited content analysis[42] conducted by Delos Wilcox, who conceded having encountered great difficulty in developing a quantitative test permitting him to differentiate the *Journal* from the *New York Evening Post*, a leading conservative (or non-yellow) daily edited by E. L. Godkin.[43] Wilcox finally decided that yellow journalism's salient characteristics were the above-average emphasis on news of crime and vice; the use of illustrations; the publications of want ads and medical advertising, and the tendency to advertise or call attention to its accomplishments.[44]

Those categories were decidedly imprecise, to be sure. Conservative titles, for example, often gave prominence to news of crime and vice. As T. T. Williams, the business manager of Hearst's *San Francisco Examiner*, observed in 1897: "The most eminently respectable newspapers in this country at times print matter that the so-called sensational paper would never dare to print—but the so-called respectable newspaper escapes uncriticised because it does not *look* sensational."[45] Moreover, Wilcox's characterization of the yellow press underemphasized the typographic exuberance and design experimentation that typified the genre.[46]

Media historian Frank Luther Mott offered a somewhat more revealing and inclusive set of defining characteristics, and usefully pointed out that yellow journalism "must not be considered as synonymous with sensationalism." Yellow journalism, Mott said, certainly reflected "the familiar aspects of sensationalism—crime news, scandal and gossip, divorces and sex, and stress upon the reporting of disasters and sports."[47] But the genre was more complex than merely sensational; its "distinguishing techniques," Mott said, included the use or appearance of:

- prominent headlines that "screamed excitement, often about comparatively unimportant news."
- "lavish use of pictures, many of them without significance."
- "impostors and frauds of various kinds," including "'faked' interviews and stories."
- a Sunday supplement and color comics.
- a "more or less ostentatious sympathy with the 'underdog,' with campaigns against abuses suffered by the common people."[48]

Mott recognized that his criteria represented "an enumeration . . . of something grotesque and vicious"—an acknowledgment of subjectivity that diminishes their value in defining and explaining yellow journalism.[49] Mott's criteria, moreover, inadequately reflect the newsgathering enterprise that characterized the yellow press and fail to recognize fully the variety of content that the yellow press typically presented.

The Defining Characteristics

This study argues for and presents a more encompassing set of defining characteristics[50] of yellow journalism, a set of characteristics derived from the close reading of issues of the *New York Journal* and *New York World* during the first half of 1897, when the term began appearing in print in New York City and beyond. This set of characteristics, moreover, acknowledges not only the complexity of yellow journalism; it recognizes the genre's aggressive flamboyance, its inclination to experiment with page design, and its eagerness to call attention to itself. Thus, in its most developed and intense form, yellow journalism was characterized by:

- the frequent use of multicolumn headlines that sometimes stretched across the front page.
- a variety of topics reported on the front page, including news of politics, war, international diplomacy, sports, and society.

- the generous and imaginative use of illustrations, including photographs and other graphic representations such as locator maps.
- bold and experimental layouts, including those in which one report and illustration would dominate the front page.[51] Such layouts sometimes were enhanced by the use of color.
- a tendency to rely on anonymous sources, particularly in dispatches of leading reporters (such as James Creelman, who wrote for the *Journal* and the *World*).
- a penchant for self-promotion, to call attention eagerly to the paper's accomplishments. This tendency was notably evident in crusades against monopolies and municipal corruption.

As defined above and as practiced a century ago, yellow journalism certainly could not be called predictable, boring, or uninspired—complaints of the sort that were not infrequently raised about U.S. newspapers at the turn of the twenty-first century.[52]

JOURNALISM FOR A LUSTY TIME

Yellow journalism was a product of a lusty, fiercely competitive, and intolerant time, when editors were known to shoot editors,[53] when editors were shot by their readers,[54] and when newspapers almost casually traded brickbats and insults.[55] The latter practice was remarkably well-developed at the end of the nineteenth century. The *Journal* and *World*, for example, were ever eager to impugn, denounce, and sneer at each other;[56] so, too, were conservative newspapers.[57] The gray, staid *Washington Post* said this about one of its conservative counterparts in 1899: "The New York Times has such abnormal keenness of vision that it is occasionally able to see that which does not exist. The ardency of its desire sometimes overcomes the coolness of its reason, so that the thing it wants to see shows up just where it wants it to be, but in so intangible a form that no other eye is able to detect, no other mind finds ground to suspect its presence."[58]

More generally, yellow journalism reflected the brashness and the widely perceived hurried pace of urban America[59] at the turn of the twentieth century. It was a lively, provocative, swaggering style of journalism well suited to an innovative and expansive time—a period when the United States first projected its military power beyond the Western Hemisphere in a sustained manner.[60] The recognition was widespread at the end of the nineteenth century that the country was on the cusp of rapid, perhaps even disruptive transformation. For example, the demographic profile had begun to swing from predominantly rural to largely urban; the population of U.S. cities expanded by nearly one third during the 1890s,[61] growth fueled in measure by incipient immigration from central, southern, and eastern Europe.[62]

The sense of change at the end of the nineteenth century went well beyond demography, however. It was more profound, more elemental.[63] "Political, commercial, social, artistic and religious customs and thoughts that have stood for many years—some for many centuries—are yielding place to new more rapidly than they have for many generations past," one commentator wrote in the spring of 1898. "Scientific discovery, popular education, free thought and business enterprise are all factors in the change."[64]

"Scientific discovery" seemed to have annihilated time and space. "Space is no intervention now between communication," an editorial writer in Cincinnati marveled in 1900. "[N]ot only do the wires of copper bind the world together in closer communication, but with the telephone it is possible to converse with friends a thousand miles away, hearing distinctly every word and recognizing the individual voice. Closer acquaintance has thus wrought vast changes in public opinions and policies. The entire civilized world has been drawn more closely together, old ideas and prejudices have been wiped out."[65]

Prejudice of course had not been excised. If anything, the late nineteenth century was a time of stunning intolerance, of prejudices renewed and deepened. In Southern states, black men were disfranchised and Jim Crow segregation became institutionalized, efforts that often were championed by local newspapers. The *Raleigh News and Observer*, for example, played a central role in North Carolina's virulent white supremacy movements which led to the severe curtailment of black suffrage at the end of the nineteenth century.[66]

The yellow press of New York felt the sting of intolerance, too, notably in a boycott by social organizations, clubs, reading rooms, and public libraries. The boycott spread quickly throughout metropolitan New York during the first months of 1897, but ultimately proved unsustainable—in no small measure because the *Journal* and the *World* were livelier, more aggressive, more insistent, and generally more appealing than their conservative rivals.[67]

To be sure, yellow journalism did not simply burst upon the media landscape of the United States in the 1890s, unique and fully formed. It was malleable and it borrowed from past practice. Pulitzer, for example, had engaged in crusades and indulged in sensationalism several years before Hearst's appearance in New York City.[68] Yellow journalism was, as contemporaneous observers noted, born before it was baptized.[69]

It was a genre keen to adapt and eager to experiment. Its distinctiveness and popularity were in no small measure attributable to a hearty embrace of established and emergent techniques and technologies. Yellow journalism cannot be explained as merely an effect or artifact of technological advances—such as the high-speed presses that cost upwards of $100,000 at the turn of the twentieth century and could print in five or even six colors.[70] The genre's boldness and its diffusion were due fundamentally to the tastes, affluence, and idiosyncrasies of individual publishers. But yellow journalism undeniably was shaped and propelled by the developments of the time, which included:

- The emergence of a "graphic revolution,"[71] marked by the popularity of half-tone photographs[72] and the rise in importance of newspapers' art departments.[73] The half-tone ultimately helped to transform the appearance, and appeal, of newspaper front pages.[74]
- The fall in the cost of pulp-based newsprint,[75] which enabled newspapers to experiment with bolder headlines[76] and to expand the page count of their daily and Sunday editions.[77] Cheaper newsprint helped make possible the six-figure daily circulations claimed by the *Journal* and *World*.[78]
- The advances in newsroom technology. Typewriters, notably, became standard[79] and were valued for their efficiency. Electric typewriters were emergent.[80] Moreover, college-educated reporters were at the turn of the twentieth century becoming "more and more of a factor" in New York City journalism.[81]
- The enhancements in delivery systems. At the end of the nineteenth century, automobiles began replacing horse-drawn carts as a principal means of distributing newspapers in New York City.[82] In addition, New York metropolitan newspapers were routinely sent by high-speed train to cities throughout the eastern United States.[83]

Despite the multiple technologies and developments that facilitated its emergence and diffusion, yellow journalism in its most flamboyant, immoderate, and self-important form could not be long sustained. By the close of the first decade of the twentieth century, it clearly had faded. The tendency to self-promotion, once so frenzied and inescapable, had subsided. The *New York American* (the *Journal*'s successor title) and the *New York World* were, by 1909, far less eager to place their names in front-page headlines than they had been ten years before.

The fading or softening of yellow journalism was also attributable to a convergence of multiple forces: Conservative competitors began to incorporate features of the genre, notably in somewhat bolder layouts. Muckraking magazines such as *McClure's*, became journalism's most prominent crusaders, exposing municipal corruption and corporate greed and misconduct. Publishers became enfeebled (as did Pulitzer) or turned toward other interests (as did Hearst, to state and national politics). Reports of sporting events migrated from the front page to discrete sections.[84]

Meanwhile, the term "yellow journalism" became tied inextricably to an improbable assortment of journalistic failings and misdeeds, notably that of provoking the war with Spain in 1898.[85] The myth of the yellow press and the Spanish-American War deepened in the 1930s with publication of studies by Joseph E. Wisan[86] and Marcus M. Wilkerson,[87] and of polemics such as Ferdinand Lundberg's hostile biography, *Imperial Hearst*.[88]

By the end of the twentieth century, the understanding of "yellow journalism" had become so distorted, so choked by myth and misunderstanding, that discussions of the genre often were little more than ill-informed caricatures. Consider, for example, the following passage from *Harper's* magazine in 1997, which discussed Hearst and the *Journal*'s reporting of the insurgency in Cuba that preceded the Spanish-American War—during what the author called "the florid bloom of crime and underwear that soon came to be known as yellow journalism":[89]

> For eighteen months, the *Journal* had been printing vivid, first-hand accounts of the cruel suffering inflicted by Spanish brutes and tyrants on the innocent, democratic, freedom-loving Cuban people. The stories were counterfeit, composed by an atelier of thirty-odd artists and writers, among them Frederick [*sic*] Remington and Richard Harding Davis, that Hearst had dispatched to Cuba to dramatize the revolution presumably taking place in the mountains. The revolution was nowhere to be found, and so Hearst's correspondents stationed themselves in wicker chairs on the terrace of the Hotel Inglaterra in Havana, where they sipped iced drinks and received news by telepathy. Borrowing from one another's adjectives, they sent word of imaginary atrocities and non-existent heroes, descriptions of battles that never occurred, fanciful but stirring tales of Spanish officers roasting Catholic priests on charcoal fires and feeding prisoners to the sharks.
>
> When all else failed, they sent an attractive Cuban girl whom they persuaded to travel north with a terrible story of how she had been violated by General Valeriano Weyler, the commander of the Spanish troops, whom the correspondents had never met but whom they routinely described as "the destroyer of haciendas," "the destroyer of families," and "the outrager of women." When the fair maiden arrived in New York, Hearst prepared for her appearance at Madison Square Garden with three concise instructions, always the same and always ready to hand, that expressed his reading of the First Amendment: "Hire military bands. Secure orators. Arrange fireworks."[90]

The errors, half-truths, and distortions in the *Harper's* account are not only spectacular: They are illustrative of the kind of routine denunciation and gratuitous misunderstanding that attaches to the yellow press and its practitioners. The *Harper's* account errs in many ways: The Spanish *did* resort to harsh measures in their failed attempt to quell the insurrection in Cuba; the *Journal* kept no "atelier" of artists and reporters on the island; Davis and Remington, whom the *Journal* dispatched to Cuba, stayed a short while but traveled beyond Havana; some *Journal* correspondents did spend time with the Cuban insurgents; the *Journal* sometimes carried extravagant atrocity stories, but so did many other

U.S. newspapers; correspondents for the *Journal* were acquainted with Weyler, the Spanish military leader in Cuba in 1896–1897; Weyler did not violate the Cuban "girl," the description of whom suggests Evangelina Cosío y Cisneros, an eighteen-year-old woman whom the Spanish imprisoned for sympathies with the insurrection and whom a *Journal* correspondent rescued from a jail in Havana and sent to a tumultuous welcome in the United States.

A TWOFOLD OBJECTIVE

This study seeks neither to laud nor apologize for yellow journalism. Its excesses were many and difficult to countenance. It was a notably impenitent genre. The *Journal*, in particular, was seldom given to acknowledge lapses and errors.[91] Its indulgence in oddities and pseudoscience,[92] moreover, lent to yellow journalism a sense of absurdity and encouraged the notion that the genre was eager "to sport with the facts."[93] While strange and improbable stories (such as "The Missing Link Found Alive In Annam,"[94] "Is the Sun Preparing to Give Birth to a New World?"[95] and "Pontius Pilate's Interview With Christ"[96]) were generally confined to Sunday supplements, they live on as blighting counterfeits.[97]

Nevertheless, it is a mistake to assess yellow journalism solely in relation to such excesses. Oddities and pseudoscience were diversions, not the principal elements of content; not all columns of the yellow press "were filled . . . with frivolities and slush."[98]

This study, while mindful of the lapses and shortcomings of yellow journalism, recognizes as well that it was a robust and searching genre, the understanding of which has been warped by myth and error. The study, therefore, pursues a twofold objective.

First, it revisits and offers fresh perspectives and interpretations about the prominent mythology of yellow journalism. The study specifically seeks to correct the record about legends and misunderstandings, such as Hearst's purported vow to "furnish the war," and about misleading claims, such as the undying notion the yellow press plunged the United States into war with Spain. Those and other myths of the yellow press are addressed in the first part of this study. The second, related objective is to assess the extent to which the defining features of yellow journalism live on in leading American newspapers. That they do live on has often been asserted by media historians[99] but never has been tested systematically. The second part of this study presents the results of a detailed content analysis of the front pages of seven leading U.S. newspapers at ten-year intervals, from 1899 to 1999. The content analysis indicates that some of the less flamboyant elements characteristic of yellow journalism have been generally adopted by leading U.S. newspapers. A separate chapter offers qualitative evidence about how the genetic material of yellow journalism can be found in various strains of activist-oriented journalism of the late twentieth century—namely, in "development journalism," a movement popular in developing countries during the 1970s and 1980s; in "public journalism," which emerged in the United States during the 1990s, and in the virulent brand of crime-busting journalism practiced by large-circulation British tabloid newspapers at the end of the 1990s.

In puncturing the myths and defining the legacies of yellow journalism, this study focuses to some degree on Hearst's *New York Journal*. Such a concentration is inescapable: Not only did the *Journal* perhaps best exemplify the accomplishments and excesses of yellow journalism, the newspaper was central to the genre's most powerful and enduring myths. More broadly, however, this study endeavors to present a nuanced and less emotional understanding of an energetic, complex, and much-maligned genre of American journalism. Yellow journalism has long awaited such treatment.

Most discussions of the yellow press, after all, have been conducted through the biographies of the figures most readily associated with the genre—of Hearst and Pulitzer, principally. A notable exception was John D. Stevens' *Sensationalism and the New York Press*, an insightful if largely descriptive account that considers the yellow press of New York City in detail. Stevens' work does not, however, examine the genre as it emerged elsewhere in the United States, nor does it explore its myths and legacies. Sidney Kobre's *The Yellow Press and Gilded Age Journalism* is a useful treatment, but is principally a descriptive survey of important figures and institutions of the press in the United States during the late nineteenth century.

This study, then, seeks to fill a significant gap in the literature. It begins with Ervin Wardman and the first sustained use of the term "yellow journalism."

NOTES

1. George B. Cortelyou, diary entry, 1 January 1901; Cortelyou papers, Library of Congress, Washington, DC.

2. Langdon Smith, "'The Journal, the First Newspaper of This Century'—McKinley," *New York Journal* (2 January 1901): 1. McKinley was quoted in Smith's article as tersely offering thanks for the newspaper and the silver case. The *Journal* sent the second copy of its 1 January 1901 edition to Vice President-elect Theodore Roosevelt, and the third to New York Governor-elect Benjamin B. Odell Jr. For another account of the *Journal*'s first issue of the twentieth century, see "Greeting to the Century," *Fourth Estate* (5 January 1901): 5. Smith reported on the Spanish-American War for the *Journal* and, in 1899, was nearly lured away by the rival *New York World*, the managing editor of which was impressed by the "vivid description" that characterized Smith's prose. See Bradford Merrill,

letter to Don C. Seitz, 6 July 1899, 1899 file, *New York World* papers, Butler Library, Columbia University, New York.

3. The term "reformed yellow journalism" was proposed in 1902 by a former editor of the *New York Journal*, Samuel E. Moffett. He said that "respectable" newspapers need not eschew large headlines and illustrations, or avoid criticizing powerful interests. Moffett suggested making "accuracy instead of record-breaking celerity the supreme requirement in your news-room." The suggestions were cited in "Are Yellow Journals as Bad as They Are Painted?" *Literary Digest* 25, 5 (2 August 1902): 132.

4. For example, the trade journal *Fourth Estate* said: "The advent of young Hearst is an event of the greatest importance, for he means what he says, says what he means and states that he is here to stay. . . . Hearst is young and ambitious. He is worth watching. He wants to prove that he has more than his millions to back him. He is in New York to hustle and not to buy gold bricks. If he can, as he intends to, push the *Journal* into the first rank, he will have proved the power of his purpose and achieved his ambitions." See "W. R. Hearst Here," *Fourth Estate* (10 October 1895): 1. *Fourth Estate* added: "The result of new blood in metropolitan journalism will be watched with the deepest interest, not only in New York, but throughout the country" (2). See also, "Who Will Be Next?" *Fourth Estate* (7 November 1895): 1.

5. James Creelman, *On the Great Highway: The Wanderings and Adventures of a Special Correspondent* (Boston: Lothrop Publishing, 1901), 177–178.

6. The purported exchange has often been invoked by journalists and media historians. See, among many others, Clifford Krauss, "Remember Yellow Journalism," *New York Times* (15 February 1998): 4, 3, and Michael Schudson, *Discovering the News: A Social History of American Newspapers* (New York: Basic Books Inc., 1978), 61–62. Many biographers of Hearst have repeated the anecdote, some of them without qualification. See, for example, Ferdinand Lundberg, *Imperial Hearst: A Social Biography* (New York: Equinox Cooperative Press, 1936), 68–69.

7. Philip Seib, *Headline Diplomacy: How News Coverage Affects Foreign Policy* (Westport, CT: Praeger Publishers, 1997), 1–13. See also, W. A. Swanberg, *Citizen Hearst: A Biography of William Randolph Hearst* (New York: Charles Scribner's Sons, 1961), 144.

8. Another enduring myth is that the yellow press was decidedly and intentionally downscale, that it appealed primarily to the poor, to newly arrived immigrants, and to people with an uncertain command of English. But the contrary evidence, both quantitative and qualitative, is persuasive: The yellow press most likely was read across the social strata in New York and elsewhere, as will be discussed in Chapter Two.

9. See Schudson, *Discovering the News*, 89, 91.

10. Gunther Barth, *City People: The Rise of Modern City Culture in Nineteenth-Century America* (New York: Oxford University Press, 1980), 101. Barth argued: "Yellow journalism reduced newspapers to a tool of power politics in the hands of news barons with concern for news reporting as an instrument of communication forged by the interaction of journalism, the modern city, and its residents."

11. Sociology studies have tended to emphasize that point. See, for example, Robert E. Park, "The Yellow Press," *Sociology and Social Research* 12 (1927–1928). Park wrote that Hearst's "appeal was frankly not to the intellect but to the

heart. The newspaper was for him first and last a form of entertainment" (10). See also, Carroll DeWitt Clark, "News: A Sociological Study," *Abstracts of Theses, University of Chicago Humanist Series* 9 (1930–32): 244.

12. See, notably, Swanberg, *Citizen Hearst*, 162. See also Lundberg, *Imperial Hearst*, 54–57.

13. The yellow press covered local news with vigor, too. John D. Stevens wrote of the *New York Journal* and *New York World*: "If they titillated, the yellow papers also told New Yorkers what was going on, what forces were shaping their lives. Each issue bulged with news accounts and feature stories which were little parables about life in the big city." Stevens, *Sensationalism and the New York Press* (New York: Columbia University Press, 1991), 99–100.

14. John H. Holmes, "The New Journalism and the Old," *Munsey's Magazine* (April 1897): 78. Holmes, then the editor of the *Boston Herald*, wrote: "Another feature characteristic of the 'new [yellow] journalism' is the liberality with which its promoters expend money in the furtherance of their aims. . . . Many journalists conceive great undertakings, but refrain from executing them on account of the expense involved. The 'new journalist' is not troubled with hesitation on that score. Like the general who orders guns to be trained in position where effective service can be rendered, he does not stop to count the cost." *Munsey's* returned to this theme a few years later, stating that "when all is said and done, the fact remains that the 'yellow journals' are the progressive newspapers, those which spend the largest sums to get the latest and best news and to present it most attractively and forcefully." See Hartley Davis, "The Journalism of New York," *Munsey's Magazine* 24, 2 (November 1900): 233.

15. "Just One Small Fact," *New York Journal* (21 January 1902): 14.

16. "'Truth' about the Old Journalism," *New York Journal* (2 February 1897): 6. "Old journalism" was the *Journal*'s dismissive term for newspapers also known as "conservative." They included the *New York Sun* of Charles A. Dana. "New journalism" was a precursor term for "yellow journalism."

17. "Full Text of the Venezuelan Treaty: Final Draft of the Arbitration Now Published for the First Time," *New York Journal* (6 December 1896): 1. The *Journal* congratulated itself for what it called "one of the most notable achievements of journalism in recent years." See "The Venezuelan Treaty," *New York Journal* (7 December 1896): 6.

18. "First Publication of Paris Protocols and Peace Treaty: The Journal Makes Public the Private Documents Recording the Proceedings of the Peace Commission," *New York Journal* (1 January 1899): 25.

19. "Extraordinary Example," *Fourth Estate* (24 November 1898): 4. For other occasions when *Fourth Estate* commended the *Journal*'s enterprise, see "The Fiercest of Fights," *Fourth Estate* (25 March 1897): 6; "Enterprise Tells: The New York Journal's Notable Achievements," *Fourth Estate* (27 October 1900): 3; and "'Print the News at Any Cost,'" *Fourth Estate* (8 June 1901): 8.

20. The *Journal* also inveighed against the disruption created by the reconstruction of water and sewer mains along New York City's Fifth Avenue in 1897. The newspaper's principal target was Charles Collis, the city's public works commissioner, whom the *Journal* assailed for his "wicked negligence." See "Good Work Accomplished by the Journal in the Public Interest," *New York Journal* (2 October 1897): 3.

21. "Ice Trust Shareholders: Van Wyck, 8,000 Shares! Carroll, 5,000 Shares!" *New York Journal* (15 May 1900): 1. John F. Carroll was a Tammany Hall leader.

22. "Put an End to the Criminal Extortion of the Ice Trust," *New York Journal* (8 May 1900): 1.

23. See "Van Wyck in Maine with Ice Trust Man," *New York Journal* (4 May 1900): 4, and "Mayor Van Wyck Sees Ice Kings of Maine," (6 May 1900): 1. Van Wyck would not say why he was visiting the Ice Trust properties, reticence that no doubt fueled the *Journal*'s suspicions.

24. "Van Wyck Inspects Properties of 'Ice Trust,'" *New York Journal* (5 May 1900): 1.

25. See, for example, "The Journal to Democrats," *New York Journal* (28 October 1897): 8, and "Great Triumph for Democrats," *New York Journal* (3 November 1897): 1.

26. Sydney Brooks, "The American Yellow Press," *Fortnightly Review* 96 (December 1911): 1136–1137.

27. For a discussion of the *Journal*'s use of injunctions to thwart what it called "giveaways" and "grabs" by powerful corporations, see "The Development of a New Idea in Journalism," *New York Journal* (3 October 1897): 38–39.

28. Hearst was twice elected early in the twentieth century to Congress from a New York City district, but failed in subsequent bids to win the presidency of the United States, the governorship of New York, and the mayoralty of New York City.

29. "Comment," *Harper's Weekly* (20 October 1906). Hearst was running for New York governor at the time. The commentary paraphrased remarks by Hearst's opponent in the gubernatorial campaign, Charles E. Hughes.

30. For a brief but revealing discussion about how *Citizen Kane* "has for generations suborned our perceptions" and left a "distorted portrait" of Hearst, see Harold Evans, "Press Baron's Progress," *New York Times Book Review* (2 July 2000): 7, 4.

31. The motion picture includes a scene in which Charles Kane, played by Orson Welles, receives a telegram from a correspondent with the word "there is no war in Cuba." Kane's reply: "You provide the prose poems. I'll provide the war."

32. See, for example, Gene Wiggins, "Sensationally Yellow!" in Lloyd Chiasson Jr., ed., *Three Centuries of American Media* (Englewood, CO: Morton Publishing Company, 1999): 155.

33. See "Wise Limitations of the War Power," *New York Tribune* (18 February 1897), 6.

34. Will Irwin, "The American Newspaper: The Spread and Decline of Yellow Journalism," reprinted in Will Irwin, *The American Newspaper* (Ames, IA: Iowa State University Press, 1969).

35. Edwin A. Grozier, the *Boston Post*'s editor and publisher, conceded that the practice of placing prominent advertising on the front pages gave the city's press a "somewhat provincial" appearance. Cited in "Front Page Advertising," *Fourth Estate* (8 February 1902): 10.

36. *Fourth Estate* quoted James Creelman, formerly a correspondent for the *New York Journal* and the *New York World*, as saying in 1902 that the difficulty for people who sought "to seriously deal with yellow journalism, rather than approach it in a spirit of levity or wanton malice . . . is the lack of definition of yel-

low journalism acceptable to both sides in the debate." See "Strong Features of the 'Yellow Journals,'" *Fourth Estate* (3 May 1902): 8.

37. Cited in "Hearst Defends So-called Yellow Journals," *Fourth Estate* (13 September 1902): 4. The *Fourth Estate* account included comments by Hearst that had appeared in the *London Express*.

38. Cited in "'Yellow Journalism' Defined," *Editor and Publisher* (20 January 1917): 14.

39. "Fall of Yellow Journalism," *New York Press* (28 March 1897): 6. The *Press* editorial was written during a well-publicized boycott of the *Journal* and *World* by clubs, social organizations, and reading rooms in metropolitan New York. The boycott dissolved in failure a few months after the *Press* predicted in the editorial of 28 March 1897 that yellow journalism would soon "practically disappear from newsstands. Goodby to it, and no regrets!"

40. Brooks, "The American Yellow Press," 1131.

41. Delos F. Wilcox, "The American Newspaper: A Study in Social Psychology," *Annals of the American Academy of Political and Social Science* 16 (July 1900): 56–92.

42. Wilcox for the most part drew his conclusions by examining only one issue of each of the 147 newspapers in his study. See Wilcox, "The American Newspaper," 78.

43. Wilcox, "The American Newspaper," 77.

44. Wilcox, "The American Newspaper," 77. Conservative newspapers, Wilcox said, were characterized by an emphasis on political and business news, letters and exchange material, and "miscellaneous advertisements."

45. Cited in *American Journalism From the Practical Side* (New York: Holmes Publishing Company, 1897), 314. Emphasis added.

46. The typographic flamboyance of yellow journalism was noted in many contemporaneous accounts. For example, Hartley Davis wrote in *Munsey's Magazine* in 1900: "The presentation or 'playing up' of news is one of the important features of modern journalism in New York. It is the distinguishing mark of the so-called 'yellow journalism,' because 'yellow journalism' consists principally of huge head lines of a startling nature, big and striking illustrations, and heavily leaded type in which the facts are presented in the most interesting style." Davis, "The Journalism of New York," 220–221. See also, Holmes, "The New Journalism and the Old," 77–78.

47. Frank Luther Mott, *American Journalism: A History: 1690–1960*, 3d ed. (New York: Macmillan, 1962), 539.

48. Mott, *American Journalism*, 539.

49. Mott, *American Journalism*, 539. Mott noted that his criteria contained the "germs of newspaper techniques which are certainly defensible and which have since been developed into general and respectable features."

50. These features were the central elements of a content analysis discussed in Chapter Five.

51. See, among many other examples, "Remington and Davis Tell of Spanish Cruelty," *New York Journal* (2 February 1897): 1. The front page was almost entirely devoted to a sketch by Frederic Remington to illustrate a dispatch by Richard Harding Davis about a Cuban rebel's execution by Spanish firing squad.

52. See, for example, Sharyn Wizda, "Breathing Life into Newsprint," *American Journalism Review* (November 1999): 49–50, and Michael Kelly, "The

Know-Nothing Media," *Washington Post* (10 November 1999): A39. Kelly's characterization was especially harsh: "Reporters like to picture themselves as independent thinkers. In truth, with the exception of 13-year-old girls, there is no social subspecies more slavish to fashion, more terrified of originality and more devoted to group-think."

53. Two New Orleans newspapers editors were reported to have shot and badly wounded each other in 1899 in a dispute arising from publication of a cartoon depicting one of them as a dog on a leash. See "Editors Shoot Each Other," *Fourth Estate* (12 October 1899): 4.

54. Frederic G. Bonfils and Harry H. Tannem, owners and editors of the *Denver Evening Post*, were shot and wounded in their offices by a lawyer in 1900. Both men recovered from their wounds. See "Assassin Visits the Post," *Denver Evening Post* (13 January 1900): 1.

55. The exchange of insults sometimes led to blows, as in Clinton, IL, in 1903, when rival editors brawled in public. See "Editors Come to Blows," *Fourth Estate* (20 June 1903): 3.

56. See "Fiercest of Fights." The *Fourth Estate* editorial deplored the brickbats and said of the *Journal-World* enmity: "When two newspapers find their time chiefly occupied in exaggeration of one another's faults, it is then time to consider whether journalism is doing justice to its high estate."

57. There were exceptions, however. Edwin A. Grozier, editor and publisher of the *Boston Post*, insisted that no employee speak badly of competing newspapers. See untitled editorial page comment, *Fourth Estate* (11 April 1895): 6. By 1905, newspapers generally were less inclined to exchange insults and brickbats in print. See "Decline of Bad Temper," *Fourth Estate* (8 April 1905): 6. The *Fourth Estate* comment said: "Close observers have remarked with pleasure the decline of bitterness and personal attack in newspaper controversies. Of course, the controversies go on, but the days when one editor could not differ with another without calling him names are over."

58. "Seeing Nonexistent Things," *Washington Post* (18 June 1899): 6. The *Post* was referring to the *Times*' opinion (mistaken, as it turned out) that the appeal of William Jennings Bryan as a Democratic presidential candidate was fading. Bryan was the party's presidential nominee in 1896 and in 1900.

59. For example, *Fourth Estate* described the dawn of the twentieth century as "these days of rush and hurry." See "The Twentieth Century," *Fourth Estate* (5 January 1901): 8. The trade journal noted on another occasion that "society hurries because it wants to hurry, wants to do things quickly and get them out of the way; and the railroads and the telegraphs have been called into existence to meet its need." See "Modern Journalism," *Fourth Estate* (2 August 1900): 14.

60. The extension of U.S. influence to Asia, it has been argued, was a largely unintended consequence of the Spanish-American War. For a brief but persuasive discussion on this topic, see Ivan Musicant, *Empire by Default: The Spanish-American War and the Dawn of the American Century* (New York: Henry Holt and Company, 1998), 590–591.

61. "Table 80—Population 1900, 1890, and 1880," *Abstract of the Twelfth Census 1900* (Washington, DC: Government Printing Office, 1902), 100.

62. Nell Irvin Painter, *Standing at Armageddon: The United States, 1877–1919* (New York: Norton, 1987), xxxiv.

63. *Fourth Estate* referred to the late nineteenth century as "this remarkable time of transition, transformation and triumph." See "A Look at the Future," *Fourth Estate* (18 July 1895): 6. The trade publication declared: "Modes of locomotion and of living are changing, and man has become a nobler animal, with abilities that seem supernatural and ambitions almost too great for attainment."

64. David A. Curtis, "Yellow Journalism," *The Journalist* 23, 1 (23 April 1898): 19.

65. "The Century's Place in History," *Cincinnati Times-Star* (1 January 1900): 4.

66. W. Joseph Campbell, "'One of the Fine Figures in American Journalism': A Closer Look at Josephus Daniels of the *Raleigh News & Observer*," *American Journalism* 16, 4 (Fall 1999): 37–56.

67. The *Journal* was not just a victim of intolerance, however. It campaigned vigorously against Chinese immigration early in the twentieth century, asserting: "The Chinaman remains always a Chinaman. He cannot, like other foreigners, be made over into an American. . . . We have one race problem [in] the South. Shall we deliberately invite another to harass us and our posterity?" "Keep Out the Chinese!" *New York Journal* (29 January 1902): 16.

68. Innovations in journalistic practice have tended to come gradually rather than dramatically and abruptly. Moreover, as John Stevens noted: "It is tempting to overstate the originality of Joseph Pulitzer's contributions to journalism. The truth is that he invented nothing, but by adapting and demonstrating so many techniques he set new standards for the business. Certainly he was not the first to exploit sensational news or to gear content to women." Stevens, *Sensationalism and the New York Press*, 68.

69. See Brooks, "The American Yellow Press," 1130.

70. "The Cost of a Big Daily," *Fourth Estate* (30 November 1901): 12.

71. Daniel J. Boorstin, *The Image: A Guide to Pseudo-Events in America* (New York: Harper and Row Publishers, 1961), 13.

72. *Fourth Estate* noted in 1897 that a "distinct passion for half-tones has been developed during the past few weeks throughout the country." See "Note and Comment," *Fourth Estate* (11 March 1897): 7. A little more than a year later, *Fourth Estate* declared it "interesting to note the extraordinary proportions which the pictures are attaining in the daily newspapers." See "War News Rapidly Developing Color Printing," *Fourth Estate* (28 April 1898): 1. The trade publication had credited the *New York Tribune* with "a novelty in newspaper accomplishments" in making use on 21 January 1897 of a half-tone photograph of U.S. Senator Thomas Platt. See "Half-tones for Perfecting Presses," *Fourth Estate* (28 January 1897): 6. However, two newspapers in Minnesota claimed to have used half-tones much earlier, prompting *Fourth Estate* to ask: "Who Holds the Half-tone Record on Fast Presses?" *Fourth Estate* (11 February 1897): 7. The two newspapers were the *Minneapolis Times* and the *St. Paul Dispatch*.

73. Holmes, "The New Journalism and the Old," 78. The art department, Holmes wrote in 1897, "is now as much a portion of a newspaper outfit as are the presses themselves. Every event has to be set off with 'cuts,' the more numerous and the more startling the better."

74. The enthusiasm for half-tones in the late 1890s was well described by Bradford Merrill, the *World*'s managing editor, who observed in a letter to Pulitzer in 1899: "The tendency is to use half-tones and actual photographs in all edi-

tions, and the improvement in process is working three important results: First, it gives absolute accuracy; second, it saves space by making the pictures small; and last but not least, the tendency will be greatly to reduce expenses because photographers are cheaper than draughtsmen." Merrill, letter to Joseph Pulitzer, 13 June 1899, *New York World* papers, 1899 file, Butler Library, Columbia University.

75. The price fell to less than two cents a pound in 1896. See "Below Two Cents," *Fourth Estate* (8 October 1896): 1.

76. See "Newspapers and Headlines," *Fourth Estate* (6 October 1898): 4.

77. See "The Extinction of Newspapers," *Scribner's Magazine* 32 (October 1902): 507–508. The article noted: "It is the cheapness of the paper that makes it possible for the publisher of a metropolitan journal to put 150 tons of 'wood-pulp' into a single Sunday issue" (508).

78. During the Spanish-American War, the *Journal* claimed daily sales of as many as 1.6 million copies.

79. "A New Time Saver," *Fourth Estate* (21 December 1899): 7.

80. "Electric Typewriter," *Fourth Estate* (28 September 1901): 4.

81. Davis, "The Journalism of New York," 228. The emphasis on recruiting college graduates was exploitative. *Fourth Estate* noted in 1900: "The tendency each year seems to be to drop the high-priced, experienced men for young fellows, fresh from college, who are ready to work for just enough to pay their expenses. The number of the latter is so large that the ranks are kept full at all times." See "Journalistic Kindergarten," *Fourth Estate* (5 May 1900): 6.

82. See "Delivery by Automobiles," *Fourth Estate* (24 March 1900): 5. The article said: "The New York Journal has successfully introduced the automobile in its newspaper delivery department. The machines are heavily built in order to stand the strain of moving rapidly over rough pavements. They can carry more papers than the ordinary wagons, can be run at a high rate of speed, and seem to be admirably adapted to the hard work they are expected to do. . . . The Journal is the first of the Manhattan newspapers to adopt these admirable machines in its circulation department."

83. Davis, "The Journalism of New York," 232.

84. For a brief discussion of sports coverage in the yellow press, which credits the *New York Journal* as the "first to develop the modern sports section," see John Rickards Betts, "Sporting Journalism in Nineteenth-Century America," *American Quarterly* 5, 1 (Spring 1953): 56.

85. See Brooke Fisher, "The Newspaper Industry," *Atlantic Monthly* 89 (June 1902): 751.

86. Joseph E. Wisan, *The Cuban Crisis as Reflected in the New York Press (1895–1898)*, (New York: Octagon Books, reprint edition, 1965).

87. Marcus M. Wilkerson, *Public Opinion and the Spanish-American War, A Study in War Propaganda*. (Baton Rouge, LA: Louisiana State University Press, 1932).

88. Lundberg, *Imperial Hearst*, 66–82.

89. Lewis H. Lapham, "Notebook: The Consolations of Vanity," *Harper's Magazine* (December 1997): 11.

90. Lapham, "Notebook," 11.

91. Similar criticism was raised about the American press at the end of the twentieth century as well. See, for example, Robert J. Haiman, *Best Practices for*

Newspaper Journalists: A Handbook for Reporters, Editors, Photographers and Other Newspaper Professionals On How to be Fair to the Public (Arlington, VA: The Freedom Forum, 2000), 13. Haiman wrote: "There is a broad feeling in the public that newspapers not only make too many mistakes, but that they also are unwilling to correct them fully and promptly."

92. See, for example, "Can Scientists Breed Men from Monkeys?" *New York Journal* (22 August 1897): 13. Other yellow journals carried bizarre tales as well. See, for example, "Is Our Earth Alive—Has It a Soul?" *San Francisco Examiner* (25 April 1909): 18.

93. Brooks, "The American Yellow Press," 1128.

94. "The Missing Link Found Alive In Annam," *New York Journal* (6 December 1896): 33. Annam is in what now is central Vietnam.

95. "Is the Sun Preparing to Give Birth to a New World?" *New York Journal* (12 September 1897): 20–21.

96. "Pontius Pilate's Interview With Christ," *New York Journal* (7 November 1897): 17.

97. Such features probably were not taken altogether seriously by readers. *Fourth Estate* said that it suspected the oddities were seen as "wildly ludicrous to people of moderate sense and education." See "Past and Present Sensationalism," *Fourth Estate* (18 November 1897): 6.

98. Brooks, "The American Yellow Press," 1135.

99. See, for example, Mott, *American Journalism*, 539.

Part One

Puncturing the Myths

1

First Use: The Emergence and Diffusion of "Yellow Journalism"

"Yellow journalism" is the sneering pejorative perhaps most frequently associated with misconduct in newsgathering. Indeed, for more than 100 years, it has served as a derisive shorthand for denouncing journalists and their misdeeds, real and imagined. It is an evocative term that has been diffused internationally, in contexts as diverse as Greece and Nigeria, as Israel and India. The precise origins of the phrase have, however, long been murky[1] and its derivation has been a source of periodic dispute among scholars.

Many media historians credit Ervin Wardman, the stern-looking editor of the long-defunct *New York Press*, for having coined the term,[2] presumably late in 1896. According to the most common version of the etiology of the phrase, Wardman derived "yellow journalism" to characterize the rivalry between William Randolph Hearst and Joseph Pulitzer, particularly in their contest for the services of R. F. Outcault. Outcault was the artist who drew a witty and colorful cartoon that depicted the antics and the friends of a character commonly called the Yellow Kid, an irreverent, jug-eared child of the New York City tenements.

In October 1896, Outcault moved from Pulitzer's *New York World* to Hearst's *New York Journal*, taking the popular "Yellow Kid" feature with him.[3] Pulitzer countered by authorizing another artist, George Luks, to draw rival yellow kid characters. It was this very public battle between Hearst and Pulitzer—the leading practitioners of what then was called "the new journalism"—that inspired Wardman to coin "yellow journalism." Or so say historians such as Frank Luther Mott,[4] chroniclers of New York City journalism such as Allen Churchill[5] and Frederick Palmer,[6] admirers of Pulitzer such as Don C. Seitz,[7] and biographers of Hearst such as W. A. Swanberg,[8] John Tebbel,[9] and John K. Winkler.[10]

Left unstated by these sources is precisely when, and under what specific conditions and circumstances, Wardman first invoked the term.

The timing and circumstances are more than merely matters of trivial interest, and they are important for reasons beyond correcting and redressing the historical record.[11] As this chapter will show, the term emerged amid disdain and overt intolerance for the "new journalism" represented by Hearst and Pulitzer. The emergence and spread of "yellow journalism," moreover, coincided with a vigorous, well-publicized but little remembered and ultimately failed campaign in metropolitan New York to exclude the *New York Journal* and *New York World* from public and university libraries, reading rooms, social organizations, clubs, and other institutions. "Yellow journalism" was in fact the emotional and rhetorical centerpiece for the crusade, to which Wardman and other conservative editors lent ardent endorsement.

Understanding the circumstances of the first published use of "yellow journalism" thus offers fresh insights into *fin de siècle* New York City journalism, a lusty time when editors were often vigorous partisans, often eager to trade brickbats and insults, and not disinclined to urge or suggest the suppression of their rivals. It was also a time of angry debate about the flamboyant "new journalism" represented by Hearst and Pulitzer—and "new journalism" came to be called "yellow journalism."

This chapter presents compelling evidence that the first published reference to "yellow journalism" was, indeed, in Wardman's *New York Press*, but that the rivalry over the Outcault's "Yellow Kid" was *not* the immediate inspiration for the term. The first published use of "yellow journalism" came in January 1897, three months *after* Hearst and Pulitzer had begun publishing their rival "Yellow Kids."

Wardman seized upon "yellow journalism" not in commenting upon the Hearst-Pulitzer cartoon rivalry but after experimenting with at least one other turn of phrase in a search for a pithy and insulting substitute phrase for "new journalism." Wardman had offered "nude journalism," a term clearly derived from "new journalism" to suggest the absence of dignity and moral standards that supposedly defined the newspapers of Hearst and Pulitzer. But once Wardman settled on "yellow journalism," he invoked the term relentlessly in his editorial comments assailing the *Journal* and the *World*. Newspapers in New York and beyond soon took note. The *New York Tribune* borrowed the term in mid-February 1897—and credited the *Press* for having developed such a telling and felicitous phrase.[12] By mid-April 1897, the term had appeared in newspapers in Chicago, San Francisco, Richmond, and Providence, Rhode Island.

This chapter—which draws in part upon an examination of all issues of the *New York Press* from August 1896 to August 1987—also suggests that Wardman may not have been the very first to write or utter "yellow journalism." Close approximations of the term were in use by early 1897, as indicated in the letters of Richard Harding Davis, the war correspondent who at the time was on assignment for the *Journal* in Cuba. But the best case for the first *published* use of the phrase—and certainly the first sustained use of the phrase—goes to Wardman, an ascetic, Harvard-educated editor who in January 1897 had just turned thirty-one.

RIVAL VERSIONS

Before turning to Wardman and the emergence of "yellow journalism," it is important to address rival claims to first use of the phrase. There are three specific versions:

- That the term originated with an editorial written by Charles A. Dana, the venerable editor of the *New York Sun*.[13]
- That the term originated with Edward Oliver Wolcott, a United States senator from Colorado, who invoked the phrase at an after-dinner speech.[14]
- That the term originated with Wardman, in "an editorial blast" 2 September 1896, dismissing Hearst's attention-grabbing transcontinental bicycle relay race.[15]

Dana: Not the First

The case for Dana was stated in an article published in the magazine *Nineteenth Century* in August 1898, ten months after the editor's death. The author, Elizabeth L. Banks, described herself as a former writer for a yellow journal and characterized the genre as "a power for evil."[16] Without reference to sources, Banks described the supposed origins of the term this way: "The application of the term 'yellow' to a certain style of American journalism originated with Mr. Charles A. Dana, the late proprietor and editor of the *New York Sun*. . . . Dana, a journalist of the old school, who hated sensational journalism, wrote an editorial in the *Sun*, in which he noted the transfer of the 'Yellow Kid' to its new quarters, referring to the two papers as 'yellow journals' and their style of journalism as the 'yellow journalism.' Thereafter the *World* and *Journal* and all other sensational newspapers became known as 'yellow journals.'"[17]

Banks gave no date for the purported first use of the term, but suggested it was in mid-October 1896, when Outcault took the "Yellow Kid" from the *World* to the *Journal*. However, a thorough review of the *Sun* from late August 1896 to early May 1897 uncovered no reference in the newspaper's editorials to "yellow journalism" or analogous phrases. Dana did condemn the frenzied competition between Hearst and Pulitzer, writing in October 1896: "There was never before anywhere on earth such a rivalry, and, God willing, there never will be again after Mr. Pulitzer is dead or has gone mad, or after Mr. Hearst is tired out or has reluctantly come to his senses. It is a positive relief to turn to the *Journal of Commerce* or the *Evening Post*, without a picture except in the advertisements."[18] But his editorial page did not invoke "yellow journalism."

The term appeared occasionally in the headlines and news reports of the gray, conservative-looking *Sun* beginning in March 1897,[19] but the newspaper's editorials routinely invoked "new journalism" to describe the practices of Hearst and Pulitzer—and continued to do so weeks after Wardman had seized upon "yellow journalism."[20] If anything, Dana's *Sun* appears to have been a belated convert to the term. And Banks' claim that Dana was first to invoke the term cannot be sustained.[21]

Wolcott: Not the First

The case for Edward Wolcott was made casually, in a book of reminiscences by George Presbury Rowell, a longtime advertising agent. Rowell wrote that the "Yellow Kid" comic "was exploited so much, so voluminously and so continuously, that it became famous and led the papers that exploited it to be referred to by an after-dinner speaker somewhere as the 'Yellow Journals.' I think Senator Wolcott, of Colorado, was the man."[22]

Rowell's vague and modest claim finds no support from Wolcott's biographer, Thomas Fulton Dawson, who wrote that the senator "could be as sarcastic and caustic as any public man who lived, and he seemed to delight in speaking at the expense of the press, knowing of course that the press had at least an equal opportunity to reply in kind. . . . The yellow press was his especial aversion."[23] Dawson, however, neither claimed nor hinted that Wolcott coined or popularized the term.

The second volume of Dawson's biographic treatment of Wolcott includes the texts and lengthy excerpts from several of the senator's speeches, including his remarks about sensational journalism made 22 December 1897 to the New England Society of New York at Delmonico's restaurant. Dawson characterized Wolcott's comments about sensational journalism as "almost classic in their force, terseness, and cleverness." The senator on that occasion said: "The continued friction is largely generated both East and West by a certain modern type of newspaper. The plague may have started here, but it has spread and sprouted like the Canada thistle until it is a blight in Colorado, as it is a curse here and wherever it plants itself. . . . It knows no party, no honor, no virtue, and appeals only to the low and the base. It calls itself journalism, but its name is Pander and its color is yellow."[24]

The dinner in December 1897 may well have been the after-dinner speech to which Rowell referred in his reminiscences, and it probably represented Wolcott's first public reference to yellow journalism. In any event, it came eleven months after Wardman invoked "yellow kid journalism" in the *New York Press*. It seems unlikely that an attentive biographer such as Dawson would have overlooked, or have failed to mention, his subject's having originated a memorable and widely used term. Moreover, Wolcott's papers at the Colorado Historical Society offer no supporting evidence that he coined the term or invoked "yellow journalism" before January 1897. Therefore, Rowell's claim for Wolcott cannot be substantiated.

Not in September 1896

The remaining rival version is more specific. It was advanced in 1995 by Bill Blackbeard, an authority on the history of cartooning, in a book celebrating the centenary of the Yellow Kid. Blackbeard wrote that Wardman's first use of "yellow journalism" came "in an editorial blast leveled at the *Journal* on September 2, 1896," [25] near the end of a San Francisco-to-New York City bicycle relay sponsored by Hearst. The relay riders, Blackbeard wrote, were dressed in yellow, from head to toe. Thus the inspiration for Wardman, who "garnered the plaudits of his fellows by coining the term" yellow journalism.[26]

However, thorough and repeated searches of the contents of the *New York Press* on 2 September 1896—and for all dates that month—uncovered no "editorial blast," or any other story or commentary that invoked "yellow journalism," "yellow kid journalism" or a similar phrase.[27] Wardman, moreover, appears to have ignored the cross-country bicycle relay, which ended in New York City 7 September 1896.[28] There is, moreover, no evidence that editors of other conservative newspapers in New York City cheered Wardman or the *Press* for any deft turn of phrase in September 1896. A search of the issues of the *New York Sun* and the *New York Times* that month revealed no such commendation. The *New York Tribune* did applaud the *Press* for having "so felicitously" invoked "'yellow journalism',"[29]—but that comment was published in mid-February 1897, soon after Wardman had unleashed his barrage against the *Journal* and *World*.

Asked about the discrepancies, Blackbeard conceded in an interview with the author that he had no "direct referential verification" that the phrase "yellow journalism" had appeared in the *Press* 2 September 1896, as he had written. Blackbeard said it was his understanding that the reference appeared in an edition of the *Press* that was not preserved on microfilm. Blackbeard further said that he had been informed "on a third hand basis" about the existence of a clipping from the *Press* from that date—a clipping that supposedly contained the elusive reference to "yellow journalism." Blackbeard said he had asked for a copy of the clipping but was told it could not be located. "It would," Blackbeard said, "be awful nice to have" that clipping.[30]

Blackbeard's claim about the timing of first use is, therefore, unsubstantiated. The account also can be challenged on grounds that it is implausible. If Blackbeard's version is correct, it means that Wardman coined but then promptly and inexplicably abandoned a colorful and evocative term. It means that from September 1896 until late January 1897, Wardman inexplicably avoided his own inspiration because, throughout that period, he and his newspaper invoked "new journalism," not "yellow journalism," to deride the excesses of the *Journal* and the *World*.[31]

It seems exceedingly unlikely that Wardman would have invoked such a colorful phrase as "yellow journalism," immediately abandon its use, only to return to it months later—and then frequently and with gusto. Blackbeard's claim, therefore, cannot be supported.

AN EDITOR FORGOTTEN TO NEW YORK JOURNALISM

Although Wardman is a figure now largely lost to New York newspaper history, he was for a time a modest force in the city's journalism. The *New York Press*, which was founded in 1887, was vigorous in its pro-Republican, high-tariff stands.[32] Wardman was suspicious about immigrants from eastern and southern Europe, [33] warning about the potential loss of jobs to the newcomers.[34] Wardman also prevailed in a test of wills with the state legislature in 1905, refusing demands to reveal his newspaper's sources about a state judge whom the legislature had tried for misconduct in office.[35] He was quoted as telling legislators, who pressed him: "I refuse to answer. I refuse to commit that dishonor."[36]

Wardman was born in Salt Lake City on Christmas, 1865, and educated at Phillips-Exeter Academy and Harvard University.[37] He enrolled at Harvard in the fall of 1885, several months after Hearst was expelled,[38] and was graduated in 1888, a year ahead of his class.

While it is unlikely the two men crossed paths at Harvard, Wardman's disdain for Hearst seemed profound. A source for the enmity may have been partisan rivalry: The men were at odds, politically. Wardman's *Press*, for example, backed William McKinley, the Republican candidate for president in 1896 while Hearst's *Journal* backed William Jennings Bryan, the Democrat. Wardman's disdain also may have been grounded in Hearst's rumored overtures in 1896 to buy the *Press* for its Associated Press franchise.[39]

In any event, Wardman—who was described as tall, grim-jawed and showing his "Calvinistic ancestry in every line of his face"[40]—did little to conceal his dislike for Hearst and Hearst's journalism. Hostility was routinely apparent in the columns of the *Press*, which Wardman joined as managing editor in 1895.[41] He became editor in chief the next year[42] and took to taunting Hearst, Hearst's mother, and Hearst's support for Bryan in the 1896 election. Hearst's *Journal* was virtually alone among large-city Eastern newspapers in supporting Bryan's "free silver" candidacy,[43] which advocated the continued coinage of silver. Wardman disparaged Hearst as a mama's boy, as "Billy," and as "little Willie." He called Hearst's newspaper "our silverite, or silver-wrong, contemporary."[44]

Reacting in September 1896 to the *Journal*'s having published an illustration showing Anna Held, a dark-haired French actress with a "nymph-like form," posed in a negligee,[45] Wardman asserted: "Surprised is a mild term; amazed we are, in very sober truth, at the spectacle of such a refined and religious woman, as Mrs. Hearst is known to be, permitting little Willie, her son, to publish such a picture and such an account."[46] Wardman added: "If any man on The Press, the Sun or the Tribune had printed such a page as this his resignation would have required no deliberation. We are moved, therefore, to inquire whether there is any subtle connection between Free Silver and Free Salacity and, in the interests of 'new journalism,' to advise Mrs. Hearst to keep her maternal eye more closely fixed on her Willie-boy."[47]

The *New York Press'* lively daily gossip column, "On the Tip of the Tongue," taunted Hearst as the wealthy but unimaginative imitator of Pulitzer's methods and editorial positions:

> The funny thing about Hearst is that he came here to teach new journalism to Pulitzer, and that after dropping two millions he is trotting along admiringly behind Pulitzer, as if he had been trained to it all his life. If the World comes out for a beer tax on Monday, Willie follows him for a beer tax on Tuesday. It's the same way with trusts, police abuses, special commissioners, baby shows, and everything else. Willie has become a crazy Free Trader now. If Pulitzer should advocate an American emperor, Willie would say amen. And his leg-pullers would make him believe that was the way to put another nail in Pulitzer's coffin.[48]

Wardman found the "Yellow Kid" cartoon repellent but the Hearst-Pulitzer rivalry over the feature appears not to have been the immediate inspiration for his invoking the phrase, "yellow journalism." Indeed, the *Press*, in its first comment about the appearance of rival "yellow kids" in the *Journal* and *World*, quipped: "One of the kids was still-born, the other was stolen."[49] Late in 1896 Wardman assailed the *Journal* and the *World* as "fake mongers, chambers of horrors, cesspools, sloughs, purveyors of mendacity."[50] But the phrase "yellow journalism" had yet to appear in the *Press*.

FROM "NEW" TO "NUDE" TO "YELLOW" JOURNALISM

Wardman appears to have been especially disturbed by the appearance of the "Yellow Kid" on the *Journal*'s editorial page in a succession of slang-filled articles purporting to be excerpts from the character's diary as he toured Europe and the Middle East. "The 'new journalism,'" Wardman wrote in early January 1897, "should make an effort to keep the Yellow Kid off its editorial page."[51] Wardman by then had begun experimenting with other pithy turns of phrase. "The 'new journalism,'" he wrote in early January "continues to think up a varied assortment of new lies."[52] Later in the month, Wardman asked in a single-line editorial comment: "Why not call it nude journalism?"[53] It clearly was a play on "new journalism" and meant to suggest the absence of "even the veneer of decency."[54] Before long, however, Wardman seized upon the phrase "yellow-kid journalism," which soon was abbreviated to "yellow journalism."

On 18 January 1897, the *World* commented about reports of "bubonic plague" in India, suggesting the disease represented a threat to Europe "and it may even be communicated to America."[55] The *Journal* suggested in an editorial a few days later that while Europe might be threatened, "We have little to fear from the disease in the United States, where all the conditions of living are so antagonistic to its possible progress."[56] The following day, Wardman wrote: "No one need be disturbed over the 'new journalism' clamor about the possibility of the Indian plague ravaging these shores. The plague could not live an hour in this climate at this time of year."[57] He revisited the "clamor" on 23 January 1897, writing: "After an attack of yellow-kid journalism New Yorkers are not going to worry about the Bombay plague."[58]

The phrase "yellow-kid journalism" was soon modified, appearing eight days later as "the Yellow Journalism" in a small headline on the *Press*' editorial page, above an exchange item from a newspaper in Galveston, Texas. The item read: "When a Philadelphia man attempts to read a rank New York newspaper it makes him drunk." The headline was: "Victory for the Yellow Journalism."[59] The phrase also appeared that day in the *Press*' editorial page gossip column, "On the Tip of the Tongue."[60]

Precisely how Wardman and the *Press* landed on the term is not clear. The newspaper's own, brief version of the term's origins was unrevealing: "We called them Yellow because they are Yellow," it stated in 1898.[61] The reference may have been to decadence, given that the color yellow was sometimes associated with depraved literature in the 1890s.[62] Moreover, pejorative expressions approximating "yellow journalism" were circulating among newspaper correspondents in early January 1897.[63] Richard Harding Davis, then on assignment to Cuba for the *New*

York Journal, complained in a letter to his mother, dated 10 January 1897, about the "yellow kid school" of journalists.[64] He mentioned "the new school of yellow kid journalists" and "yellow kid reporters" in a letter dated 16 January 1897—a week before Wardman's first published use of "yellow-kid journalism."[65] Frederic Remington, the artist who accompanied Davis on the assignment to Cuba, wrote to a friend in late January 1897 about the poor reproduction quality of his illustrations "in a Yellow Kid journal."[66]

The casual use of such phrases by Davis and Remington—neither of whom claimed to have coined "yellow journalism"—makes it clear that approximations of "yellow journalism" or "yellow-kid journalism" were in use among newsmen about the time Wardman landed upon the term. But even if Wardman did not coin the phrase, the evidence is persuasive that he was the first to publish it—and was certainly the first to invoke "yellow journalism" in a sustained manner.

THE *PRESS* POUNDS AWAY

After landing on the pithy, evocative description, Wardman turned to it often during the first half of February 1897, as suggested by the following sequence of quips and commentaries that appeared in the *Press*:

- "The Yellow Journalism is now so overripe that the little insects which light upon it quickly turn yellow, too."[67]
- "The tint of a broiled-alive crustacean is an impotent understudy to the ever-deepening hues of the Yellow Journalism."[68]
- "Even if real color photography has at last been discovered, the Yellow Journalism won't have use for it."[69]
- "The Yellow Journalism finds a parallel in the bubonic plague. Even the vultures that feed on it are dying from it."[70]
- "To some it will be a matter of profound regret to learn that the Spaniards have captured only one of the Cuban correspondents of the Yellow Journalism."[71]

Wardman capped the barrage against "yellow journalism" with an editorial titled "Yellow Lies." It read: "So far we have not observed that yellow journalism has found any difficulty in convicting itself of all the crimes it charges against itself. Indeed, the task has been so easy that we wonder [why] yellow journalism takes the trouble to gather so much proof of its turpitude. It would be far less troublesome and quite as convincing for it to head the first page every day with a conspicuous 'display' line like this:

YELLOW JOURNALISM
IS A LIAR AND WE ARE IT.[72]

At times it appeared as if Wardman took specific aim at Hearst in denouncing "the Yellow Journalism." For example, Wardman alluded to readers of "the Yellow Journal" in this editorial comment in late February:

> It now requires so much space in the columns of the Yellow Journalism to explain that the features of the preceding issue were made up of bogus news and forged interviews that the Yellow Journal readers have a right to demand, it seems to us, that a special edition should be issued daily to give some of the news for which there is no room in any of the regular editions of the Yellow Journalism.[73]

But were he troubled by Wardman's assaults, Hearst failed to show it, at least not in the editorials of the *Journal*. Hearst in early 1897 was far more eager to poke fun at the *Sun* and its venerable editor, Dana. For example, the *Journal* published a cartoon taunting Dana as asleep in bed while the enterprising *Journal* gathered news about the sinking of a French steamer off the East Coast in March 1897. "If you see it in the Sun," the *Journal*'s caption read, "you're lucky."[74]

BACKLASH AGAINST THE YELLOW PRESS

Meanwhile, a broad backlash against the *Journal* and the *World* was gathering force, a movement doubtless sustained and bolstered by Wardman's frequent denunciation of yellow journalism. The makings of a boycott against the yellow press appeared with the appointment in December 1896 of a committee of the New York Ministers' Association; the panel was charged with considering ways of countering "the pernicious influence of the so-called 'New Journalism.'"[75] The committee's report in late January 1897 deplored newspapers that were "so low in moral tone as to make their toleration and success a reproach upon the community" and underscored "the importance of patronizing only such newspapers as manifestly aim to be clean and wholesome."[76] While the report stopped short of proposing specific measures against the *Journal* and the *World*, the next, short step would be to boycott the yellow journals as corrupting forces.[77] The first to take such a step was the Newark Free Public Library. On the recommendation of the librarian, Frank P. Hill, the trustees voted 4 February 1897 to ban the *Journal* and the *World* and removed the newspapers from the library's files.[78]

The *Press* applauded the library's move to designate the newspapers a public menace: "In expelling from its reading room and files the New York exponents of yellow journalism the Newark Public Library has begun a reform which doubtless will be continued by similar bodies in other cities. In decent public esteem yellow journalism occupies the same place as brothels."[79] It is clear that the *Press* expected the boycott to spread, that "many other moral and respectable institutions [will follow] the example of the Newark Public Library."[80] The *Sun* likewise predicted the boycott would "be pursued by decent institutions . . . generally. It is a movement whose natural impulse is in the disgust and indignation which have been increasing in all quarters against the licentiousness, the vulgarity, and the criminal spirit exhibited by those shameless papers with an effrontery almost without example in the history of journalism."[81]

The boycott did intensify, spreading swiftly to other public and university libraries, reading rooms, clubs, and social organizations in New York City, New Jersey, and Connecticut. By mid-March, the *Journal* and *World* had been banned from the Century Club and the Merchants' Club in New York, the New York Yacht Club, the reading room of the New York City Mission and Tract Society, the Harlem Branch of the YMCA, the Montauk Club of Brooklyn, the Flatbush Young Republican Club in Brooklyn, the Public Library in Bridgeport, Connecticut, [82] as well as the reading room at Yale University Library.[83] "Hardly a day passes now but some library or some club joins the revolt," the *Sun* reported. "In many institutions where the *World* and *Journal* are still admitted they have been for some time . . . kept under lock and key, to be brought out on the express demand of adults only."[84]

The boycott seemed dizzying in its speed and impressive in its sweep.[85] The trade journal *Fourth Estate* called it a "battle royal . . . a tornado of hard breathing and a whirlwind of dust."[86] By early May 1897, nearly ninety libraries, reading rooms, and other organizations had, by the *Press*' count, "quarantined their members and patrons from the contagion."[87] Wardman cheered such developments and predicted the boycott would signal "the fall of yellow journalism." [88] "The places where Yellow Journals are admitted," he wrote, "are rapidly narrowing down to prisons, dives and brothels."[89] The public, he exclaimed, "has discovered the surest and swiftest way to put down the infamy of Yellow Journalism. It is to expel the Yellow Journals from reputable society."[90] As for the *Press*, he wrote, "We want no Yellow readers."[91]

It was hardly a salutary time for tolerance and free expression. The Rev. Dr. W.H.P. Faunce, speaking at the twenty-fifth anniversary dinner of the New York Society for the Suppression of Vice, declared, "Would to God the exclusion [of the yellow press] might become universal and extend to every family in the land."[92] But murmurs of dissent percolated about the tactic of banning newspapers. One New York clergyman warned that the boycott could backfire. "To denounce them in the pulpit, to sweep them out of clubs and reading rooms, only gives them a free advertisement," he said of the yellow journals. "You cannot touch their sense of decency. They are too cynical."[93] The *New York Times* reported the Union Club was reluctant to join the boycott, in part because Hearst was a member. The *Times* quoted the organization's vice president as saying, "If Mr. Hearst is good enough to be a member of the Union Club, I do not see why his paper should not be good enough to be read in the club."[94]

At least a few newspapers deplored the movement. In Kansas, the *Topeka State Journal* scoffed at the "prudish library managers [who] have shut out certain New York newspapers from their files." The New York yellow press, the *State Journal* said, "has its faults as all good things have, but it also gets important and invaluable news which the other little bankrupt whining New York papers can't get."[95] *Fourth Estate* was tentative in its appraisal of the boycott noted: "The idea that it is not proper to read a paper is a dangerous one to have abroad, and, undoubtedly, both of these papers will soon or later eliminate the sort of matter which has led to their expulsion."[96]

But as the boycott spread, the yellow journals turned to countermeasures, some of them quite clever. The *World* was far more confrontational than the *Journal* in answering the boycott, dismissing it as a "malicious but impotent assault."[97] Rival newspapers that cheered the boycott were ridiculed as "doomed rats"[98] motivated by their "jealousy" of the *World*'s "splendid success."[99] The *Journal*, on the other hand, generally avoided direct counter-attacks and instead wrapped itself in the cloth, notably on Sundays when its editorial columns were opened to clergymen. Topics such as these were discussed on the *Journal*'s editorial pages on Sundays in May 1897: "The Church and the Mass,"[100] "Biblical Criticism in Latter-Day Pulpits,"[101] "The Right to Think,"[102] and "The Parable of Spring."[103] Few if any of the clergy's editorials addressed the boycott or the press of New York City. In another shrewd move, the *Journal* arranged for Mark Twain to join its coterie of writers covering Queen Victoria's diamond jubilee in June 1897.[104] Twain may have been unaware that the *Journal*'s anti-boycott offensive "was to feature some eminent authors" in its columns.[105]

In the end, it was the vigor and attraction of its newsgathering that permitted New York's yellow press to outlast the boycott. The *Journal* and the *World*, though bitter enemies, were brighter, more aggressive, more colorful, and on the whole far more interesting than their conservative rivals. It is difficult to read the issues of the *Journal* and the *World* from the first half of 1897 and not be struck by their enterprise and their lusty self-promotion. They devoted considerable resources to reporting the major events that spring and summer—the brief war between Greece and Turkey over Crete,[106] the heavyweight boxing championship match between Robert Fitzsimmons and James Corbett, Victoria's jubilee in

London, the Klondike gold rush, and a mystery—eventually solved by the *Journal*—of the dismembered male body that washed up in the East River in June 1897.[107]

To be sure, the *Journal* published a fair amount of material that appears frivolous more than 100 years later. Outcault's "Yellow Kid" was depicted in the *Journal* as taking a rollicking, round-the-world trip during the first half of 1897, calling on the likes of Bismarck[108] and frolicking at the Louvre with the Venus de Milo.[109] The *Journal*'s Sunday supplement, where most of its oddball articles appeared, included such unlikely reports as the purported discovery of the "last will and testament of Job,"[110] and the supposed receipt of messages from Mars.[111] It also published drivel that questioned whether modern photography incited women to commit brutal crime.[112]

But conservative papers of the time carried a fair amount of oddball material as well. Sea serpents were a particular fascination of the time.[113] Wardman's *Press* reported in October 1896 the capture of such a creature and accompanied the article with a five-column illustration of a bug-eyed monster and its menacing, spear-like tongue.[114] The decidedly conservative *Washington Post* published in 1899 a three-column illustration supposedly showing "fossilized remains of a gigantic sea serpent."[115]

In any event, predictions that the boycott would end with the repudiation of yellow journalism went unfulfilled. The yellow journals effectively overwhelmed the boycott with energetic and aggressive newsgathering. The boycott, moreover, fell victim to its self-limiting nature: After banning the *Journal* and the *World*, what else could the libraries and clubs and social organizations do to punish the newspapers? There was simply no next step. The successive bans did for a time project a sense of rapidly gathering momentum. But once the protest was made, it permitted no opportunities for additional measures. The boycott withered.[116]

Ironically, the boycott may have provided a small *stimulus* to sales of the *Journal* and *World*.[117] *Fourth Estate* reported that many people "who had read them in the clubs [began] buying them for their personal use. The crusade of the clubs soon collapsed, and there has been nothing more heard of it in a long time." [118]

Wardman, too, ultimately relented. The editorial assaults on yellow journalism came less frequently in May and June 1897,[119] and the *Press* seemed finally to surrender on 1 July 1897. The *Journal* and *World* were at that time vigorously pursuing their respective inquiries into the torso murder mystery, a sensation that Wardman found macabre. He wrote:

> The Yellow Journals are at it again harder than ever. For a few weeks after they were banished from decent society, they clothed their repulsive bodies with respectable raiment and reeked with sanctimonious hypocrisy. Like the habitual drunkard who falls back into the gutter after a temporary "reform," however, or the wanton who fails to be illicit only because of lack of opportunity, they have

plunged into new debaucheries, more frightful than anything that sullied them previous to their "conversion." . . . Bah! It turns the stomach. But perhaps it is better to have them so. Down in their filth they can pollute only those who go down to them. They cannot repent. They cannot clean themselves. So let them stay down where they always have belonged and always will belong.[120]

THE DIFFUSION OF "YELLOW JOURNALISM"

Though it dissolved in quiet failure, the boycott did leave a lasting contribution, that of helping to secure a place for "yellow journalism" in the lexicon of American journalism.[121] The term was swiftly adopted.[122] First to do so was probably the *New York Tribune*,[123] which commented favorably on the *Press*' use of "yellow journalism"[124] and soon began calling the *World* "the senior yellow" and the *Journal* the "younger yellow."[125] Readers also took note of the evocative phrase. "I feel indebted to you for the editorial criticisms that you are making on 'Yellow Journalism,'" said a letter writer to the *Press*. "I have read at sundry times enough of this 'stuff' thoroughly to disgust me. . . . 'Yellow journalism' is to morals as yellow fever is to life. . . . Keep on, you are doing good work and your principles will prevail and be respected when 'Yellow Journalism' has long ceased to be a living stench in the nostrils of respected and respectable American citizens."[126]

By mid-March, a reference to "yellow journalism" had appeared in the *San Francisco Call*. "They call it 'Yellow Journalism' in New York," the newspaper said, "but from the noise it makes 'yullen' would be better."[127] The *Providence Journal* in Rhode Island discussed possible consequences of the boycott for what it called "the yellow journals," predicting that advertisers would withdraw their patronage and "then will come a sudden end to the new journalism."[128] The *Richmond Dispatch* also took note of the "great reaction taking place against the sort of 'yellow' journalism that is typified by two New York papers" and declared that the boycott had "come none too soon. May it be blessed with complete success, and thereby benefit not only the chief sinners, but the general public."[129] The *Chicago Times-Herald* offered a variation of the term "yellow journalism" in taking note of the boycott against "the journalistic bleached blondes of Gotham. This is not a good year for peroxide journalism."[130]

The diffusion of "yellow journalism" was secured when the *Journal* embraced the term in an editorial in mid-May 1898, during the Spanish-American War. In doing so, the *Journal* identified itself with patriotic icons:

Every innovator the world has known for its good has been 'yellow' to what Draper describes as 'that mass of common men who have impeded the progress of civilization in every country in every age. Caesar was yellow to the plutocrats of the Roman Senate. Napoleon was yellow to the traditional strategists whom he routed by scorning their rules. Washington was yellow to the Tories, and so were Jefferson and Franklin and Paine, and all the bold men who created this republic. The United States is doing an extremely yellow thing in waging this war to help another people instead of to fill its own pockets. And the sun in heaven is yellow—the sun which is to this earth what the *Journal* is to American journalism.[131]

CONCLUSION

This chapter has offered specific and compelling evidence about the date and the context of what likely was the earliest published use of the term "yellow journalism": It appeared first in Ervin Wardman's *New York Press* in late January 1897. Wardman, before seizing upon "yellow journalism," had experimented with at least one other phrase—specifically, "nude journalism"—to replace "new journalism", which at the time was commonly associated with the newspapers of Hearst and Pulitzer. "Yellow journalism" was undeniably a more evocative, more clever, and more disparaging term than "new" or "nude" journalism, and such characteristics doubtless contributed to its swift diffusion.

Establishing the date and circumstances of the first published use of "yellow journalism" should prove useful in several respects. For one, it is inherently valuable to set straight the historical record, to resolve the rival and conflicting versions about the emergence and etiology of "yellow journalism." After all, references to Blackbeard's unsubstantiated version have appeared in the news media.[132]

In addition, fixing the date and circumstances of the first published use of "yellow journalism" should enable media historians to avoid committing small but annoying errors related to the origins of the term. Swanberg, for example, wrote that Hearst, in organizing the San Francisco-to-New York bicycle relay in late summer 1896, sought "to blow up a hurricane of publicity, turning the term 'yellow journalism' from opprobrium to praise."[133] But as this chapter has demonstrated, the term "yellow journalism" had yet to appear in print at the time of the 1896 transcontinental bicycle relay.

More significantly, ascertaining the context of the first published use is important because it makes clear that the emergence and diffusion of "yellow journalism" was *not* directly associated with the Hearst-Pulitzer rivalry over the "yellow kid" cartoon. Indeed, the first sustained use of "yellow journalism" came three months after Hearst and Pulitzer began offering readers the rival "yellow kids." Rather, the appearance and spread of the term coincided with what became a vigorous effort in metropolitan New York to denigrate and marginalize the *Journal* and the *World*, to exclude them from clubs and reading rooms. It was a campaign to which conservative newspapers invested great hope. As such, this chapter has demonstrated that incivility, coarse exchanges, and manifest intolerance were features of New York City newspapering at the end of the nineteenth century.

The ultimate futility of the 1897 boycott against the yellow press also signaled the more general difficulty of sustaining organized efforts to counter Hearst's flamboyant style of journalism. Nearly forty years later, a small group calling itself the League Against Yellow Journalism was established in San Francisco. There were in the League's objectives clear if unintended echoes of the 1897 boycott: It described itself as "devoted entirely to educating people to demand truthfulness and decency from the daily press and to coordinate protest against yellow journalism in general, and the Hearst newspapers in particular."[134] It accused Hearst of endeavoring "to create war hysteria, particularly against Japan," of supporting fascism, fostering racial hatred, and using "his newspapers and magazines . . . to stimulate morbid curiosity in murders, seductions, drunken brawls and all phases of immorality."[135]

The League, though severely underfunded,[136] envisioned itself a statewide force. It proposed to support its activities by the sale of stamps that proclaimed: "I Don't Read Hearst."[137] It also arranged to sell copies of *Imperial Hearst: A Social Biography*, a polemic by Ferdinand Lundberg published in 1936.[138] By mid-1939, however, the League Against Yellow Journalism had lapsed into inactivity.[139]

Wardman, meanwhile, kept a modest profile for most of his career.[140] He served in the Army during the Spanish-American War, enlisting as a private and gaining promotion to first lieutenant before his discharge.[141] He returned to edit the *Press* until its was folded by Frank A. Munsey into the *Sun* in July 1916. Wardman was the *Sun*'s publisher until Munsey merged the title with the *Herald* in 1920.[142] He was a vice president in the Sun-Herald Corp. at the time of his death in 1923 from complications of pneumonia.

"Like many another anonymous worker in journalism," the *New York Times* said in a posthumous editorial tribute to Wardman, "his name was not often conspicuously before the public, and he was content to sink his personality in that of the papers he served."[143] The *Times* added: "While broad-minded and always courteously considerate of the opinions of others, he had strong convictions of his own and stood up for them with entire directness and fearlessness. . . . He could hit hard, but was always ready for a friendly handclasp afterward."[144]

Ironically, perhaps, Wardman's contribution of "yellow journalism" was little remembered at his death. Obituaries in the *New York Times*, *New York Herald*, and Hearst's *New York American*[145] made no mention of Wardman's having popularized the term. The *Tribune* remembered, however. "Mr. Wardman," it said, "coined the phrase 'yellow journalism' and fastened it into the language of the late '90s when he was writing many editorials on the subject. He was a well-informed writer and a pungent and aggressive one."[146]

NOTES

1. The origins of the term were the source of speculation as long ago as 1898. See, for example, "Note and Comment," *Cincinnati Times-Star* (12 March 1898): 4. The editorial stated in part: "How such despicable methods [of journalism] came to be termed yellow has not been fully established. A yellow flag designates a quarantined district, a disease infected district and other places to be avoided. Yellow fever is accompanied by black vomit. . . . Sulphur is yellow and the yellow journalists may be homesick and seeking to establish the environment of Hades. . . . And last but not least, yellowness means jealousy. Jealous because it cannot get the actual happenings, a yellow journal makes its own news."

2. See, for example, Donald Paneth, *The Encyclopedia of American Journalism* (New York: Facts on File Publications, 1983), 506.

3. The first appearance of the yellow kid cartoon in the *Journal* was Sunday, 18 October 1896. See "McFadden's Row of Flats," *New York Journal* (18 October 1896): 5.

4. Mott wrote: "The figure of the silly [Yellow Kid] fellow, with his toothless, vacant grin and his flaring yellow dress, struck some of the critics of the new sensationalism represented by the *Journal* and the *World* as symbolical of that type of journalism; Ervin Wardman, of the *Press*, referred to New York's 'yellow press' . . . it stuck, and eventually became an accepted term in the language. See Frank Luther Mott, *American Journalism: A History: 1690–1960*, 3d ed. (New York: Macmillan, 1962), 526.

5. Allen Churchill, *Park Row* (New York: Rinehart and Company, 1958), 82. He wrote: "Like everyone else on Park Row, Ervin Wardman, editor of the New York Press, watched with fascination as the rival Yellow Kids slugged it out. Wardman one day went further by characterizing the contest between the World and the Journal as Yellow Journalism, a description so completely apt that it has remained to this day. When the sensitive Pulitzer heard this designation, he cringed. Hearst was delighted." Hearst and his supporters ultimately embraced the term. See, among others, James Creelman, *On the Great Highway* (Boston: Lothrop, 1901), 176–178.

6. Frederick Palmer, "Hearst and Hearstism," *Collier's* (29 September 1906): 16.

7. Don C. Seitz, *Joseph Pulitzer: His Life and Letters* (New York: Simon and Schuster, 1924), 232. Seitz was the *World*'s business manager.

8. W. A. Swanberg, *Citizen Hearst: A Biography of William Randolph Hearst* (New York: Charles Scribner's Sons, 1961), 82. Swanberg wrote: "With Outcault now drawing yellow kids for the *Journal* and another artist, George Luks, drawing yellow kids for the *World*, the term 'yellow journalism' was born.

9. John Tebbel, *The Life and Good Times of William Randolph Hearst* (New York: E. P. Dutton and Company Inc., 1952), 120–121. Tebbel wrote: "While the battle of the Yellow Kids went on, to the increasing profit of both Hearst and Pulitzer, the other New York papers, whose motives were certainly far from unselfish, sneered loftily at the struggle. Ervin Wardman, editor of the *New York Press*, a paper subsidized by a group of high-tariff Republicans, and naturally a

bitter opponent of the Democratic low-tariff *Journal*, characterized the contest as 'yellow journalism,' thereby contributing a phrase to the language which far outlasted its inventor."

10. John K. Winkler, *W. R. Hearst: An American Phenomenon* (New York: Simon and Schuster, 1928), 109–110.

11. Some descriptions of the emergence of the phrase "yellow journalism" are in error. See, for example, the entry for "yellow journalism" in Mitchel P. Roth, *Historical Dictionary of War Journalism* (Westport, CT: Greenwood Press, 1997), 357. Roth wrote: "The term 'yellow journalism' refers to the *New York World*'s use of a yellow-ink cartoon strip on its front page." The cartoon appeared in the *World*'s Sunday supplement.

12. "Wise Limitations of the War Power," *New York Tribune* (18 February 1897): 6.

13. See Elizabeth L. Banks, "American 'Yellow Journalism,'" *Nineteenth Century* 44 (August 1898): 328–329.

14. George Presbury Rowell, *Forty Years An Advertising Agent: 1865–1905* (New York: Printer's Ink Publishing Co., 1906), 432.

15. Bill Blackbeard, "The Yellowing of Journalism: The Journal-Examiner Bicycle Marathon versus the Yellow Kid (1896)," in Richard F. Outcault, *The Yellow Kid: A Centennial Celebration of the Kid Who Started the Comics* (Northampton, MA: Kitchen Sink Press, 1995), 59.

16. Banks, "American 'Yellow Journalism,'" 330.

17. Banks, "American 'Yellow Journalism,'" 328–329.

18. "Notes on the New Journalism," *New York Sun* (21 October 1896): 6.

19. See "Vile Newspapers Put Out," *New York Sun* (10 March 1897): 1, and "Yellow Journalism Denounced," *New York Sun* (23 March 1897): 1.

20. See, for example, "A Bill to Suppress Outrage," *New York Sun* (27 February 1897): 6, and "The Outcasts," *New York Sun* (22 March 1897): 6.

21. Banks' claim that Dana "hated sensational journalism" cannot be supported either. The *Sun* in early 1897 often published above the fold on its front page articles such as these: "Suicides Due to Women," *New York Sun* (2 January 1897): 1; "Bullets Reform A Thief," *New York Sun* (10 March 1897): 1; "New Husband Slew Her," *New York Sun* (14 March 1897): 1; "Arrested for Playing Marbles," *New York Sun* (17 March 1897): 1; "Explosion in a Bathhouse," *New York Sun* (22 March 1897): 1; "Quay Tackled a Panther," *New York Sun* (23 March 1897): 1; "Suicide Found in a Boat," *New York Sun* (30 March 1897): 1; and "Office Cashier Arrested," *New York Sun* (1 May 1897): 1.

22. Rowell, *Forty Years An Advertising Agent*, 432.

23. Thomas Fulton Dawson, *The Life and Character of Edward Oliver Wolcott*, vol. 1 (New York: Knickerbocker Press, 1911), 478.

24. Dawson, *The Life and Character of Edward Oliver Wolcott*, 500–501. See also, Dawson, *The Life and Character of Edward Oliver Wolcott*, vol. 2 (New York: Knickerbocker Press, 1911), 553. See also, "Senator Wolcott's Address," *New York Times* (23 December 1897): 2, and "Wolcott's Plea for the West," *New York Herald* (23 December 1897): 6.

25. Blackbeard, "The Yellowing of Journalism," 59.

26. Blackbeard, "The Yellowing of Journalism," 59.

27. The author and three research assistants conducted separate searches of the contents of the *New York Press* from August 1896 to January 1897. None of the searches uncovered a reference to the phrase before 23 January 1897.

28. It is unlikely that Wardman would have delivered such "an editorial blast" several days *before* the relay reached New York City. The *Journal*, moreover, reported the last leg of the relay on an inside page. See "Welcome to the Last Courier in the Relay," *New York Journal* (8 September 1896): 3.

29. "Wise Limitations of War Power," *New York Tribune*.

30. Bill Blackbeard, telephone interview with author, March 2000.

31. See, for example, "Journalistic Indecency," *New York Press* (22 September 1896): 4; untitled editorial page comment, *New York Press* (11 December 1896): 6; untitled editorial page comment, *New York Press* (3 January 1897): 6; untitled editorial page comment, *New York Press* (4 January 1897): 4, and untitled editorial page comment, *New York Press* (16 January 1897): 4.

32. In its inaugural issue, the *Press* promised to be "'a newspaper for busy people, a fair paper to all people, a clean paper, and a straightforward, outspoken Republican paper.'" See "Note and Comment," *Fourth Estate* (9 December 1897): 6. See also, "New York Press in New Home," *Fourth Estate* (26 April 1902): 4.

33. See, for example, "Socialism and Immigration," *New York Press* (8 February 1897): 4.

34. See "More Work, Not Less, Wanted," *New York Press* (18 February 1897): 6. The editorial stated: "What the American people want now is more work, not less. They can get it by restricting in our market the competition of goods made by cheap labor abroad and by restricting the immigration of that cheap labor which, pouring into our country, drives out of employment American citizens."

35. See Wardman's obituary, "Ervin Wardman, Publisher, Dies," *New York Times* (14 January 1923): sec. 2, p. 6. See also, "Some Events of the Year," *Fourth Estate* (13 January 1906): 14.

36. "Will Not Commit Dishonor," *Fourth Estate* (22 July 1905): 11.

37. "Ervin Wardman, Publisher, Dies," *New York Times*.

38. See Swanberg, *Citizen Hearst*, 32–33.

39. See "One Cent World," *Fourth Estate* (13 February 1896): 1. The report said: "The rumor that Hearst will buy, or has bought, the New York *Press* is revived and denied. The fact that he would undoubtedly like an Associated Press franchise . . . is given as the foundation of the report that is denied." Hearst's *Journal* gained an Associated Press franchise in 1897 by acquiring the fading *New York Advertiser*.

40. "Ervin Wardman, 'Sun'-'Herald' Executive, Dies," *New York Tribune* (14 January 1923): 6.

41. Wardman began his career in 1888 as a reporter for the *New York Tribune*. See "Ervin Wardman, 'Sun'-'Herald' Executive, Dies," *New York Tribune*.

42. See "The Year's Record, " *Fourth Estate* (7 January 1897): 4. The trade journal described Wardman as "one of the brightest of the young men of the profession."

43. Swanberg, *Citizen Hearst*, 84–85.

44. See "Journalistic Indecency," *New York Press* (22 September 1896): 6.

45. See "Mlle. Anna Held Receives Alan Dale Attired in a 'Nightie,'" *New York Journal* (20 September 1896): 35. The illustration was not especially reveal-

ing: Held was shown in a rather chaste pose, her hands clasped in front of her chest. The illustration was not prominently displayed in the *Journal*, appearing on a page inside a Sunday supplement. A week earlier, the *Journal* devoted a page to reports about novelties in night gowns and chemises. See, "Fall Fashions in Underclothes," *New York Journal* (13 September 1896): 27.

46. "Journalistic Indecency," *New York Press*.

47. "Journalistic Indecency," *New York Press*.

48. "On the Tip of the Tongue: Me, Too, Willie," *New York Press* (22 January 1897): 4.

49. "On the Tip of the Tongue: The Yellow Kids," *New York Press* (26 October 1896): 6. The item also stated: "The most serious affair of modern colored journalism is the conflict of the yellow kids in the World and Journal. Each is merely kidding the other. The unfortunates who read these Sunday magazines of fiction are the sufferers. There never was any wit in 'Say!' and 'See?'"

50. "Sunday Newspapers," *New York Press* (12 December 1896): 6.

51. Untitled editorial page comment, *New York Press* (8 January 1897): 6.

52. Untitled editorial page comment, *New York Press* (3 January 1897): 6.

53. Untitled editorial page comment, *New York Press* (21 January 1897): 6.

54. "On the Tip of the Tongue: Flayed Alive," *New York Press* (16 February 1897): 6.

55. "The Menace of the Plague," *New York World* (18 January 1897): 6. The editorial also said, "But neither Europe nor America, now that both are tolerably clean, will ever suffer again the ravages wrought in earlier and more ignorant centuries."

56. "The Bubonic Plague in India," *New York Journal* (21 January 1897): 6.

57. Untitled editorial page comment, *New York Press* (22 January 1897): 4.

58. Untitled editorial page comment, *New York Press* (23 January 1897): 4.

59. "Victory for the Yellow Journalism," *New York Press* (31 January 1897): 6.

60. "On the Tip of the Tongue: Beginning Low," *New York Press* (31 January 1897): 6. The item referred to a young man named Adam who was seeking work and "would be willing to start very low. I do not know how he could possibly start lower than by obtaining employment in yellow journalism."

61. "On the Tip of the Tongue: Where 'Yellow Journalism' Came From," *New York Press* (1 March 1898): 6. The *Press* claimed on another occasion to have "enriched the language with the term Yellow Journalism." See "Cowardice as a Philosophy," *New York Press* (14 March 1898): 6.

62. The literary magazine *Yellow Book*, which first appeared in April 1894, was seen to embody the sense of *fin de siècle* decadence. See Larzer Ziff, *The American 1890s: Life and Times of a Lost Generation* (Lincoln, NE: University of Nebraska Press, 1966), 132–133. Moreover, the *New York Press* in late September 1896 noted that "the favorite color this season" was yellow, adding: "Notwithstanding that it is the hue of jealousy, of decadent literature, of biliousness and other unpleasantness, the American woman has decided she will wear yellow this autumn and winter." See "Yellow Is To Prevail," *New York Press* (27 September 1896): 26. Interestingly, during a cool and rainy summer more than 100 years later, some New Yorkers took to wearing what the *New York Times* called "sunny yellow"—a cheery response to the gloomy weather. Bill Cunningham, "Making Like the Sun," *New York Times* (6 August 2000): 5, 6.

63. Journalists may have referred to each other as "yellow dog" years before the emergence of "yellow journalism." *Fourth Estate* said in 1898: "The term 'yellow' which has been applied to progressive journalists of various sorts antidates by centuries the seemingly ancient custom of speaking of a fellow journalist as a yellow dog." See "Note and Comment," *Fourth Estate* (30 June 1898): 7.

64. Richard Harding Davis, letter to Rebecca Harding Davis, 10 January 1897, Richard Harding Davis Collection, Alderman Library of American Literature, University of Virginia.

65. Davis, letter to Rebecca Harding Davis, 16 January 1897, Richard Harding Davis Collection, Alderman Library.

66. Frederic Remington, letter to Poultney Bigelow, 28 January 1897, cited in Allen P. Splete and Marilyn D. Splete, *Frederic Remington – Selected Letters* (New York: Abbeville Press, 1988), 219.

67. Untitled editorial page comment, *New York Press* (2 February 1897): 4.

68. Untitled editorial page comment, *New York Press* (5 February 1897): 4.

69. Untitled editorial page comment, *New York Press* (6 February 1897): 4.

70. Untitled editorial page comment, *New York Press* (9 February 1897): 4.

71. Untitled editorial page comment, *New York Press* (14 February 1897): 6. The reference was to the arrest of the *World*'s Sylvester Scovel, who was accused of communicating with the Cuban insurgents. His arrest was prominently reported in the *World* and in many other U.S. newspapers. Scovel was released in March 1897. For an account of Scovel's arrest and time in jail, see Joyce Milton, *The Yellow Kids: Foreign Correspondents in the Heyday of Yellow Journalism* (New York: Harper & Row, 1989), 146–152.

72. "Yellow Lies," *New York Press* (20 February 1897): 6.

73. Untitled editorial page comment, *New York Press* (24 February 1897): 6.

74. "If You See It in the Sun, You're Lucky," *New York Journal* (20 March 1897): 3. The caption was a play on the *Sun*'s motto, "If you see it in the *Sun*, it's so."

75. See "The Duty of the Press," *New York Times* (26 January 1897): 12.

76. Cited in "The Duty of the Press," *New York Times*.

77. Wardman later wrote, "It was the ministry which first sounded the alarm against the evils of Yellow Journalism. To the assistance of the church have come now the public libraries, the schools, and even the judges of our higher courts." See "Fighting Yellow Journalism," *New York Press* (7 March 1897): 6. However, the *New York Times* reported in March 1897 that members of various social and literary clubs in New York had been weighing for some time "a movement . . . to prohibit the further introduction of copies of these [yellow] sheets in the club buildings." See "Freak Journals Reprobated," *New York Times* (3 March 1897): 10.

78. See "Freak Journals Reprobated," *New York Times*. See also "'World' and 'Journal' Tabooed," *Newark* [NJ] *Evening News* (25 February 1897), included in the Newark Free Public Library scrapbook, 1889–1900. The *New York Sun* quoted Hill as saying about the ban, "We consider that for young men and women and boys and girls to read those papers was to do themselves harm, and we have concluded to remove, as far as we might, a cause of harm from our younger patrons." See "Leprous New Journalism," *New York Sun* (undated), included in the Newark Free Public Library scrapbook, 1889–1900.

79. Untitled editorial page comment, *New York Press* (26 February 1897): 6.

80. Untitled editorial page comment, *New York Press* (27 February 1897): 6. The *Press* later described the decision of the Newark Free Public Library officials as "moved simply by their own disgust, and [they] did not know they were acting in accord with a widespread public sentiment." See "Yellow Journalism Denounced Everywhere," *New York Press* (3 May 1897): 5.

81. See "The End is Approaching," *New York Sun* (10 March 1897): 6. The *Sun* also said: "These publications are no more competitors of decent journals than dealers in pornographic literature are competitors with the regular, decent, and honorable book trade."

82. These decisions were all reported on the front page of the *New York Sun*. See "World and Journal Put Out," *New York Sun* (7 March 1897): 1; "World and Journal Cast Out," *New York Sun* (9 March 1897): 1; "World and Journal Cast Out," *New York Sun* (11 March 1897): 1; "World and Journal Kicked Out," *New York Sun* (14 March 1897): 1; "World Barred at Yale," *New York Sun* (15 March 1897): 1; "World and Journal Shut Out," *New York Sun* (17 March 1897): 1.

83. "'New Journalism' at Yale," *New York Times* (15 March 1897): 1.

84. "Vile Newspapers Put Out," *New York Sun* (10 March 1897): 1.

85. During the second half of March, the boycott had spread to the University Club and the Union Club in New York City, the American Whig Literary Society, the New Haven Public Library in Connecticut, the New York Military Academy, the YMCA in New Brunswick, NJ, and the Young Men's Catholic Literary Union in Orange, NJ. The *Sun* reported on all of those decisions. See "Casting Out the World," *New York Sun* (22 March 1897): 1; "World and Journal Excluded," *New York Sun* (23 March 1897): 1; "World and Journal Cast Out," *New York Sun* (25 March 1897): 1; "The World Excluded," *New York Sun* (30 March 1897): 1; "University Club Drops the World," *New York Sun* (7 April 1897): 1; "The World Kicked Out," *New York Sun* (1 May 1897): 1; "The World Barred Out," *New York Sun* (6 May 1897): 1.

86. "The Fiercest of Fights," *Fourth Estate* (25 March 1897): 6.

87. "Yellow Journalism Denounced Everywhere," *New York Press*.

88. "Fall of Yellow Journalism," *New York Press* (28 March 1897): 6. See also, "A Shrinking Yellow Thing," *New York Press* (15 March 1897): 4, and "Yellow Journalism Madness," *New York Press* (23 March 1897): 6. Charles Dana's *Sun* also predicted the boycott would lead to the collapse of the *Journal* and *World*, stating: "The unanimity with which decent institutions are excluding them is only the first step toward their downfall. The revulsion of the members of these institutions against their vileness and devilishness is a symptom of the rising of the public sentiment which always sooner or later lays such journals low." See "The End is Approaching," *New York Sun*.

89. "Barring Yellow Journals," *New York Press* (10 March 1897): 1.

90. "Banishing Yellow Journals," *New York Press* (12 March 1897): 6.

91. "Our Growing Circulation," *New York Press* (25 June 1897): 6.

92. "New Journalism and Vice," *New York Times* (3 March 1897): 2.

93. The Rev. Edwin C. Bolles, quoted in "Ethics of Newspapers," *New York Times* (25 March 1897).

94. "Views of New Journalism," *New York Times* (4 March 1897): 3.

95. "New Journalism," *Topeka* [KS] *State Journal* (13 March 1897): 4.

96. "Note and Comment," *Fourth Estate* (11 March 1897): 7. The *Washington Post* said of the boycott: "The newspaper that thinks it necessary to attack the

methods of its contemporaries is generally experiencing trouble at home." Untitled editorial page comment, *Washington Post* (18 March 1897): 6.

97. See "Has the Old Man No Friends?," *New York World* (23 March 1897): 6.

98. "Fear," *New York World* (28 March 1897): 6. The editorial read: "Fight on, poor rats! The thumbs above you are all turned down. . . . Keep your tails to the wall and your teeth to The World and pray that the last, merciful bite may come soon." The *Sun*'s Charles Dana was a frequent target of the *World*'s counterattacks. The *World* wrote 23 March 1897 that Dana's "shriveled hands sought the mud bucket again yesterday with another outburst of dotard rage." The *New York Press* was derided as "the little fry." See "The World and Its Enemies," *New York World* (21 March 1897): 6.

99. "The Derelicts of Journalism," *New York World* (28 March 1897): 10–11.

100. J. Fred W. Kitzmeyer, "The Church and the Mass," *New York Journal* (2 May 1897): 50. Kitzmeyer was identified as the pastor of Bethany Lutheran Church of New York.

101. Maurice H. Harris, "Biblical Criticism in Latter-Day Pulpits," *New York Journal* (9 May 1897): 50. Harris was identified as rabbi of the Harlem Hebrew Temple.

102. Frank M. Goodchild, "The Right to Think," *New York Journal* (16 May 1897): 50. The writer was identified as affiliated with the Central Baptist Church in New York.

103. J. B. Remensnyder, "The Parable of Spring," *New York Journal* (23 May 1897): 40. The writer was identified as pastor of the St. James English Lutheran Church.

104. Mark Twain, "Mark Twain's Pen Picture of the Great Pageant in Honor of Victoria's Sixtieth Anniversary," *New York Journal* (23 June 1897): 1.

105. Louis J. Budd, "Color Him Curious About Yellow Journalism: Mark Twain and the New York City Press," *Journal of Popular Culture* 15, 2: 31–32.

106. See James Creelman, "Journal Correspondent in Camps of Greek and Turk," *New York Journal* (15 March 1897): 3; James Creelman, "Greece's King Threatens War," *New York Journal* (27 March 1897): 1; and Harriet Boyd, "A Journal Woman on the Battlefield in Greece," *New York Journal* (9 May 1897): 25.

107. The *Press* grumbled about the *Journal*'s crime-solving coup: "It may make feeble feints at news of war and politics, but Yellow Journalism is only really at home with a dripping and dismembered cadaver." Untitled editorial page comment, *New York Press* (5 July 1897): 4.

108. "Yellow Kid Calls on Prince Bismarck: A Leaflet From the Yellow Kid's Diary," *New York Journal* (5 April 1897): 6. See also, "The Yellow Kid Sees the German Kaiser," *New York Journal* (12 April 1897): 6.

109. "Around the World with the Yellow Kid," *New York Journal* (28 February 1897).

110. "Found! The Last Will and Testament of Job," *New York Journal* (14 March 1897): 31.

111. "Messages from Mars," *New York Journal* (17 January 1897): 25.

112. Winifred Black, "Does Modern Photography Incite Women to Brutality?" *New York Journal* (30 May 1897): 17.

113. See J. B. Montgomery-McGovern, "An Important Phase of Gutter Journalism: Faking," *Arena* 19, 99 (February 1898): 253.

114. "Caught a Baby Sea Serpent: His Papa Had Towed a Vessel Out to Sea," *New York Press* (25 October 1896): 33.

115. "Genuine Sea Serpent," *Washington Post* (18 June 1899): 22.

116. Frank P. Hill, the librarian at the Newark Free Public Library who set in motion the boycott, made no mention of the ban of the *Journal* and *World* in his annual reports for 1897 and 1898. See Frank P. Hill, "Ninth Annual Report of the Librarian," Newark Free Public Library (1 January 1898), and Hill, "Tenth Annual Report of the Librarian," Newark Free Public Library (2 January 1899).

117. The *World*'s business manager during the boycott claimed that "all the hullabaloo did not check circulation, which kept on mounting," but left Pulitzer shaken. See Seitz, *Joseph Pulitzer: His Life and Letters*, 230.

118. "The Past Year: Crusade of the Clubs," *Fourth Estate* (6 January 1898): 3. A letter writer to the *World* also noted that the boycott had an unintended effect, in that club members were "compelled . . . to buy The World for themselves to get the news, and thus to take several hundred copies of the paper where previously they had taken only one. Great heads in those clubs!" "The Gain of a Loss," letter to the *New York World* (19 March 1897): 6.

119. In what perhaps was a burst of wishful thinking, the *Press*' gossip column, "On the Tip of the Tongue," reported in June 1897 that Hearst's losses at the *Journal* were such that "he thinks seriously of giving up the paper. . . . Men in the know say the Journal will go up in less than six months. The drain and strain are too great." "On the Tip of the of the Tongue: Hearst Tired Out," *New York Journal* (14 June 1897): 4.

120. "Yellower Than Ever," *New York Press* (1 July 1897): 6.

121. One measure of the term's swift diffusion was that the *New York Tribune* included an entry for "yellow journalism" in its index of articles for 1897. The *Tribune*'s index includes no entry for "yellow journalism" before then.

122. It is possible the diffusion of the term was propelled by the members of the American Newspaper Publishers' Association, who met in New York in February 1897 while Wardman was regularly berating "yellow journalism." *Fourth Estate* reported that the ANPA meeting was attended by few New York City publishers, however. See "Characteristics of a City," *Fourth Estate* (25 February 1897): 6.

123. The *Press* said as much in March 1898: "Shortly after we re-baptised them [as yellow journals] the New York Tribune complimented us on our selection of a name. . . ." See "On the Tip of the Tongue: Where 'Yellow Journalism' Came From," *New York Press*. William Randolph Hearst's eldest son later wrote that the phrase "originated at the *Tribune* and the *Press*, both of which were losing considerable circulation to the *Journal* and *World*. It was born of professional antagonism and perhaps jealousy." See William Randolph Hearst Jr. with Jack Casserly, *The Hearsts: Father and Son* (Niwot, CO: Roberts Rinehart Publishers, 1991), 41.

124. "Wise Limitations of War Power," *New York Tribune*.

125. See, for example, "The Yellow War," *New York Tribune* (19 February 1897): 6.

126. "Yellow Journalism. As Bad for Morals as Yellow Fever Is for Life," letter to *New York Press* (27 February 1897): 6.

127. Cited in "Nasty and Noisy: From the San Francisco Call," *New York Press* (14 March 1897): 6.

128. Cited in "The Handwriting on the Wall: From the Providence Journal," *New York Press* (24 March 1897): 6.

129. Cited in "The Anti-Yellow Reaction: From the Richmond Dispatch," *New York Press* (26 March 1897): 6.

130. Cited in untitled editorial page comment, *New York Press* (12 April 1897): 6.

131. "A Large Observer of a Large Thing," *New York Journal* (13 May 1898): 10. The editorial described the use of "yellow journalism" as "the bitter groan of the defeated and envious, or the smirk of a mere prig. It is the cry of that mindless conservatism which is shocked by what is new, whatever is vigorous, whatever is not made safely respectable by familiarity."

132. See Jay Maeder, "R. F. Outcault Polychromous Effulgence," *New York Daily News* (25 April 1999): 42. Maeder wrote: "Actually, as historian Bill Blackbeard has noted in his definitive 1995 chronicle of The Kid's life and times, the term [yellow journalism] was in use before Outcault ever left Pulitzer" in October 1896.

133. Swanberg, *Citizen Hearst*, 88.

134. "The League Against Yellow Journalism, Circular No. 3," undated pamphlet, Bancroft Library, University of California-Berkeley, Peter Gulbrandsen papers.

135. "The League Against Yellow Journalism," undated pamphlet, Bancroft Library, Gulbrandsen papers.

136. The League's secretary, Leila L. Thompson, wrote to the treasurer, Peter Gulbrandsen, in 1936, saying she worried "that we won't even pay the printer's bill. . . . I have eleven dollars on hand. . . ." Thompson, letter to Gulbrandsen, 19 July 1936, Bancroft Library, Gulbrandsen papers.

137. "The League Against Yellow Journalism," undated pamphlet, Bancroft Library, Gulbrandsen papers.

138. Ferdinand Lundberg, *Imperial Hearst: A Social Biography* (New York: Equinox Cooperative Press, 1937).

139. Kay Knapp, letter to Peter Gulbrandsen, 26 June 1939, Bancroft Library, Gulbrandsen papers. Knapp, the editor of the *Liberal Survey*, wrote in part: "From your report we gather that the organization is no longer active."

140. *Fourth Estate* wrote in 1916: "Mr. Wardman's newspaper life has been a rather steady day-by-day affair." See "The Sun's New Publisher," *Fourth Estate* (15 July 1916): 3.

141. "Editor and Soldier," *Fourth Estate* (8 September 1898): 1.

142. "Ervin Wardman Dies in 58th Year," *New York Herald* (14 January 1923): 3.

143. "Mr. Ervin Wardman," *New York Times* (15 January 1923): 14.

144. "Mr. Ervin Wardman," *New York Times*.

145. The *Journal* was renamed the *American* in 1902.

146. "Ervin Wardman, 'Sun'-'Herald' Executive, Dies," *New York Tribune*.

Yellow journalism's most prominent practitioners were William Randolph Hearst of the *New York Journal* (left) and Joseph Pulitzer of the *New York World* (right).

The term "yellow journalism" first appeared in print in late January 1897 in the *New York Press*, edited by Ervin Wardman (above). The term became the rhetorical centerpiece of a movement that year to boycott the *New York Journal* and the *New York World*.

The antics of the "Yellow Kid"—a popular comic character invariably linked to yellow journalism—were featured in color in the *New York World* and, later, in the *New York Journal*. For a time in 1896 and 1897, the newspapers ran rival versions of the comic. In this cartoon, published in the *World* in May 1896, the "Yellow Kid" is the diminutive figure gesturing at the wagon. Reproduced from the Collections of the Library of Congress.

The "Yellow Kid" was drawn by R. F. Outcault, who worked for the *World* before Hearst lured him to the *Journal* in October 1896. Outcault's defection was emblematic of Hearst's raids on the *World*'s staff. This cartoon was published in the *World* in April 1896; the "Yellow Kid" is in the center, bat in hand. Reproduced from the Collections of the Library of Congress.

MAIL EDITION.

NEW YORK JOURNAL AND ADVERTISER.

NEW YORK, SUNDAY, APRIL 4, 1897.—70 PAGES.

WHY THE JOURNAL LEADS THE AMERICAN PRESS.

Timely Review of a Great Newspaper's Achievements and Claims to Public Respect.

Enterprise Which Has Been Recognized By an Elevenfold Increase of Circulation in Fifteen Months.

The Morning Advertiser.

FAMOUS ECCLESIASTICS WHO HAVE CONTRIBUTED TO THE JOURNAL.

REV. DR. CHARLES H. PARKHURST.

REV. WILLIAM S. RAINSFORD.

NEW YORK JOURNAL AND ADVERTISER.

NEW YORK, THURSDAY, JUNE 10, 1897.—16 PAGES.

M'KINLEY'S CUBAN MESSAGE OUTLINED IN ADVANCE.

The Journal Gives the Principal Points of the Ultimatum to Spain Which the President Is Now Preparing.

A "JOURNAL" VICTORY FOR PUBLIC DECENCY

The Sharkey-Maher Slugging Match Stopped by the Police in the Seventh Round at the Palace Athletic Club.

All of the Principals and Jimmy Colville, the Referee Arrested and Taken to the Police Station by Inspector McLaughlin's Men.

NEW YORK JOURNAL AND ADVERTISER.

GENERAL LEE HOLDS SPAIN RESPONSIBLE FOR RUIZ'S DEATH.

The Journal Gives the Full Text of His Official Report to Secretary Sherman on the Killing of the American.

SPAIN IS BLAMED FOR RUIZ' FATE.

ASSEMBLYMAN HORTON'S STATEMENT TO THE JOURNAL.

Secretary Fishback Doesn't Understand How It Got Out.

The yellow press indulged in self-promotion—and no newspaper did so more eagerly or routinely than the *New York Journal*, as these front pages suggest.

NEW YORK JOURNAL, FRIDAY, JANUARY 29, 1897.

JOURNAL RELIEF WAGONS BRINGING HELP THROUGH THE STORM TO THE POOR OF A GREAT CITY.

The arrival of the Journal relief wagon in Monroe Street.

Bringing food to the Starving Sheridans 105 Orchard Street

HUNGRY AND COLD FED AND WARMED.

The Journal Provides More Food and Fuel for the Most Miserable of the City's Poor.

Five Wagons Busy All Day Carrying to the Starving and the Sick Edibles to Which They Have Long Been Strangers.

Harrowing Instances of Distress and Dire Destitution. The Relief Fund Grows, One Generous Giver Subscribing $1,000.

LYNN'S LAW OF KINDNESS.

Yellow journalism was infused by an ethos of activism. The *New York Journal* frequently injected itself as an agency bringing aid and comfort to victims of natural disasters and disruptive snowstorms.

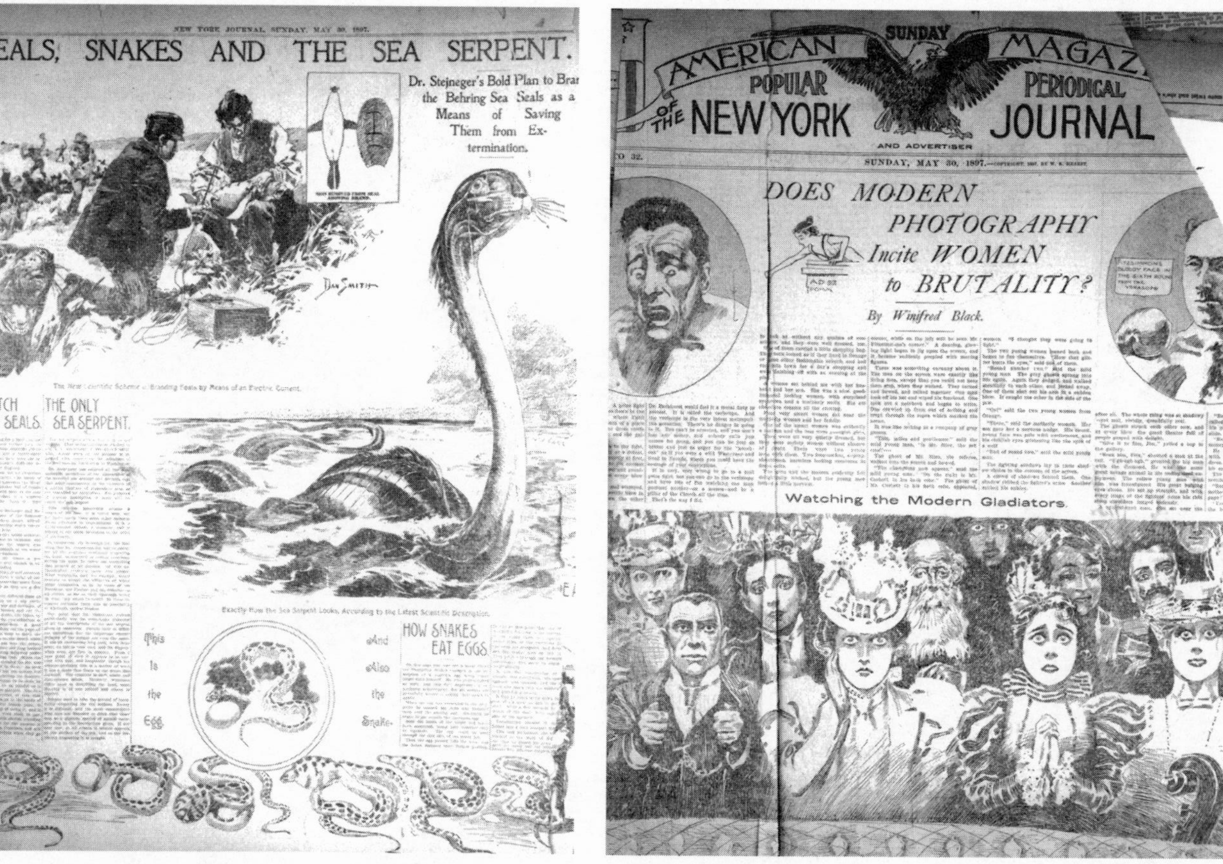
NEW YORK JOURNAL, SUNDAY, MAY 30, 1897.

SEALS, SNAKES AND THE SEA SERPENT.

Dr. Stejneger's Bold Plan to Brand the Behring Sea Seals as a Means of Saving Them from Extermination.

The New Scientific Scheme of Branding Seals by Means of an Electric Current.

TO SCOTCH OUR SEALS.

THE ONLY SEA SERPENT.

Exactly How the Sea Serpent Looks, According to the Latest Scientific Description.

This is the Egg.

And Also the Snake.

HOW SNAKES EAT EGGS.

SUNDAY AMERICAN MAGAZ[INE]

POPULAR PERIODICAL

OF THE NEW YORK JOURNAL

AND ADVERTISER

SUNDAY, MAY 30, 1897.

DOES MODERN PHOTOGRAPHY Incite WOMEN to BRUTALITY?

By Winifred Black.

Watching the Modern Gladiators.

The *Journal*'s indulgence in oddity and pseudo-science in its Sunday supplement encouraged the notion that in the yellow press, accuracy was subordinate to the absurd and the bizarre.

NEW YORK JOURNAL

NEW YORK, THURSDAY, MARCH 18, 1897.—14 PAGES.

STEAMER SINKS AT SEA; SEVENTY-SIX ARE LOST.

Only Four Brought Back to Port to Tell How the Ville de St. Nazaire Foundered in a Storm Off the Carolina Coast.

Women and Children Crowded Into the Boats While Mountainous Waves Tore the Leaking Vessel Apart Beneath Their Feet.

One Longboat at Sea Six Days a Father Saw His Wife and Children Die, and One by One Twenty-nine Men Perish, the Survivors Casting Their Bodies Into the Waters.

When the Schooner Hilda Picked Up This Wandering Craft There Were Four Living, Four Dead, Lying in the Bottom Together—The Steamer's Leak Started One Day Out from This Port for the West Indies on March 7.

VILLE DE ST. NAZAIRE LOST WITH SEVENTY-SIX PERSONS.

THE GREAT FIGHT DESCRIBED BY INGALLS.

Realistic Picture of the Terrible Knock-Out Blow and Fitz's Fiendish Smile When the Deed Was Done.

To the Ex-Senator All the Members of This National Convention of Pugilists and Their Constituents, Except Fitzsimmons, Seemed to Lack Earnestness, and Brutality Did Not Suggest Itself.

By John J. Ingalls.

CHAMPION FITZSIMMONS.

NEW YORK JOURNAL

NEW YORK, THURSDAY, FEBRUARY 11, 1897.—14 PAGES.

THE GREAT BALL PORTRAYED BY PEN AND PENCIL.

Major sporting and society events were frequently given prominent treatment in the yellow press. The *Journal* gave top billing to a heavyweight boxing match and devoted its front page to an illustration of a society ball in 1897.

NEW YORK JOURNAL

NEW YORK, FRIDAY, MARCH 5, 1897.—14 PAGES.

HOW PRESIDENT M'KINLEY WAS INAUGURATED.

The Nation's New President Took the Oath Amid the Wild Cheers of Many Thousands.

All Were Anxious to See the Aged Mother Whose Son Has Reached the Highest Office in the Land.

The Day Was Fine, the Parade Brilliant, the Enthusiasm Unbounded and Not a Hitch in Any Portion of the Ceremonies.

Illustrated by Pictures Made on the Spot and Brought to New York on a Special Train That Broke the Record.

The Journal's Special Commissioner, Ex-Senator Ingalls, Describes the Inaugural.

Patriotic Decorations, Sunshine and a Mighty Multitude Made a Scene of Unprecedented Splendor.

The New President, McKinley, Appeared at His Best. His Address Indicates That Innovations Will Not Be Introduced.

PRESIDENT M'KINLEY TAKING THE OATH OF OFFICE.

FROM WASHINGTON TO NEW YORK IN 4 HOURS.

Two Hundred and Twenty-eight Miles in Two Hundred and Forty-nine Minutes, Breaking All Previous Records—That's What the Journal's Special Inauguration Train Did Yesterday.

NEW YORK JOURNAL AND ADVERTISER.

NEW YORK, TUESDAY, APRIL 6, 1897.—14 PAGES.

Look Out for It!

Easter Stories.

Next Sunday

LIVES AND LAND WASTED BY THE YELLOW RIVER'S FLOOD

DEMOCRATIC MAYORS ELECTED.

They Are Successful in Cincinnati and Many Other Cities.

CLEVELAND IN LINE.

Cox-Foraker Gang Completely Overthrown in the Queen City.

DID MARK HANNA VOTE?

This Question Will Soon Cause a Very Lively Fight in Ohio.

Sad Story of Ruin to Men and Homes Caused the Greatest Overflow in the History of the Mississippi.

Desperate Struggles to Hold Soaked Levees Against Pounding Waters End in Crevasses and Inundations of Many Counties.

LOSS OF LIFE AND PROPERTY

GOV. TAYLOR'S TALE OF RUIN

GOV. M'LAURIN ON BROKEN LEVEE

THE FLOODED MISSISSIPPI FROM ST. PAUL TO THE GULF.

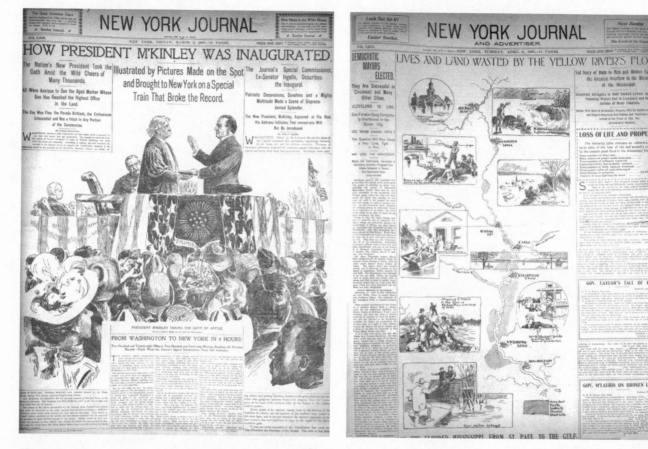

The yellow press was noticeably inclined to experiment with page design, as suggested by the illustrations that accompanied the *Journal*'s coverage of President William McKinley's first inauguration and the flooding in the Midwest.

In this 1899 illustration, the *Journal* likened itself to a cop on the beat, bringing a corrupt business trust to justice. Such characterizations were in keeping with the *Journal's* advocacy of what it called "the journalism of action." Reproduced from the Collections of the Library of Congress.

AND THE TRAIN WENT BY.

New York City journalism in the late 1890s was characterized by fierce rivalries. Here the *Journal* touts itself as the vanguard of "new journalism," leaving behind such veteran editors as Charles A. Dana of the *New York Sun* and Joseph Pulitzer. Dana is depicted as the dog chasing the train. "New journalism" was a predecessor phrase of "yellow journalism."

2

The Yellow Press and the Myths of Its Readership

Just as the term "yellow journalism" spread swiftly from New York City during the late 1890s, the diffusion of conspicuous elements of the genre was similarly swift. For a time at least, yellow journalism was an influential model. While no reliable quantitative studies about the spread of yellow journalism were conducted at the time,[1] several contemporaneous accounts say the diffusion of the practice was astonishingly rapid. Will Irwin hyperbolically likened the spread of yellow journalism to "a prairie fire," in that it influenced to some degree "nineteen out of twenty metropolitan newspapers."[2]

"Now that the yellows had shown the way," Irwin wrote, "other publishers fell in and imitated them wholly or in part."[3] *Atlantic Monthly* described yellow journalism in 1902 as "running wild and luxuriant"[4] while the trade journal *Fourth Estate* observed that "in several if not all of our large cities there are yellow sheets."[5] Senator Edward Oliver Wolcott of Colorado, an outspoken foe of yellow journalism, deplored the diffusion. "The plague may have started here," he told an audience in New York City in December 1897, "but it has spread and sprouted like the Canada thistle until it is a blight in Colorado, as it is a curse here and wherever it plants itself."[6] An editorial writer at the *Times-Star* in Cincinnati, no doubt referring to local rivals, remarked in 1898: "When speaking of yellow journalism it is well to remember that New York is not the only aching tooth in the nation."[7]

While such characterizations are decidedly impressionistic, their cumulative effect is to underscore the appeal and the adoption of elements of the practice of yellow journalism. This is not to say, however, that newspapers outside New York City were duplicates of the archetypal yellow journals, Hearst's *New York Journal* or Pulitzer's *New York*

World. There were differences in typography and content between Hearst's newspapers in New York and San Francisco,[8] as there were between Pulitzer's titles in New York and St. Louis.[9] Rather, the diffusion of yellow journalism appears to have been idiosyncratic, marked typically by the adoption of typographic or content elements that were more flamboyant than those customarily appearing in conservative newspapers: Bold, multicolumn headlines and generous use of illustrations were two of the most widely embraced signal features of yellow journalism.[10]

Non-yellow newspapers also were known to modify their appearance and content in response to the emergence of a new title employing characteristic features of yellow journalism. A notable example came in Chicago, where Hearst in July 1900 launched the *Chicago American*. In anticipation of the newcomer, some Chicago newspapers introduced large headlines on their front pages or added color supplements in their Sunday editions.[11] "It was quite natural that the coming of Mr. Hearst into the Chicago field should stir up the other Chicago publishers to greater effort," *Fourth Estate* noted.[12]

Although yellow journalism was much derided, its techniques were appealing and emulated for several reasons. Foremost, perhaps, was that the techniques were seen as stimulants to circulation.[13] Moreover, yellow journalism *was* exciting journalism: Its crusades against privilege and powerful interests were widely admired.[14] Its exposure of corruption in municipal government probably encouraged the rise of magazine muckraking in the early twentieth century. Additionally, leading practitioners of yellow journalism had achieved a measure of professional standing and respect. Hearst, for example, was not everywhere despised. The *New York Herald* praised the *Journal* and its editors for enterprising reporting from the Klondike goldfields in 1897.[15] Josephus Daniels, editor of the conservative *Raleigh News and Observer*, called the *Journal* "America's greatest newspaper," saying: "It is not because the people like stories of crime that they take the 'yellow journals.' It is because they want the news. They know that the Journal hires the ablest correspondents and spends the most money to get the fullest news."[16] *Fourth Estate* often commented favorably about the *New York Journal* and its enterprising reporting,[17] and Hearst was described in the inaugural issue of *Editor and Publisher* as "the foremost figure in American journalism."[18]

Propelled by a combination of factors, the genre's practices spread. They had become extensive enough in the United States that a British observer lamented early in the twentieth century: "No civilized country in the world has been content with newspapers so grossly contemptible as those which are read from New York to the Pacific Coast. The journals . . . are known as Yellow."[19]

Even though characteristic components of yellow journalism proved popular, the view took hold (and became accepted among media scholars) that yellow journalism—notably in its characteristic bold headlines and generous display of illustrations—appealed essentially to the little-educated masses and, in particular, to immigrants and illiterates. The yellow press supposedly enabled them to acquire a taste for reading and, in turn, a command of English. Frank Luther Mott wrote, for example: "The yellow journal, with its pictures, sensation, and easy editorials, brought the immigrant more and more into the newspaper audience."[20] Sidney Kobre maintained that "immigrants influenced particularly the press in eastern metropolitan areas, with some newspapers printing large headlines, primer-like texts and many pictures."[21] Willard Grosvenor Bleyer claimed that immigrants, because of their "limited knowledge of the English language and of American institutions," were "attracted by large, striking headlines, sensational news stories, diagrammatic illustrations, and well-displayed editorials."[22] Newcomers to the United States, Bleyer claimed, represented "a considerable part of the total number of readers of the 'yellow journals.'"[23] More recently, William A. Hachten wrote of the *Journal* and the *World*: "To maximize circulation meant targeting news to the masses, often recent immigrants, whose tastes and interests affected the newspapers' content. Despite its faults, yellow journalism did much to help the new arrivals off Ellis Island learn about and adjust to a strange, new land."[24]

Contemporaneous accounts also associated the yellow press with rough-hewn, little-educated readers—or to what one advertising agent called the "lower million of the populace."[25] The appeal of sometimes lurid, often provocative yellow journalism supposedly was quite powerful for immigrants and for people without a command of English. "One thing only," the British observer wrote in 1907, "can explain the imbecility of the Yellow Press: it is written for immigrants, who have but an imperfect knowledge of English, who prefer to see their news rather than to read, and who, if they must read, can best understand words of one syllable and sentences of no more than a dozen words."[26] The yellow journals were also said to "serve yellow people" who, supposedly, had no taste for the sophisticated fare of *Atlantic Monthly* and the *Nation*.[27] A letter writer to the *New York Times* in 1898 said of the yellow journals: "They are issued more for the amusement and excitement of a certain class of ignorant and uncultivated readers than for public enlightenment, and are the result of a morbid craving on the part of the lower order of mankind for sensational reading and illustrations."[28]

Such unflattering and condescending views about the readers of the yellow press were not at all uncommon. "On the whole," wrote a critic in *Bookman* magazine in 1906, "the banality and sensationalism of the bad papers are a shade above the banality and coarseness of the people who read them. The scandalous stories are about as harmful as the gossip of the village women and much less filthy than the conversation exchanged by the men who pay Mr. Hearst or some other publisher a cent every morning."[29]

The yellow press was not without its perceived beneficial effects, despite its supposed down-market appeal. It was frequently claimed, in fact, that the yellow journals "made new readers."[30] Yellow journalism, moreover, was seen as a powerful democratizing force, encouraging not only literacy in English but the embrace of American values. As one defender of the genre wrote early in the twentieth century:

> Altogether, the foreign and the ignorant comprise the bulk of the American people. The principal problem that confronts us in our struggle to develop an American democracy is the education and uplifting of this vast mass. . . . Theories of every sort are constantly advanced; but the one institution that is successfully coping with this problem, day after day, is the yellow journal. It gives the people what they want—sensation, crime and vulgar sports—thus inducing them to read. But having secured its audience, it teaches them, simply, clearly, patiently, the lessons they need. Undeniably the yellow journals are not nice and proper. But neither are the people they are intended to reach.[31]

The assertions about the effects, attributes, and audiences of the yellow press tend not only to be condescending, but impressionistic[32] and highly anecdotal. They rarely are buttressed by quantitative data or by analyses of the environments that proved particularly hospitable to yellow journalism. In important respects, these data do not exist: Demographic profiles about newspaper readers at the turn of the twentieth century were not meaningfully or systematically collected, in part because urban dailies of the time relied heavily on sales by newsdealers or by newsboys. A crude survey announced by the *Boston Journal* in 1897 is suggestive of the generally limited understanding metropolitan newspapers had about their readers. The newspaper undertook what was called a "most novel" attempt to overcome the data gap by asking readers to complete and return questionnaires that inquired about the occupation of the person buying the newspaper and the number of readers per issue. The newspaper said it wanted "to know its readers better—their names, their occupations, and their tastes."[33]

While readership data systematically gathered are elusive, the federal Census of 1900—taken when yellow journalism was at or near its zenith in popularity[34]—does offer invaluable and revealing, though seldom-examined, quantitative data about the demographic makeup of the places where the genre took hold and flourished. This chapter draws upon the Census data in an attempt to discern whether shared demographic variables accounted for yellow journalism's emergence. Specifically, the chapter addresses whether the yellow press appeared most commonly in fast-growing U.S. cities that had higher-than-average numbers of foreign-born and foreign-born illiterate populations. Was there a clear demographic profile or pattern that characterized the places where the yellow press most dramatically emerged? Were the critics accurate in claiming that the yellow journals were read by immigrants and the poorly educated?

In addressing those questions, this chapter also examines qualitative evidence about the yellow press, particularly the claims and characterizations it made about its readers and the measures it undertook to seek a wide audience. The chapter also considers the importance of foreign-language newspapers to newly arrived immigrants at the turn of the twentieth century, and concludes that the appeal of yellow journalism extended well beyond the émigré and the illiterate, that the yellow press in 1900 was more a part of mainstream America than is generally understood. The 1900 Census data make clear that yellow journalism took hold in a *variety* of urban settings at the end of the nineteenth century: It flared in fast-growing *and* in slow-growing cities, in places where foreign-born populations exceeded and fell below the national urban average, in cities where foreign-born illiterate populations were numerous and comparatively small. Yellow journals appeared in highly competitive as well as fairly stable newspaper markets.

The demographic profile commonly attributed to the rise of yellow journalism in urban America is inadequate in explaining the genre's diffusion. The demographic factors that were present in New York City in 1900 were not matched or uniformly shared in Boston, Chicago, Denver, and other urban centers where yellow journalism emerged. This chapter concludes that the diffusion of yellow journalism was due more to the idiosyncratic tastes and decisions of individual publishers than it was to the weight or force of any set of demographic variables. In short, the yellow press was doubtless read across the urban social strata in the United States at the turn of the twentieth century. The yellow press said as much about itself, and undertook specific campaigns to accomplish that objective.

METHOD

Central to this chapter are data from the 1900 federal Census for cities recognized by historians as hospitable to yellow journalism, and for cities where the genre made scant or no impact. In all, Census data were examined for eleven cities, all of which were among the country's twenty-five most populous cities in 1900. Eight of the ten largest U.S. cities were included in the analysis.[35]

Seven cities in the study were, historians and other researchers concur,[36] places where the genre flourished or gained prominence, often alongside more conservative competitors. Those cities were:

- **New York**, home to Hearst's *New York Journal* and Pulitzer's *New York World*.

- **Boston**, home to the *Boston Post*, an assertive, self-promoting daily edited by Edwin A. Grozier, formerly an editor at Pulitzer's *World*.[37] Mott accurately described the *Post* as "a leader among the yellows."[38]

- **Chicago**, home to Hearst's *Chicago American*, which brought yellow journalism to the city.

- **Cincinnati**, home to the *Enquirer* and the *Evening Post*, which were described as being "just as sensational as they look." [39] By 1900, the *Times-Star* also made frequent use of bold, multicolumn headlines and large illustrations.

- **Denver**, home to *Evening Post*,[40] which Kobre likened to "the Rocky Mountain outcropping of Hearst"[41] and which Irwin called "super-yellow."[42]

- **St. Louis**, home to the *Chronicle*,[43] which adopted the frequent use of bold, banner headlines by 1900 and was given, occasionally, to self-promotion. Pulitzer's *Post-Dispatch* exhibited some features characteristic of yellow journalism and St. Louis, overall, was described as a notable center of the genre.[44]

- **San Francisco**, home to Hearst's *Examiner*. Irwin reported that the other San Francisco newspapers, including the *Chronicle*, "fell universally" to the influence of yellow journalism.[45]

The four other cities in the study were those where, historians say, the yellow press was little seen. Those cities were: Baltimore, Kansas City, New Orleans, and Philadelphia.[46]

URBAN DEMOGRAPHIC DATA, 1900

By 1900, 160 cities in the United States had populations of 25,000 people or more and, on average, those cities had grown by nearly one third since 1890. Population growth in New York City exceeded the national urban average, but not all yellow-press cities grew so rapidly. Indeed, many of them failed to match the average national urban growth rate, as Table 2.1 shows. Notably, Cincinnati and San Francisco fell substantially behind the national urban average in that category.

As Table 2.1 also shows, the percentage of foreign-born residents in New York City, Boston, Chicago, and San Francisco exceeded the U.S. urban average in 1900. However, other cities amenable to yellow journalism—including Cincinnati, Denver, and St. Louis—lagged significantly behind the national urban average. The non-yellow cities all trailed the national urban average in foreign-born populations.

Moreover, nearly twelve percent of the country's foreign-born urban population older than ten years of age was illiterate. New York City exceeded the national urban average in this category as well. But in other cities hospitable to the yellow press, foreign-born illiterate populations tended to fall far short of the national urban average. In Denver and San Francisco, notably, slightly more than five percent of foreign-born residents were illiterate in 1900. On the other hand, illiteracy among foreign-born residents of non-yellow cities in this study often *surpassed* the rates in many centers of yellow journalism, as Table 2.1 shows.

Table 2.1
Urban demographic data (1900)
Cities where yellow journalism took hold are in italics.

City	Population growth[47] (%)	Foreign born[48] (%)	Foreign-born illiterate[49] (%)
New York	37.1	37.0	13.9
Boston	25.1	35.0	11.3
Chicago	54.4	34.6	8.2
Cincinnati	9.8	17.8	8.9
Denver	25.4	18.9	5.7
St. Louis	96.8	19.4	9.8
San Francisco	14.6	34.1	5.6
Baltimore	17.2	13.5	12.9
Kansas City	23.4	11.2	8.8
New Orleans	18.6	10.6	18.3
Philadelphia	23.6	22.8	12.1
U.S. average	**32.5**	**26.0**	**11.6**

Moreover, the 1900 Census data are inconsistent and unrevealing as to whether competition for newspaper readers (as measured by number of daily titles) was a factor explaining the diffusion of yellow journalism. The number of daily newspapers declined slightly in New York City, Cincinnati, and St. Louis from 1890 to 1900, but increased during that period in Boston, Chicago, Denver, and San Francisco, as Table 2.2 shows. A similarly uneven pattern was apparent in non-yellow cities.

Table 2.2
Daily newspapers, 1900 and 1890 [50]
Cities where yellow journalism took hold are in italics.

City	1900	1890	Trend
New York[51]	53	55	▼
Boston	16	12	▲
Chicago	37	27	▲
Cincinnati	13	14	▼
Denver	7	5	▲
St. Louis	13	15	▼
San Francisco	23	21	▲

Baltimore	9	7	▲
Kansas City	9	9	◄
New Orleans	9	9	◄
Philadelphia	21	24	▼

Thus, key urban statistical data from the 1900 federal Census permit a direct challenge to the view that yellow journalism found its most hospitable environment in fast-growing cities having sizable foreign-born populations, many of whom were unable to read and write. The quantitative evidence presented in this chapter points to considerable differentiation in the demographic profiles of cities that gave rise to yellow newspapers.

The demographic elements that coincided with the emergence of yellow journalism in New York City—which in 1900 exceeded national urban averages in population growth, in foreign-born residents, and in foreign-born illiterates—were not uniformly matched in other yellow cities. No other major city that gave rise to yellow newspapers exceeded the national urban averages in each of those critical categories. The data for Kansas City—a city where the yellow press failed to make notable inroads—were consistently below the national averages in those three categories, but they also were consistently below the national averages in Cincinnati and Denver, two cities where the yellow press was in evidence. In short, there appears to be no single set of decisive demographic variables that signal or help explain why the yellow press took hold where it did, as Table 2.3 shows.

Table 2.3
No common pattern
This table shows how each of the eleven cities examined here compared to national averages in the three key demographic variables. A=above national average, B=below national average. Cities where yellow journalism took hold are in italics.

City	Population growth	Foreign born	Foreign-born illiterate	Overall
New York	A	A	A	AAA
Boston	A	A	B	AAB
Chicago	A	A	B	AAB
Cincinnati	B	B	B	BBB
Denver	B	B	B	BBB
St. Louis	A	B	B	ABB
San Francisco	B	A	B	BAB
Baltimore	B	B	A	BBA
Kansas City	B	B	B	BBB
New Orleans	B	B	A	BBA
Philadelphia	B	B	B	BBB

The yellow press was an easy and ready target for critics and would-be reformers, who regarded such newspapers as a public menace best banned or boycotted.[52] But the results of this study suggest that the yellow press in 1900 was more a part of mainstream America than is generally recognized.

To characterize yellow journalism as catering to, and drawing sustenance principally from, the foreign-born and the illiterate is to fundamentally misstate the broader appeal of the yellow press in the United States. The demographic profiles of the places where yellow journalism took hold and flourished 100 years ago were, this study has shown, quite varied and differentiated. The yellow press no doubt was widely appealing, attracting its readers from across the social strata.

"THE WORLD IN LITTLE"

Indeed, that is how the yellow journals viewed themselves, as being widely appealing. While they surely attracted a host of working-class readers—small traders, longshoremen, clerks, laborers, and factory workers[53]—the yellow press sought a large and diverse readership. The *Journal* claimed for a newspaper to be recognized as truly great, it had to be inclusive, or "broad and catholic in its character. It must be, in a word, the world in little—the world of literature, art, science, and human action. All that men do must be reflected in its columns."[54] Pulitzer's *World* expressed similar sentiments: "To make a newspaper for a class is comparatively an easy task," it said in 1899. "To make a publication acceptable to the mass is quite another and infinitely more difficult problem. And it is in doing this that The World has long been pre-eminent."[55]

To be sure, the claims to wide readership were not infrequently exaggerated and self-aggrandizing—much like many claims of expanding circulations. The *Denver Post*, for example, once called itself "your paper and the people's paper, and the paper of Colorado, Wyoming, Montana, Utah, Idaho, Nevada, Arizona, New Mexico, Northern Texas, Oklahoma, Western Kansas and Nebraska and the Dakotas."[56] The gaudy *New York Evening Journal*, on the first anniversary of its founding, described itself without a hint of irony as "pre-eminently . . . a home and family paper."[57]

But the broad appeal of the yellow press was more than a matter of overblown, self-serving rhetoric. The newspapers pursued marketing tactics clearly intended to attract broad-based audiences. One method adopted during the weeks following Hearst's acquisition of the *Journal* in 1895 was the door-to-door distribution of sample copies "'in all parts of New York and Brooklyn and in near-by towns and cities.'"[58] In fact, the yellow press of New York circulated throughout much of the eastern United States, further evidence of its broad appeal. By 1900, for example, the *Journal* was on sale in all towns "within several hundred miles of New York."[59] Arrangements also were made for the *Journal* and the *World* to arrive daily by train in Washington, D.C., by 8 a.m.[60] Such broad distribution would have been unlikely—and impractical—had the newspapers appealed only to lower classes of New York City.

Other marketing techniques intended to attract a broad base of readers included sending thousands of Valentine's Day greetings to would-be female readers, calling their attention to the *Journal*'s women's page.[61] Such measures were taken in recognition of the growing importance of female readers, who often selected the goods and services for the household.[62]

Nor did the yellow press stint on matters of direct interest to its affluent readers. The *Journal* and the *World* often gave prominence to reports about high society, fashion, and the theater[63]—topics that were, arguably, of distant, vicarious interest to the lower classes. Such news certainly lay beyond their immediate, day-to-day concerns. Moreover, some advertising in the yellow press was clearly intended for upscale readers. The *Journal* in early June 1897 published five pages of advertisements for summer resorts, including upscale hotels and cottages in the Catskills and elsewhere in upstate New York. The spread was so impressive that *Fourth Estate* remarked: "The summer resort supplement of the New York *Journal* last Sunday is without question the neatest thing of its kind which has ever been published by a daily paper."[64] In the early twentieth century, moreover, the *Journal* on Sundays carried listings for what it termed "high-class apartments" in mid-town Manhattan.[65]

It is probable that the yellow journals drew a fair number of upscale readers who were simply curious or who sought diversion from their grayer, somber rivals—much as readers of high-brow publications in London at the turn of the twentieth century are said to have sought out the then-emergent tabloid newspapers because, said one, "'they keep me from thinking.'"[66] "The curious thing," a writer said about the tabloid press in London, "is that the reading is no longer confined to the class for which it was originally intended, as the people of greater intelligence are not ashamed to acknowledge that they are addicted to tabloidism."[67] Because they were colorful, self-promoting, assertive, and enterprising, the New York yellow journals assuredly had their fair share of readers among "the people of higher intelligence."

IMMIGRANTS AND THE YELLOW PRESS

Immigrants certainly were not ignored in the columns of New York's yellow press,[68] but their arrivals and their struggles to adjust to America were not preoccupying issues. The immigrants themselves were probably ambivalent about English-language American newspapers, given that they tended to adapt "pragmatically and selectively to life in the United States, vigorously asserting their right to cultural autonomy."[69] As such, they were likely not to turn first to the yellow press but to publications in the language of their native countries[70]—publications that could be counted upon to cover the local immigrant community far more closely and perceptively than the yellow journals.[71] Moreover, foreign-language newspapers offered recent and assimilating immigrants invaluable guidance about navigating their new surroundings.[72] They also helped acquaint them with the English language. In New York, for example, the Yiddish daily newspaper *Tageblatt* included a page of news in English from 1897 to 1907.[73]

Census data also are illustrative of the importance of foreign-language publications to newcomers: Immigrants from southern, eastern, and central Europe began arriving in the United States in numbers after 1890—an influx reflected in the expansion of Italian- and Polish-language publications during the closing decade of the nineteenth century.[74] Such data, Robert Park wrote in *The Immigrant Press and Its Control,* directly "point to the fact that the [foreign-language] press is a phenomenon of immigration."[75] He also wrote: "In the main, the [foreign-language] immigrant press is read by the more recent arrivals of each immigrant group. They have not learned the English language, and because of this isolation find themselves particularly dependent upon their own tongue for news of this country as well as of their native country and their own people."[76]

Despite the claims that the yellow journals were important agencies for the integration of newcomers—and that they were "written for immigrants"[77]—they no doubt were subordinate to foreign-language newspapers and to local organizations. Mutual aid societies, places of worship, and other agencies were vastly more useful, and accessible, to newly arrived immigrants than the yellow journals in helping them "adjust to a strange, new land."[78] Social and religious organizations were looked to for pertinent advice about adjusting to life in urban America.[79] They were critical in the process of adjusting or assimilating to life in America. As one contemporaneous report noted: "The immigrant must, of course, go through a more or less lengthy process of adjustment on his own account, but this process may be hastened by conditions in the environing group."[80]

To be sure, not all immigrant populations of the late nineteenth century and early twentieth century were inclined or eager to incorporate themselves into American society. Many immigrants from Italy, notably, came to the United States intending to make enough money to buy land back home.[81] These temporary immigrants tended to guard their cultural and ethnic identities, and the yellow press likely appealed to them marginally, if at all.

Moreover, anecdotal evidence from the early twentieth century suggests that at least some immigrants in New York City were suspicious of the yellow press and its attempts to position itself as an advocate for the masses. A writer in 1907 reported seething hostility to Hearst and his newspapers:

Some time ago, down in the heart of the Ghetto, I attended a mass meeting of tenants at a time when the whole East Side had been roused by the preconcerted attempt of tenement landlords to raise all the rents, though the last raise had come only two years before. The dimly lit hall was jammed with dark, angry faces. All at once the meeting was thrown into an uproar. A *Journal* reporter had come to assure them of the hearty support of his paper and to contribute money to the expense of the movement. The uproar rose. Some wanted to accept the money. But the overwhelming majority, young men with radical views, were for rejecting it. "Who is this man Hearst?" they shouted. "Is he a workingman? What has he to do with us? Why is he always helping? . . . No! Send back his money! We want to manage ourselves!"[82]

CONCLUSION

Media historian John D. Stevens, in his study about sensationalism and New York City journalism, noted that it is "tempting to caricature the yellow papers as being edited for janitors and clerks." But in fact they "published a fair amount of sober financial, political, and diplomatic information." The *Journal* and the *World*, Stevens concluded, "probably were read by people in all social classes."[83] That view finds support in an incisive essay published in 1910: "The new journalism wants not some readers but all—all classes, both sexes, and nearly all ages."[84]

Such claims to broad readership are supported by the evidence presented in this chapter. Indeed, an impressive and persuasive variety of quantitative and qualitative data signals that the yellow press was more a part of the mainstream newspaper readership 100 years ago than is generally understood. It was not published for, nor read exclusively by, immigrants and the poor. The yellow press was lively, compelling, and entertaining, and there is no reason to believe its appeal would have been so confined or circumscribed. That the yellow press took hold in a variety of settings in turn-of-the-century urban America suggests as much.

The diffusion of yellow journalism appears to have been highly idiosyncratic, due more to the initiative, affluence, and inclination of individual publishers than to forces exerted by any set of shared or defining demographic variables. The idiosyncratic factor was often in evidence at the end of the nineteenth century and during the first years of the twentieth century, as these examples indicate:

- In Denver, a transplanted New Yorker named W. H. (Billy) Milburn advised the *Post*'s owners "'to make this paper look different. Get some bigger headline type. Put red ink on page one. You've got to turn Denver's eyes to *The Post* every day, and away from the other papers.'"[85]

- In Philadelphia, Adolph Ochs, the owner of the *New York Times*, presented detailed instructions to the staff of the *Philadelphia Times* after acquiring the newspaper in 1901.[86] Ochs' instructions in effect warned against the practices and features of yellow journalism: "No red ink. No pictures. No double column heads. No freak typography. No free advertisements. No free circulation. . . . No Bryanism. No coupon schemes. . . . No personal journalism. No pessimism. No friends to favor. No enemies to punish. No drinking by employees."[87]

- In New York, Joseph Pulitzer instructed the *World*'s editors to tone down the newspaper, typographically, after the Spanish-American War[88] and by 1903 was said to be "growing more and more conservative every year."[89]

The turn of the twentieth century was a time of great difference in the appearance and content of urban newspapers in the United States,[90] from the typographical exuberance of the *New York Journal* and the *Denver Post* to the gray, illustration-free appearance of the *New York Times* and the *Kansas City Star*. It was the inclination of *publishers*—not the weight of demographic variables—that accounted for such wide variety.

The evidence presented in this chapter signals the broader importance of reassessing conventional wisdom about a much-maligned genre of American journalism. To characterize yellow journalism as appealing principally or exclusively to downscale readers not only is elitist: It misrepresents the broad appeal of the genre and, in turn, serves to perpetuate a myth about a dynamic and influential force in American journalism. Myths and misunderstandings abound about yellow journalism, and they die hard.

The purported exchange of telegrams between Hearst and Frederic Remington—in which Hearst supposedly promised "to furnish the war" with Spain—is, as we shall see, routinely repeated by journalists and media historians even though no evidence exists that such messages were ever sent. Hearst denied sending the telegram[91] and the original source of the story, James Creelman,[92] was in Europe at the time the purported messages were sent. We turn next to a detailed examination of that anecdote, one of the most famous in American journalism.

NOTES

1. A crude content analysis, published in 1900, attempted to quantify the diffusion of the yellow press. See Delos F. Wilcox, "The American Newspaper: A Study in Social Psychology," *Annals of the American Academy of Political and Social Science* 16 (July 1900): 56–92. The study reported that of 147 newspapers examined in 21 U.S. metropolitan areas, 47 were distinctly yellow and 55 others exhib-

ited some characteristics of the genre. The remaining 45 were conservative, or decidedly non-yellow. The study also reported finding three or more yellow journals in the New York, Boston, Chicago, and St. Louis metropolitan areas (78). However, the study was methodologically flawed, in that the author drew conclusions by examining, for the most part, just one issue of each newspaper in the study. The author also reported that "the definition of a yellow journal is a matter of some difficulty" and said that he had encountered "considerable trouble in getting a quantitative test which would make the *New York Journal* yellow and the *New York Evening Post* conservative" (76–77). Despite the study's flaws, its results often have been cited by journalism historians. Frank Luther Mott, for example, referred to Wilcox's work as "a careful study." See Mott, *American Journalism: A History, 1690–1960*, 3rd ed. (New York: Macmillan, 1962), 539. A contemporaneous account noted Wilcox's methodological difficulties but nonetheless concluded that "with all its limitations, the method pursued brings out interesting contrasts." See "Shades of Yellow Journalism," *Outlook* 65 (25 August 1900): 947.

2. Will Irwin, "The American Newspaper: The Spread and Decline of Yellow Journalism," reprinted in Will Irwin, *The American Newspaper* (Ames, IA: Iowa State University Press, 1969). Another observer, writing in 1900, noted that "those very journals which have hitherto most bitterly attacked [the yellow newspapers] are now quietly adopting many of the most successful yellow methods." See "The Other Side of Yellow Journalism," *Independent* (29 March 1900): 786.

3. Irwin, "The Spread and Decline of Yellow Journalism."

4. Brooke Fisher, "The Newspaper Industry," *Atlantic Monthly* 89 (June 1902): 745.

5. "Newspapers Analysed," *Fourth Estate* (19 April 1902): 10.

6. Thomas Fulton Dawson, *The Life and Character of Edward Oliver Wolcott*, vol. 2 (New York: Knickerbocker Press, 1911), 553. See also, "Senator Wolcott's Address," *New York Times* (23 December 1897): 2, and "Wolcott's Plea for the West," *New York Herald* (23 December 1897): 6.

7. Untitled editorial page comment, *Cincinnati Times-Star* (8 March 1898): 4. The *Times-Star* itself had adopted important features of the yellow press, notably multicolumn headlines and large illustrations of the front page.

8. As will be discussed in Chapter Five, the *San Francisco Examiner* at the end of the nineteenth century was less inclined than the *New York Journal* to use front-page banner headlines or to call attention to its reportorial accomplishments.

9. The *New York World* in 1899 exhibited far more features characteristic of yellow journalism than did the *St. Louis Post-Dispatch*, as will be discussed in Chapter Five.

10. See Irwin, "The Spread and Decline of Yellow Journalism." See also, Mott, *American Journalism*, 540.

11. "Hearst's American Sets a Lively Pace for Other Chicago Papers," *Fourth Estate* (7 July 1900): 7, and "The Year's Record: Hearst's Chicago American," *Fourth Estate* (12 January 1901): 3.

12. "The Year's Record: Hearst's Chicago American," *Fourth Estate*. See also, Willard Grosvenor Bleyer, *Main Currents in the History of American Journalism* (Boston: Houghton Mifflin Co., 1927), 387. Bleyer wrote: "The advent of a

Hearst newspaper in a city often resulted in the adoption of Hearst methods by rival papers, in the belief that they could thus meet the competition. These attempts, however, scarcely ever proved successful, because the individual papers lacked the resources in the way of special news and feature services that a Hearst paper could command. Nevertheless, the ensuing competition often modified the character of the rival papers."

13. Bleyer, *Main Currents*, 387.

14. Irwin, "The Spread and Decline of Yellow Journalism."

15. Cited in "Note and Comment," *Fourth Estate* (29 July 1897): 6. The *New York Herald* said about Hearst and Samuel Chamberlain, the managing editor at the *New York Journal*: "Our wideawake contemporary has sent a large and able corps of special correspondents to the Klondike region and has arranged for the quick transmission of their dispatches by special couriers. This shows genuine journalistic enterprise, which entitles Messrs. Hearst and Chamberlain to unstinted praise and merits the reward of success."

16. "So Called Yellow Journalism Vindicated," *Raleigh News and Observer* (27 March 1898): 4. The editorial specifically cited the *Journal*'s coverage of the Cuban insurrection.

17. See "Enterprise Tells: The New York Journal's Notable Achievements," *Fourth Estate* (27 October, 1900): 3. The article read: "Mr. Hearst had not been running the Journal very long before New Yorkers awoke to the fact that the young man from San Francisco knew his business. As soon as he organized a competent staff Mr. Hearst's paper began to do things. Its enterprise made the newspaper owners rub their eyes." See also, "W. R. Hearst Here," *Fourth Estate* (10 October 1895): 2. The article reported Hearst's purchase of the *New York Journal* and said, "The result of new blood in metropolitan journalism will be watched with the deepest interest, not only in New York but throughout the country." See also, "Who Will Be Next? Morning Journal's Latest Acquisitions," *Fourth Estate* (7 November 1895): 1. "The *Morning Journal* is surprising everyone," the article said, in reporting the *Journal*'s hiring talent from other newspapers soon after Hearst's arrival in New York.

18. "William R. Hearst: The Foremost Figure in American Journalism," *Editor and Publisher* 1, 1 (29 June 1901): 1. In addition, the article described Hearst's *Chicago American* as "the most successful recent adventure in American journalism."

19. Charles Whibley, "The American Yellow Press: An English View," *Bookman* (May 1907): 239. Whibley also wrote of the yellow press: "Divorced completely from the world of truth and intelligence, they present nothing which an educated man would desire to read. . . . They seem to address the half-blind eye and the wholly sluggish mind of the imbecile." See also, Sydney Brooks, "The Significance of Mr. Hearst," *Fortnightly Review* 88 (December 1907): 921. Brooks noted that Hearst's *Journal* had "multiplied itself in many cities and under many aliases."

20. Mott, *American Journalism*, 598.

21. Sidney Kobre, *The Yellow Press and Gilded Age Journalism* (Tallahassee, FL: Florida State University Press, 1964), 2–3.

22. Willard Grosvenor Bleyer, *Newspaper Writing and Editing* (Boston: Houghton Mifflin Co., 1913), 337.

23. Bleyer, *Newspaper Writing*, 337.

24. William A. Hachten, *The Troubles of Journalism: A Critical Look at What's Right and Wrong With the Press* (Mahwah, NJ: Lawrence Erlbaum Associates, 1998), 52.

25. George Presbury Rowell, *Forty Years An Advertising Agent, 1865–1905* (New York: Printer's Ink Publishing Co., 1906), 337.

26. Whibley, "The American Yellow Press," 242.

27. Hamilton Holt, *Commercialism and Journalism* (Boston and New York: Houghton Mifflin Co., 1909), 90. Holt also asserted: "Formerly the masses had to choose between such papers as 'The Atlantic Monthly,' 'The Nation,' the New York 'Tribune,' and nothing. No wonder they chose nothing. In the yellow press they now have their own champion—a press that serves them, represents them, leads them, and exploits them, as Tammany Hall does its constituency."

28. W. W. Hallock, "Pernicious 'Yellow' Papers," letter to *New York Times* (28 March 1898): 5.

29. John A. Macy, "Our Chromatic Journalism," *Bookman* 24 (October 1906): 128.

30. Hartley Davis, "The Journalism of New York," *Munsey's Magazine* 24, 2 (November 1900): 233. See also, "The Uses of Yellow Journalism," *Literary Digest* 24, 17 (26 April 1902): 571. The article quotes James Creelman, an apologist for William Randolph Hearst and formerly a correspondent for Hearst's *New York Journal*, as saying: "There is something to be said about the yellow journals: They have created newspaper readers."

31. Lydia Kingsmill Commander, "The Significance of Yellow Journalism," *Arena*, 34 (August 1905): 154–155. The notion that the yellow press was a force for educating the masses was not uncommon. A detailed report about New York newspapers in 1900 noted: "Paradoxical as it may seem, the chief value of the yellow journal is as an educator." See Davis, "The Journalism of New York," 233.

32. The supposed differences between readers of the yellow press and those of conservative newspapers typically rested on impression, rather than analysis. For a further example, see "Chicago Estimate of the Value of the 'Yellow' Newspapers," *Fourth Estate* (5 December 1903): 7. *Fourth Estate* reprinted a commentary from the *Chicago Chronicle*, which declared: "In point of fact, the 'yellow' newspaper has no intelligent readers. It circulates among people who prefer hideous pictures and flaring headlines to news or who hope for the complete overthrow of existing society and a reversion to a condition of anarchy." The *Chronicle* also claimed: "It follows that the readers of the conservative newspapers are a far more discriminating and intelligent class of people than the patrons of the 'new' journalism."

33. Cited in "An Interesting Journalistic Census," *Fourth Estate* (22 April 1897): 7. The *Fourth Estate* article suggested the survey was quite unusual, stating: "The Boston *Journal* has started a most novel census of its readers, one of a sort we do not remember having heard of before."

34. Mott, *American Journalism*, 539.

35. "Table 80—Population 1900, 1890, and 1880," *Abstract of the Twelfth Census*, 100–102. The ten most populous U.S. cities in 1900 were, in order: New York, Chicago, Philadelphia, St. Louis, Boston, Baltimore, Cleveland, Buffalo, San Francisco, and Cincinnati.

36. Mott, *American Journalism*, 539–540, and Irwin, "The Spread and Decline of Yellow Journalism." See also, Kobre, *The Yellow Press*.

37. Kenneth Stewart and John Tebbel, *Makers of Modern Journalism* (New York: Prentice-Hall Inc., 1952), 362.

38. Mott, *American Journalism*, 540.

39. See "Cincinnati," in *American Journalism from the Practical Side* (New York: Holmes Publishing Co., 1897), 84.

40. It became the *Denver Post* in 1901. See Bill Hosokawa, *Thunder in the Rockies: The Incredible Denver Post* (New York: William Morrow and Co. Inc., 1976), 29.

41. Kobre, *The Yellow Press*, 244. Kobre wrote: "The two partner-publishers, Fred G. Bonfils and Harry H. Tammen, brought the yellow, crusading type of journalism to the mountain region, and, in certain instances, went beyond [Hearst,] the master-sensationalist of San Francisco and New York. The Denver publishers gave the yellow hue a coloration all their own."

42. Irwin, "The Spread and Decline of Yellow Journalism."

43. The *Chronicle* was described as seeming "to care very little about appearances and goes in for sensationalism." See *American Journalism from the Practical Side*, 226.

44. Wilcox, "The American Newspaper," 71–72.

45. Irwin, "The Spread and Decline of Yellow Journalism."

46. See Irwin, "The Spread and Decline of Yellow Journalism," and Mott, *American Journalism*, 540.

47. "Table 80," *Abstract of the Twelfth Census*, 100–102.

48. "Table 81—Population Classified by Sex, by Race, and by Nativity: 1900," *Abstract of the Twelfth Census*, 103–105.

49. "Table 85—Illiterate Population at least 10 years of age, Classified by Race and Nativity: 1900," *Abstract of the Twelfth Census*, 115–117. The data are for what the Census table identified as foreign-born whites. Overall, 5.7% of the population in the country's 160 cities was illiterate. The urban illiteracy rate among the U.S.-born white population was 0.4%.

50. "Table 30—Statistics Relating to Daily Publications in 27 Cities, 1880 to 1900, "Printing and Publishing," *Census Reports: Manufacturers, Twelfth Census of the United States*, vol. 9. (Washington, DC: United States Census Office, 1902), 1051–1052.

51. Data are for Manhattan, the Bronx, and Brooklyn.

52. See Chapter One.

53. See "Who Reads the Editorials," *Fourth Estate* (7 December 1899): 6. The trade journal noted, "Those who read editorials are not confined to college graduates or professional men. This is shown by the comments made by readers of the Journal and World in the letters published in those papers. Small traders, hucksters, porters, longshoremen, bootblacks, shop girls, clerks, operators in factories and laborers find in them warm admirers."

54. "The Newspaper of To-Day," *New York Journal* (8 December 1897): 6. *Fourth Estate* noted that illustrations and large headlines often crowded out telegraphic news reports. "Nevertheless," it stated, "the illustrated papers have the largest circulations, which would seem to indicate that the general public prefers pictures to an abundance of telegraphic news." "Note and Comment," *Fourth Estate* (13 July 1899): 4.

55. "Something For Everybody," *New York World* (18 June 1899): 6.

56. "So the People May Know," *Denver Post* (18 April 1909): 1.

57. "First Anniversary of the New Era in Afternoon Journalism," *New York Evening Journal* (28 September 1897): 3. The *Evening Journal* then claimed a daily circulation of more than 510,000. *Fourth Estate* praised the *Evening Journal* as "evidently the sort of paper the people wanted, and the kind that was bound to be bought." See "Live One-Year-Old," *Fourth Estate* (30 September 1897): 1.

58. Charles M. Palmer, the *Journal*'s business manager, quoted in *American Journalism from the Practical Side*, 26. Palmer was further quoted as saying about the newspaper's attempt to reach a variety of readers: "'Society is made up of many classes, or at least there are many men of many minds, and in making a great metropolitan newspaper you must cover all the subjects of human interest that arise in this enlightened and progressive age. If you do not give the people [such] a newspaper, you cannot obtain a large circulation."

59. "Enterprise Tells: The New York Journal's Notable Achievements," *Fourth Estate* (27 October 1900): 3.

60. "The Fast Newspaper Mail to Washington," *Fourth Estate* (14 October 1897): 1.

61. "Note and Comment," *Fourth Estate* (20 February 1896): 7.

62. See Kobre, *The Yellow Press*, 18. See also, "The Purchasing Sex," *Fourth Estate* (10 October 1895): 6. *Fourth Estate* noted: "To-day, to-morrow, and in the days to come, the wise publisher will appeal to the women, not with silly women's pages, but with live information and advertising appealing to their prejudices and preferences."

63. See, for example, "America's Richest Bride," *New York Journal* (11 June 1897): 1. See also, "Society at Newport and Elsewhere," *New York Journal* (27 June 1897): 29.

64. "Note and Comment," *Fourth Estate* (10 June 1897): 4.

65. See, for example, "Directory of High-Class Apartments," *New York Journal* (3 November 1901): 65.

66. Cited in A. Maurice Low, "'Tabloid Journalism': Its Causes and Effects," *Forum* 31 (March 1901): 58.

67. Low, "'Tabloid Journalism,'" 58.

68. See, for example "Italian Peasantry at Ellis Island," *New York Journal* (15 May 1897): 6, and "Avalanche of Girls: Ten Thousand Irish Colleens Coming to New York," *New York Journal* (16 May 1897): 27. The *Journal* prominently covered the fire that destroyed the immigration center at Ellis Island in 1897. See "Ellis Island Burns; 200 Immigrants Saved," *New York Journal* (15 June 1897): 1.

69. Steven J. Diner, *A Very Different Age: Americans of the Progressive Era* (New York: Hill and Wang, 1998), 101.

70. The 1900 Census report suggests as much: "It is reasonable to conclude that [foreign-language] publications . . . depend for support, to a large extent, upon comparatively recent arrivals and that in general, when emigration from a country decreases, the number of publications printed in the language of that country decreases, and when immigration shows an increase the number of publications also increases." See "Printing and Publishing," *Census Reports: Manufacturers, Twelfth Census of the United States*, vol. 9, 1048.

71. See Mordecai Soltes, *The Yiddish Press: An Americanizing Agency* (New York: Arno Press reprint edition, 1969), 40–42.

72. See Lisa Yaszek, "'Them Damn Pictures': Americanization and the Comic Strip in the Progressive Era," *Journal of American Studies* 28 (1994): 28.

73. Soltes, *The Yiddish Press*, 178–179. Soltes, 178, characterized the Yiddish press in the United States as "in the front rank as an Americanizing agency," through efforts such as acquainting readers with a sense of American history and encouraging them to develop a command of English. See also, "Socialistic Papers," *Fourth Estate* (3 June 1897): 5.

74. See "Table 21—Newspapers and periodicals classified according to language in which printed, 1880 to 1900," *Census Reports: Manufacturers, Twelfth Census of the United States*, vol. 9, 1048. The Census found 35 Italian-language publications in 1900 and 13 in 1890. The number of Polish-language publications increased to 33 in 1900 from 18 in 1890. German-language publications, on the other hand, dropped to 613 in 1900 from 727 in 1890.

75. Robert E. Park, *The Immigrant Press and Its Control* (Westport, CT: Greenwood Press, 1970, reprint of 1922 ed.), 326.

76. Park, *The Immigrant Press*, 314–316. Drawing on 1900 Census data, Park further noted, 316: "The countries showing the highest proportion of immigrants show a high proportion of [foreign-language] papers started; and conversely, the immigrants who are arriving in proportionately smaller numbers have started fewer papers."

77. Whibley, "The American Yellow Press," 242.

78. Hachten, *The Troubles of Journalism*, 52.

79. Alan M. Kraut, *The Huddled Masses: The Immigrant in American Society, 1880–1921* (Arlington Heights, IL: Harlan Davidson Inc., 1982), 132.

80. Mary Hallock Foote, "Our Immigrants and Ourselves," *Atlantic Monthly* 86 (October 1900): 542.

81. Diner, *A Very Different Age*, 79. Diner also noted: "Among Italians, perhaps 50 percent of those who came to America went back."

82. Ernest Poole, "New Readers of the News," *American Magazine* 65, 1 (November 1907): 45.

83. John D. Stevens, *Sensationalism and the New York Press* (New York: Columbia University Press, 1991), 98.

84. H. W. Massingham, "The Modern Press and Its Public," *Contemporary Review* 98 (October 1910): 424.

85. Cited in Hosokawa, *Thunder in the Rockies*, 24. Hosokawa wrote, 24–25, "*The Post* of the early years with good reason has been described as looking like an explosion in a type factory."

86. Ochs merged the *Philadelphia Times* with the *Philadelphia Public Ledger* in 1902. See "Ledger and Times Consolidated," *Fourth Estate* (16 August 1902): 2.

87. "A New Code for Dailies," *Fourth Estate* (22 June 1901): 9. The article noted: "Following . . . the instructions given in this codification, a total of two-and-a-half pages of objectionable advertising was thrown out in the first seven days of the new management."

88. W. A. Swanberg, *Pulitzer* (New York: Charles Scribner's Sons, 1967), 254–255.

89. See "Brilliant Year's Record in the Newspaper Field," *Fourth Estate* (3 January 1903): 4.

90. As will be discussed in detail in Chapter Five.

91. See William Randolph Hearst Jr. with Jack Casserly, *The Hearsts: Father and Son* (Niwot, CO: Roberts Rinehart, 1991), 38.

92. James Creelman, *On the Great Highway: The Wanderings and Adventures of a Special Correspondent* (Boston: Lothrop Publishing, 1901), 177–178.

3

Not Likely Sent: The Remington-Hearst "Telegrams"

"W. R. Hearst, New York Journal, N.Y.:
"'Everything is quiet. There is no trouble here. There will be no war. I wish to return.
"'Remington.'"

"'Remington, Havana:
"'Please remain. You furnish the pictures, and I'll furnish the war.
"W. R. Hearst.'"[1]

The purported exchange of telegrams between Frederic S. Remington and William Randolph Hearst undeniably ranks among the most famous anecdotes in American journalism.[2] Hearst's supposed reply has been described as his "most quoted single utterance."[3] The exchange frequently has been cited by journalists[4] and by mass communication scholars of many specialties,[5] often as compelling evidence about how the yellow press, led by Hearst's *New York Journal*, forced the United States into war with Spain in 1898.[6]

The exchange suggests not only reckless arrogance by Hearst but also speaks to the potentially powerful effects of the news media. That, indeed, was the intent of James Creelman, the sole original source for the anecdote[7] who described the purported Remington-Hearst exchange in his book of reminiscences, *On the Great Highway*, which was published in 1901. Creelman maintained that the messages were emblematic of the power and the foresight of yellow journalism. [8] (Creelman did not specify when the exchange took place, saying vaguely that it occurred "some time before the destruction of the battleship Maine in the harbor of Havana"[9] in February 1898. Remington's lone visit to Cuba during the months before the *Maine*'s destruction was in January 1897, when he and

Richard Harding Davis, a famed war correspondent, went to the island on assignment for Hearst's *Journal*.)

While some historians have expressed doubt that such an exchange ever took place,[10] the literature reveals no concerted effort to assess the veracity of the account.[11] This chapter, then, reviews the context and key evidence associated with the purported exchange and concludes that it is exceedingly unlikely such messages were ever sent. The reasons for doubting the exchange are many and go beyond Hearst's somewhat belated denial,[12] go beyond the absence of documentation supporting Creelman's account, and go beyond the fact that the telegrams Creelman described have never surfaced. These reasons—drawn from an extensive review of papers of Creelman, Hearst, Remington, and others—include:

- Creelman at the time of the exchange was in Europe, as the *Journal*'s "special commissioner," or correspondent, on the Continent. As such, Creelman could only have learned about the supposed exchange second-hand.
- Creelman's credibility was impugned on another important matter, his account of the Japanese massacre at Port Arthur in 1894. An inquiry conducted for the U.S. State Department concluded Creelman's account was sensational and highly exaggerated.
- Creelman misrepresented the context of Remington's assignment to Cuba, saying it was open-ended. In reality, Remington and Davis had agreed to a one-month stay.
- The contemporaneous correspondence of Davis contains no reference to Remington's wanting to leave because "there will be no war." Rather, Davis in his letters gave various other reasons for Remington's departure, including the artist's reluctance to travel through Spanish lines to reach the Cuban insurgents. Davis also said in his correspondence that *he* asked Remington to leave.
- The contents of the purported telegrams bear little correlation to events in Cuba in early 1897. Specifically, the passages "there will be no war" and "I'll furnish the war" are at odds with the fierce and devastating conflict in Cuba that had begun in February 1895 and had forced Spain to send 200,000 soldiers to the island.
- Hearst's supposed reply to Remington runs counter to the *Journal*'s editorial positions in January 1897. The newspaper in editorials at that time expected the collapse of the Spanish war effort and resulting independence for Cuba. The *Journal* at the time was neither anticipating nor campaigning for U.S. military intervention to end the conflict.
- It is improbable that such an exchange of telegrams would have been cleared by Spanish censors in Havana. So strict were the censors that dispatches from American correspondents reporting the war in Cuba often were taken by ship to Florida and transmitted from there.

- The pithy epigram of the purported reply to Remington seems uncharacteristic of Hearst's telegrams. While not voluble or rambling in such messages, Hearst often offered specific suggestions and instructions in telegrams to his representatives assigned to important tasks and missions. It is thus likely that if Hearst had exchanged telegrams with Remington in January 1897, his messages would have contained explicit instructions and suggestions.
- Had there been such an exchange, Remington was clearly insubordinate and, as such, risked Hearst's displeasure. Despite Hearst's supposed instruction to stay, Remington left Cuba for New York in mid-January 1897. The *Journal* subsequently gave considerable prominence to Remington's sketches—arguably not the kind of response Hearst would have made or permitted in the face of outright insubordination.

THE WAR IN CUBA

Each of the foregoing reasons for questioning Creelman's account of the Remington-Hearst exchange will be reviewed in some detail. But first, it is vital to consider the context in which the exchange supposedly took place. In late 1896, Hearst hired Remington and Davis to travel to Cuba to spend time with the rebel forces, whose insurrection by then had spread across much of the island.[13] Spain had responded to the rebellion by sending 200,000 soldiers to Cuba. Their commander in 1896 and 1897 was Captain General Valeriano Weyler y Nicolau, who insisted that "war should be answered with war."[14]

Perhaps the most severe and controversial of Weyler's tactics were his successive *reconcentración* orders directing Cuba's rural population into urban camps in an attempt to deny the insurgents support from the countryside. Tens of thousands of Cuban noncombatants were thus crowded into these camps where many of them died from disease and malnutrition.[15] Beyond the camps, the conflict produced horrors of its own.[16] Reports of atrocities on both sides were not uncommon and not always exaggerated.[17] By late 1896, the war had left "a stillness . . . over vast expenses of the Cuban countryside."[18] A stalemate had thus taken hold by the time Remington and Davis set out for Cuba: The Spanish ruled the cities, the insurgents effectively controlled the countryside.

The plans were for Remington and Davis to travel from Key West to Cuba aboard Hearst's yacht, the *Vamoose*, and make their way surreptitiously to the camp of the insurgency's commanding general, Máximo Gómez. Reaching Cuba proved frustratingly difficult, however. Inclement weather, the yacht's suspect seaworthiness, and the crew's reluctance to attempt a landing in Cuba all conspired to keep Remington and Davis in Key West for three weeks.

Davis fumed about the delay. "The *Vamoose* is the fastest thing afloat and the slowest thing to get started I ever saw," he wrote from Key

West on Christmas Day 1896. "In fact, the engineer wanted to spend Christmas on shore so he is delaying the game for that."[19] Waiting, Davis wrote 2 January 1897, "is all we do and that's my life at Key West. I get up and half dress and take a plunge in the bay and then dress fully and have a greasy breakfast and then light a huge Key West cigar . . . and sit on the hotel porch. . . . Nothing happens after that except getting one's boots polished."[20] Aborting the assignment and returning to New York was considered, but rejected. Remington was inclined to do so but, Davis wrote, "gave up the idea of returning as soon as he found I would not do so."[21]

Finally, they booked passage on a passenger steamer to Havana, arriving 9 January 1897.[22] The next day they met Weyler, the Spanish military leader in Cuba, who granted "permission to travel over the island."[23] By 15 January 1897, Remington had parted with Davis and had begun making his way back to New York. On 24 January, the *Journal* began publishing his sketches and brief descriptions about the Cuban rebellion. Davis' reports trickled in later—the most notable of which was an account of the execution of a suspected Cuban rebel by Spanish firing squad.[24] That dispatch was accompanied by an evocative sketch by Remington that dominated the *Journal*'s front page on 2 February 1897.[25]

CREELMAN, THE ANECDOTE'S SOLE SOURCE, WAS IN EUROPE IN EARLY 1897

The first account of the purported Remington-Hearst telegraphic exchange appeared more than four years later in Creelman's *On the Great Highway*. Creelman does not in that account, nor in the version he wrote for *Pearson's* magazine in 1906,[26] describe how or when he learned about the supposed Remington-Hearst exchange. Although some accounts mistakenly place Creelman with Remington in Cuba at the time of purported exchange,[27] Creelman was in fact in Europe in early 1897, as the *Journal*'s "special commissioner" on the Continent. Creelman reported during the winter of 1897 from Madrid on Spain's struggling and increasingly costly effort to prosecute the war in Cuba. He also filed dispatches from Paris and Rome.

Creelman's reports often contained little or no attribution and few named sources—not unlike those of many of his contemporaries, and not unlike the account about the Remington-Hearst telegrams that appeared in his book.[28] Creelman's dispatches were, moreover, characterized by an extravagant, breathless, and improbable quality. Extraordinary conspiracies figured in his reports to the *Journal* in early 1897. In one, he described a "hidden deal" between the outgoing administration of President Grover Cleveland and Spanish authorities to help thwart the Cuban insurgency. "It has taken me many days to trace out the astounding dealings of President Cleveland and his Administration with the Spanish monarchy, but I am now in a position to give the American public some light on the subject," Creelman asserted in a dispatch published in the *Journal* on New Year's Day 1897.[29] At the heart of this supposed conspiracy was Cleveland's refusal "to recognize the Independence of the Cuban Government or the belligerency of its arms, and at the same time calmly absolv[ing] Spain from all its responsibility for the protection of American property in the island," Creelman wrote.[30]

Later that winter, he reported from Paris that he had uncovered plans by Spain and other European powers to array themselves against the United States. "Within an hour," he wrote in February 1897, "I have learned impressive details of the Spanish conspiracy to form a league of European governments against the United States."[31] Needless to say, such a "league" never took shape. Nor could it have, given the diverse interests among the European powers, their reluctance to "risk the wrath of the United States," and Spain's pursuit of a foreign policy that had generally ignored the rest of Europe.[32]

Creelman's fondness for hyperbole, his reluctance or disinclination to cite sources, and his failure to explain how he learned about the purported Remington-Hearst exchange all serve to undercut the believability of his account about the telegrams.

CREELMAN'S DUBIOUS CREDIBILITY

Creelman's credibility had been impugned long before publication of *On the Great Highway*. A notable challenge came in December 1894, in the aftermath of his report that Japanese soldiers massacred and mutilated Chinese civilians while overrunning Port Arthur (now Lushun) in November of that year. Creelman, who at the time was writing for the *New York World*, said the slaughter was so complete that the only Chinese survivors were those needed to form burial parties.[33] The reported atrocities—although they were dismissed as "reckless sensationalism" by the *New York Tribune*[34]—provoked an uproar in the United States,[35] and the U.S. minister to Japan, Edwin Dun, investigated. He interviewed Creelman as well as American, French, and Japanese military officials and concluded in a report to the U. S. State Department that "the account sent to 'The World' by Mr. Creelman is sensational in the extreme and a gross exaggeration of what occurred."[36] Undeterred by the rebuke, Creelman in his book repeated his account of the atrocities at Port Arthur, writing that "the Japanese killed everything they saw. Unarmed men, kneeling in the streets and begging for life, were shot, bayoneted, or beheaded. The town was sacked from end to end, and the inhabitants were butchered in their own houses."[37]

Creelman invoked similarly horrific scenes in his dispatches filed from Cuba for the *World* in 1896. "The horrors of a barbarous struggle for the extermination of the native population are witnessed in all parts of the country," he wrote. "Blood on the roadsides, blood in the field, blood of the doorsteps, : blood, blood, blood! The old, the young, the weak, the crippled—all are butchered without mercy."[38] Given the guerrilla nature of the Cuban insurrection, widespread bloodshed of the kind Creelman described was quite uncommon.[39]

CREELMAN ERRED IN DESCRIBING CONTEXT OF REMINGTON'S ASSIGNMENT

Creelman's credibility is further undercut by his inaccurate description of the nature of Remington's mission. Creelman (who failed in his book to mention that Davis had accompanied Remington) described the assignment to Cuba as open-ended, that the artist had been "instructed to remain there until the war began; for 'yellow journalism' was alert and had an eye for the future."[40]

However, Davis' correspondence—the best contemporaneous record of the trip to Cuba—made clear the assignment was to last only one month. "We will stay a month with [the insurgents,] the yacht calling for copy and sketches once a week and finally for us in a month," Davis said in a letter 19 December 1896, in which he told his mother that he and Remington were going to Cuba.[41] Later, during their prolonged stay at Key West, Davis and Remington made clear to Hearst that "there was to be no delay or nonsense about picking us up [on the Cuban coast] at the end of a month."[42]

When they finally reached Cuba in January 1897, Davis told his mother of plans to spend two or three weeks traveling in the hinterland, after which "we will then be about ready to return home."[43] Remington stayed in Cuba about a week; Davis returned in early February 1897.

REMINGTON LEFT BECAUSE HE HAD ENOUGH MATERIAL—OR WAS ASKED, OR WAS FRIGHTENED

Davis' correspondence makes clear that he had little regard for the rotund, slow-moving Remington, whom he called "a large blundering bear."[44] But the letters contain no reference to Remington's having wanted to leave Cuba because the artist believed "there will be no war." Rather, Davis in his letters offers no fewer than three other explanations for Remington's departure. They were:

- Remington left because he had sufficient material for illustrating Davis' articles. Davis wrote 15 January 1897 in a letter to his mother: "Remington has all the material he needs for sketches and for illustrating my stories so he is going home. I will go on further as I have not yet seen much that is interesting."[45]

- Remington left at Davis' request. "I asked him to go as it left me freer," Davis wrote elsewhere in the 15 January letter. In a separate letter that day, Davis told his mother: "I am as relieved at getting old Remington to go as though I had won $5000. He was a splendid fellow but a perfect kid and had to be humored and petted all the time."[46]
- Remington left because he was frightened by the prospect of crossing Spanish lines to spend time with the Cuban insurgents. "Remington got scared and backed out much to my relief and I went on and tried to cross the lines," but without success, Davis wrote later in January 1897.[47]

Davis' correspondence indicates that Remington's departure came soon after they had visited Jaruco, a town near Havana where they encountered unpleasant conditions. "There we slept off the barnyard," Davis wrote, "and cows and chickens walked all over the floor and fleas all over us."[48] The hardships of that outing may have contributed to Remington's decision to return to New York. The assignment had been an exacting one for the artist. As a friend said later of Remington's time in Cuba in 1897: "The heat was terrible, the transportation bad, and his physical condition poor. He suffered."[49]

Whatever prompted Remington's departure—and it appears he was neither reluctant nor disinclined to leave—none of Davis' letters suggest that the artist wanted to return to the United States on the pretense of having found "no war" in Cuba. Davis wrote that Remington had become "very bitter over what he saw" during the assignment and intended "to stir up Washington" upon his return.[50] Davis also said the artist was "very excitable and a firebrand"[51]—hardly an apt or fitting description for someone who supposedly had found "everything is quiet" in Cuba.

Remington seemed very much the firebrand in the aftermath of his trip to Cuba. The descriptions that accompanied his illustrations in the *Journal* bristled with outrage. Remington's sketch of pro-Spanish irregular forces escorting prisoners carried this caption:

> The acts of the terrible savages, or irregular troops called "guerrillas," employed by the Spaniard, pass all understanding by civilized man. The American Indian was never guilty of the monstrous crimes that they commit. Their treatment of women is unspeakable, and as for the men captured by them alive, the blood curdles in my veins as I think of the atrocity, of the cruelty, practised on these helpless victims. My picture illustrates one case where the guerrillas saw fit to bring their captives into the lines, trussed up at the elbows, after their fashion.[52]

Such a description is totally at odds with the content of Remington's purported telegram to Hearst. While the description may have reflected the suggestions of *Journal* editors, it would have been unconscionable to have insisted that Remington attach his name and prestige to such an account—or to agree to the publication of such illustrations—if he truly believed that "everything" had been "quiet" in Cuba.

Remington also wrote to the *New York World* after his return, denouncing the Spanish administration as the "the woman-killing outfit down there in Cuba."[53] That the letter appeared in the *World* suggests that Remington's hostility to the Spanish was not artifice crafted to please editors at the *Journal*. The evidence of such antipathy after his trip makes it seem quite improbable that Remington sent Hearst a telegram with word that "there is no trouble" in Cuba.

CONTENT OF "TELEGRAMS" CONTRADICTED BY CONDITIONS IN CUBA

The content of the purported exchange—in particular, Hearst's supposed vow to "furnish the war"—bears little correlation to events in Cuba at the time, or to coverage of those events by New York newspapers. It would have been incongruous for Hearst to have promised to "furnish" a war because he knew quite well that war had been waged in Cuba since early 1895. Indeed, the ongoing war was the very reason Hearst sent Remington and Davis to Cuba.[54]

The *Journal* and its rival newspapers in New York City routinely described the Cuban insurgency as a "war" and gave prominence to reports about the fighting, low intensity though it often was.[55] When Remington returned from Cuba, for example, the *Journal* reported that he had brought "from the scene of the war . . . a sketch book full of illustrations of characters, scenes and incidents, which are making the insurrection on the island so interesting to Americans."[56]

The *New York Sun* in early 1897 referred often to an ongoing "war of extermination"[57] in Cuba. Like the *Journal*, the *Sun* assailed Weyler as a "Spanish savage" who "has made the island a place of slaughter. . . . The story of his deeds is such a one as mankind has not before heard for generations."[58] The *New York Tribune* invoked similarities between the Cuban insurrection and the American Revolution,[59] a not uncommon theme at the time. Even the *New York Herald*, a voice for diplomatic resolution to the Cuban insurrection, referred in January 1897 to the "destructive conflict in which neither side is able to vanquish the other by force."[60]

Davis was under no illusions, either, about the upheaval in Cuba. "There is war here and no mistake," he wrote from Cuba in mid-January 1897, "and all the people in the field have been ordered in to the fortified towns where they are starving and dying of disease[.]"[61] His correspondence contains graphic description of what he called the grim process "of extermination and ruin. . . . The insurgents began first by destroying the sugar mills some of which were worth millions of dollars in machinery, and now the Spaniards are burning the houses of the people and hoarding them in around the towns to starve out the insurgents and to leave them without shelter or places for food or to hide the wounded. So all day long, wherever you look you see great heavy columns of smoke rising into the beautiful sky above the magnificent palms."[62]

Davis compiled his dispatches from Cuba in a volume published late in 1897. The book, illustrated by Remington's sketches, was titled *Cuba In War Time*.[63]

CONTENT OF "TELEGRAMS" AT ODDS WITH EDITORIALS IN THE *JOURNAL*

Editorials in Hearst's *Journal* in January 1897 expressed and reiterated the view that the Cuban rebels would ultimately defeat Spain in Cuba. At the time, the *Journal*'s editorials about Cuba were not bellicose; the newspaper was not campaigning for U.S. military intervention to end the conflict. [64] Rather, the editorials reflected a view that Spain would be unable to sustain its war effort in Cuba. As such, Hearst's purported reply to Remington—"I'll furnish the war"—would have been inexplicably inconsistent with the editorial stance of his newspaper.

Moreover, the *Journal*'s editorial position *vis-à-vis* Cuba in January 1897 was clearly based on, and influenced by, Creelman's reporting from Madrid. Notably, on 4 January 1897, the *Journal* assessed "the state of Spain" in an editorial that declared the "news furnished by the Journal's special commissioner to Madrid demonstrates that Spain is hardly able to prolong much longer the struggle with its lost colony, to say nothing of undertaking to give battle to a nation vastly its superior." The editorial added: "Not even the rigidness of Weyler's censorship at Havana has prevented the news of his complete failure from reaching the mother country."[65]

At the end of January, a *Journal* editorial said the rebels needed only to persevere to prevail: "They must now know that it is but a little more battle and struggle to win, even without the help of the great Republic where dearth of action matched verbal exuberance of sympathy. . . . Whatever disposition Spain may now display, it will be belated wisdom. She has practically already lost her magnificent colony. . . . Cuba Libre will speedily cease to be a mirage if the Cubans continue loyal to their own honor and duty, and that but a little longer."[66]

CENSORS NOT LIKELY TO HAVE CLEARED THE "TELEGRAMS"

It is improbable that Spanish censors in Havana—the bane of American correspondents reporting about the insurgency—would have cleared the Remington-Hearst exchange. [67] A *Journal* correspondent sent to Cuba in 1896 referred to the Havana telegraph office as "this tomb of telegrams." He said that correspondents were "broken-hearted" to find "how ruthlessly [their] stories had been slaughtered" by the censors there.[68] The U.S. consul-general in Havana, Fitzhugh Lee, wrote in February 1897 that the "Spanish censor permits nothing to go out except formally to Spain and whenever you see a dispatch in newspapers dated Habana it is shaped to pass the censor."[69] Indeed, censorship in Cuba was "so strict that even routine dispatches had to be smuggled out of the country by boat and filed from Florida."[70] Correspondents also sent reports from Cuba through the consul-general's diplomatic pouch.[71]

The prospect of severe censorship was precisely why Remington and Davis planned to enter Cuba illicitly, to be infiltrated by Hearst's *Vamoose*. As Davis noted in his correspondence, the yacht also was to retrieve Davis' reports from Cuba and take them to Key West, thus evading the censors in Havana. The intended use of the *Vamoose* was no secret. The trade publication *Fourth Estate* reported in November 1896 the "*Journal* has planned a bold move to outwit the Spanish censor. William R. Hearst has chartered the steam yacht *Vamoose*, the fastest craft afloat in American waters. The *Journal* will carry its own dispatches from Havana to Key West. It will take the *Vamoose* but three hours to make the trip."[72]

Even if the censors had cleared the purported Remington-Hearst exchange,[73] the Spanish captain general in Cuba—regularly assailed in the *Journal* and other New York newspapers as "the Butcher" Weyler[74]—surely would have seized on the telegrams as evidence of flagrant meddling. Spanish authorities had, after all, often complained that arms and ammunition were being delivered to Cuban insurgents by American filibusters. A vow from a leading American newspaper publisher to "furnish the war" was not the kind of message that Weyler would have ignored. The general, in fact, could have been expected to exploit Hearst's message for its obvious propaganda value to the beleaguered Spanish war effort.[75]

Intercepting and publicizing the telegrams undoubtedly would have helped Weyler justify his policy of expelling or jailing American reporters who communicated with, or spent time among, the insurgent forces.[76] As early as the first months of the Cuban revolt in 1895, a Cuban-born American correspondent for the *New York World* was jailed briefly on charges of aiding the rebels.[77] A *Journal* reporter, Charles Michelson, was arrested in western Cuba and jailed for ten days in 1896.[78] A few weeks after Remington and Davis arrived in Cuba, Sylvester Scovel of the *World*, who had spent time in January with the insurgents, was arrested on charges of traveling without a military pass and communicating with the enemy.[79] Scovel was released after about a month in jail—and after the *World* campaigned vigorously for his freedom.[80]

So the risks facing American correspondents covering the war in Cuba were well-known. Hearst, by planning to use the *Vamoose* to take Remington and Davis to Cuba, had developed a plan (however ineffective in practice) to skirt Weyler's restrictions on newsgathering. Therefore, Hearst's sending a sensitive and combative message into the teeth of rigorous Spanish censorship in Havana would have been inconsistent, reckless, and quite likely dangerous for his correspondents.[81]

HEARST FILLED TELEGRAMS WITH DETAILED INSTRUCTIONS

The pithy epigram of the purported reply to Remington seems uncharacteristic of Hearst's telegrams of the time. While not necessarily expansive or wordy in such messages, Hearst often included suggestions and instructions in telegrams to those whom he had assigned important tasks or missions. For example, Hearst's numerous telegrams to Creelman in Europe during the weeks before the Spanish-American War in 1898 were replete with instructions about coverage from the Continent. Those messages make it quite clear that Hearst was an engaged editor, inclined to manage closely his special correspondents.

In the immediate aftermath of the destruction of the U.S. warship *Maine* in Havana harbor in February 1898, Hearst instructed Creelman, then in London, to "hold" an interview story that Creelman had evidently planned for the upcoming Sunday because "all interest now centered in *Maine*." Hearst also informed Creelman that the rival *World* and *Herald* were "printing good foreign interviews."[82] In a separate message, Hearst urged Creelman to prod the *Journal*'s correspondents in Europe, informing him, for example that "Madrid seems [to be] doing nothing. *Herald* has fine cable on attitude of Weyler. *Maine* is great thing. Arouse everybody."[83] Hearst's deepening displeasure with reporting from Madrid prompted another cable to Creelman: "Stir up Madrid. *World* has cabled man there to get from Spanish government statement whether mines in Havana harbor. Should have something offset this."[84] Finally, Hearst instructed Creelman to "proceed [to] Madrid immediately. Get big interviews on situation. Describe war feeling, etc."[85]

Few of Hearst's papers and letters from the late nineteenth century survive or have been made public, including those for the months before, during, and after the Spanish-American War. Nevertheless, the available record suggests his clear propensity to send, via the telegraph, explicit and detailed instructions to his far-flung representatives. Had Hearst communicated with Remington by telegraph in January 1897, it is quite likely, therefore, his messages to the artist would have contained explicit instructions and suggestions. A pithy response of the sort he supposedly made to Remington—"You furnish the pictures, and I'll furnish the war"—would have been out of character.

THE "EXCHANGE" MEANT HEARST EXCUSED INSUBORDINATION

If Remington and Hearst did exchange the telegrams Creelman described, it meant that the artist was insubordinate: He defied Hearst's order to "remain" and promptly returned to New York instead.[86] Even so, Remington's work received prominent display in the *Journal*, which suggests that if the telegrams were exchanged, Hearst ignored or overlooked flagrant disobedience by a wayward artist. Hearst, after all, was used to getting his own way[87] and was said to "rise in terrible wrath when a reporter came back empty-handed from an assignment."[88]

Perhaps Hearst believed he had little choice but to use what illustrations Remington provided. But the variety of Remington's drawings, the prominence they received, and Hearst's favorable recollections of the Remington-Davis assignment many years later all suggest that Hearst was not at all displeased with the artist or his work—and further suggest that the purported exchange of telegrams never took place.

Remington's illustrations were prominently displayed in the *Journal*. His sketches of a bedraggled Spanish scouting party, and of pro-Spanish irregulars escorting their captives, dominated the newspaper's first news pages on Sunday, 24 January 1897.[89] A headline that introduced the sketches referred to Remington as "the gifted artist" who had been assigned to Cuba "especially for the Journal."[90] A few days later, the *Journal* devoted its entire second page to a sketch by Remington that depicted Cuban troops firing at small Spanish fortifications that dotted the landscape. The illustration appeared beneath a headline that read: "Frederic Remington Sketches A Familiar Incident of the Cuban War."[91]

In recollections written years later, Hearst commented favorably about the artist's work for the *Journal*. Hearst noted that he had sent Davis and Remington to Cuba "to describe and depict the atrocities which the cruel Spaniards were inflicting upon the courageous Cubans, struggling for their liberties. These correspondents did their work admirably and aroused much indignation among Americans against 'Butcher' Weyler, the bloodthirsty Spanish general, but no urge to war."[92]

Remington, though, was none too pleased with the reproduction quality of his illustrations from Cuba. "Davis will write and I will draw," he wrote after returning home in January 1897, "but can't do much in a Yellow Kid journal—printing too bad."[93] Even so, he appears to have remained on reasonably friendly terms with Hearst. For example, Remington assured his publisher in 1898 that Hearst would not object to the use in a forthcoming book of illustrations the artist had drawn for the

Journal. "There is no doubt," Remington wrote, "that I can get his permission."[94]

COULD THE "TELEGRAMS" HAVE BEEN SENT, NONETHELESS?

The preponderance of evidence is that the Remington-Hearst exchange described by Creelman—and repeated many times by journalists and media historians—never took place. Even so, there may have been an opportunity for Remington to have communicated with Hearst by telegram, without Davis' knowledge.

Davis' correspondence indicates that he and Remington parted ways 15 January 1897 in Matanzas, east of Havana. The artist was escorted to Havana by an interpreter named Otto.[95] Remington probably spent at least a day there before obtaining the required exit visa from Spanish authorities,[96] time enough to send Hearst a message announcing he was on his way home—and perhaps justifying his return on the pretext, "Everything is quiet. . . . There will be no war." Remington, under such a scenario, may then have boarded the steamer from Havana without receiving or waiting for Hearst's reply. Davis, in Matanzas, would not have known immediately about the telegram.

But even such a scenario is implausible in that it fails to explain why Spanish authorities declined to exploit the purported reply by Hearst. The scenario also fails to explain why and how Creelman, across the Atlantic, learned of such an exchange. If his sources were Spanish authorities in Madrid, why would they have shared the evidence of a Hearstian *faux pas* exclusively with Creelman, a correspondent and apologist for Hearst? Why would they not have publicized such a prize? Why would they not have shared it with one of the many bitter newspaper rivals to Hearst and his *Journal*?

The far more plausible and persuasive explanation is that the purported exchange of telegrams never took place. The more plausible and persuasive explanation is that Remington, rather than finding "everything [to be] quiet" in Cuba, grew impatient with a frustrating and physically demanding assignment that had been slow to unfold, and with a fellow correspondent, Davis, who could barely tolerate the artist's presence.[97]

LINGERING QUESTIONS

Despite the preponderance of evidence, a few matters remain unresolved, including that of Remington's silence about the purported exchange. He appears to have said nothing about it, after Creelman's book appeared in 1901 and after the matter became the subject of a brief controversy in 1907.

So why did Remington not deny the exchange? Perhaps he wanted to avoid reminders of the assignment to Cuba, on which he said he "saw more hell . . . than I ever read about."[98] The immediate aftermath of the trip proved controversial and embarrassing, because of Remington's wildly inaccurate and imaginative sketch of Spanish authorities conducting a strip-search of a young Cuban woman aboard an American passenger vessel, the *Olivette*. The sketch accompanied Davis' report about the search and was published in the *Journal* in February 1897[99]—and was quickly exposed as exaggerated.[100] Perhaps by keeping a silence, Remington sought to avoid revisiting awkward issues that surrounded the trip to Cuba.[101]

A Remington scholar, Allen P. Splete, maintains that Remington was more inclined to confront challenges to his artistic reputation than he was to address controversies surrounding his personal conduct. That inclination, Splete suggests, may help explain Remington's reticence about the purported exchange with Hearst.[102]

Davis, on the other hand, was unlikely to have kept silent had he known first-hand about the exchange of telegrams. After all, the trip to Cuba had left Davis embittered and disgusted with Hearst and vowing never to work for him again. He blamed Hearst for failing to follow through on plans to infiltrate him and Remington into Cuba. He accused Hearst of thwarting his plans to join the Cuban insurgents by publishing an erroneous report in mid-January 1897 that said Davis and Remington had linked up with the rebels. Davis complained about those lapses in a letter to his mother, writing: "Twice [Hearst] has prevented me from doing what I set out to do."[103] Davis also tried to distance himself from Hearst's journalism, telling his mother in another letter: "I am not writing for the *Journal*, the Journal is printing what I write."[104]

More than four years after the assignment to Cuba, Davis received from Creelman a copy of *On the Great Highway*. Davis replied promptly, thanking Creelman and praising the book as "entertaining" and "full of information."[105] Davis, however, did not comment or raise questions about the chapter in which Creelman related the Remington-Hearst exchange. Perhaps he failed to realize that Creelman was referring in *On the Great Highway* to the same, star-crossed assignment in which Davis and Remington had traveled to Cuba together. Creelman's account, after all, fails to say that it was a joint assignment and Creelman's contextual error—that Remington was instructed to stay in Cuba "until the war began"—may well have caused Davis to believe that Creelman was discussing another assignment entirely.

Why, then, wasn't Hearst more insistent in denying the purported exchange of telegrams? Perhaps it was because Creelman's account was meant not to be damning but *flattering*, to illustrate the power and effectiveness of yellow journalism. Creelman was indeed expansive in defense of the genre, writing in *On the Great Highway*:

> How little they know of "yellow journalism" who denounce it! How swift they are to condemn its shrieking headlines, its exaggerated pictures, its coarse buffoonery, its intrusions upon private life, and its occasional inaccuracies! But how slow they are to see the steadfast guardianship of public interests which it maintains! How blind to its unfearing warfare against rascality, its detection and prosecution of crime, its costly searchings for knowledge throughout the earth, its exposures of humbug, its endless funds for the quick relief of distress![106]

The purported Remington-Hearst exchange, moreover, appears not to have been particularly important or newsworthy at the time: It was cited only infrequently in reviews[107] of *On the Great Highway*.[108] Nor did the anecdote about the telegrams appear in obituaries about Creelman, who died in 1915.[109] The anecdote seems to have provoked almost no discussion or controversy until a correspondent for the *Times* of London mentioned it in a dispatch from New York in 1907. He wrote: "Is the Press of the United States going insane? . . . A letter from William Randolph Hearst is in existence and was printed in a magazine not long ago. It was to an artist he had sent to Cuba, and who reported no likelihood of war. 'You provide the pictures,' he wrote, 'I'll provide the war.'"[110]

Hearst, indignant about the report, replied in a letter to the *Times*. He described as "frankly false" and "ingeniously idiotic" the claim "that there was a letter in existence from Mr. W. R. Hearst in which Mr. Hearst said to a correspondent in Cuba: 'You provide the pictures and I will provide the war,' and the intimation that Mr. Hearst was chiefly responsible for the Spanish war.

"This kind of clotted nonsense could only be generally circulated and generally believed in England, where newspapers claiming to be conservative and reliable are the most utterly untrustworthy of any on earth. In apology for these newspapers it may be said that their untrustworthiness is not always to intention but more frequently to ignorance and prejudice."[111]

Nor does it seem likely that Hearst quietly allowed the legend of the telegrams to take hold and grow, as emblematic of his influence and power. Rather, the record suggests that Hearst rejected the notion his newspapers fomented the Spanish-American War and pointedly blamed Spain instead. "Any informed and unprejudiced person knows that the one cause of the Spanish war was Spain, and that from the time of the blowing up of the Maine in Havana Harbour war was inevitable," he wrote in his letter to the *Times* of London in 1907.[112] In a column written in 1940, Hearst asserted that it was the *Maine*'s destruction that "precipitated the conflict" with Spain.[113]

CONCLUSION: WHY IT MATTERS

This chapter, in addressing and challenging an enduring anecdote of yellow journalism, finds little if any evidence that Remington and Hearst exchanged the telegrams, as Creelman described. Because the evidence is so persuasive that the purported exchange *did not* take place, the anecdote deserves relegation to the closet of historical imprecision—at least until proved otherwise. Journalists and historians clearly are ill served by repeating the anecdote, by presenting a fanciful story as factual.

They likewise are ill served by presenting the anecdote as illustrative of some "greater truth" about Hearst's supposed warmongering—that he was intent on provoking war over Cuba between the United States and Spain. As this chapter has shown Hearst's *Journal* at the time of the supposed exchange with Remington was anticipating the collapse of Spain's war effort in Cuba, and was not campaigning for armed intervention by the United States. In taking such an editorial stance, the *Journal* relied heavily on Creelman's reporting from Madrid about Spanish views and opinion. Rather than reflecting and confirming Hearst's intentions at that time, the purported telegram to Remington, if sent, would have been incongruous and contradictory.

By repeating the colorful anecdote about the Remington-Hearst telegrams, journalists and historians risk falling victim to the distorting effects of "the aesthetic fallacy," a condition in which facts and details are used to construct "a beautiful story"—a story that distorts or supplants empirical truths.[114] The Remington-Hearst anecdote is indeed "a beautiful story," a succinct and delicious tale, one rich in hubris and swaggering recklessness. It is, however, a story altogether dubious and misleading. It suggests power that the press, including Hearst's *Journal*, did not possess, that of propelling the country into war it did not want. We will turn next to an examination of the reasons why the yellow press could not have fomented the Spanish-American War.

NOTES

1. James Creelman, *On the Great Highway: The Wanderings and Adventures of a Special Correspondent* (Boston: Lothrop Publishing, 1901), 177–178.

2. That point is made by Arthur Lubow in *The Reporter Who Would Be King: A Biography of Richard Harding Davis* (New York: Scribner's Sons, 1992), 139–140.

3. John K. Winkler, *William Randolph Hearst: A New Appraisal* (New York: Hastings House, 1955), 95. Historians have given various versions of the pur-

ported Remington-Hearst exchange. One variation was: "You make the pictures, and I'll make the war," see Oliver Carlson and Ernest Sutherland Bates, *Hearst: Lord of San Simeon* (New York: Viking, 1936), 97, and Oliver Carlson, *Brisbane: A Candid Biography* (New York: Stackpole Sons, 1937), 120. The purported exchange has sometimes been presented as "you provide the pictures, I'll provide the war."

4. See, for example: Mark Dawidziak, "Remembering America's 'Splendid Little War,'" *Plain Dealer* [Cleveland, OH] (23 August 1999): 3E; Michael Taylor, "The Reign of S.F.'s 'Monarch of the Dailies,'" *San Francisco Chronicle* (7 August 1999): A9; Clifford Krauss, "Remember Yellow Journalism," *New York Times* (15 February 1998): 4, 3; "Forget the *Maine!*" *Economist* 346 (3 January 1998): 32. The anecdote also has appeared in several books by journalists. See, for example, David Halberstam, *The Powers That Be* (New York: Dell Publishing Company Inc., 1980), 295; Allen Churchill, *Park Row* (New York: Rinehart and Company, 1958), 104; and Willis J. Abbot, *Watching the World Go By* (Boston: Little, Brown and Company, 1933), 217.

5. The anecdote appears in surveys of mass communication as well as in more specialized treatments. For an example of its appearance in surveys, see, among others, Ray Eldon Hiebert and Sheila Jean Gibbons, *Exploring Mass Media for a Changing World* (Mahwah, NJ: Lawrence Erlbaum Associates, 2000), 151. See also, Michael Schudson, *Discovering the News: A Social History of American Newspapers* (New York: Basic Books Inc., 1978), 61–62. Foreign policy analysts have likewise cited the purported exchange. See, for example, Philip Seib, *Headline Diplomacy: How News Coverage Affects Foreign Policy* (Westport, CT: Praeger Publishers, 1997), 5. The anecdote was cited as well in a study of 1920s journalism. See Simon Michael Bessie, *Jazz Journalism: The Story of the Tabloid Newspapers* (New York: E. P. Dutton and Company, 1938), 59–60. It also appeared in a 1998 Spanish-language study of the press and the Spanish-American War. See Félix Santos, *1898: La prensa y la guerra de Cuba* (Bilbao, Vizcaya: Asociación Julián Zugazagoitia, 1998), 42.

6. See, for example, Hiley H. Ward, *Mainstreams of American Media History: A Narrative and Intellectual History* (Boston: Allyn and Bacon, 1997), 279, and John Tebbel, *The Compact History of the American Newspaper* (New York: Hawthorn Books Inc., 1963), 202.

7. Creelman's account is the earliest reference to the purported exchange that has been found. Leading media history texts that discuss the exchange cite Creelman's book as the original source. See, for example, Frank Luther Mott, *American Journalism: A History: 1690–1960,* 3d ed. (New York: Macmillan, 1962), 529. See also John D. Stevens, *Sensationalism and the New York Press* (New York: Columbia University Press: 1991), 96. Stevens wrote: "Creelman's memoir is the only evidence for the infamous anecdote about Hearst's cabling Remington that he would provide the war."

8. Creelman, *On the Great Highway,* 177. He wrote that Hearst "was as good as his word" in bringing about the war with Spain.

9. Creelman, *On the Great Highway,* 177.

10. See, for example, Carlson and Bates, *Hearst: Lord of San Simeon,* 97; Stevens, *Sensationalism and the New York Press,* 92; and Joyce Milton, *The Yellow Kids:*

Foreign Correspondents in the Heyday of Yellow Journalism (New York: Harper and Row, 1989), xii.

11. Some historians have characterized the anecdote as "legend" but have repeated it nonetheless. See, for example, Jean Folkerts and Dwight L. Teeter Jr., *Voices of a Nation: A History of Mass Media in the United States*, 3d ed. (Boston: Allyn and Bacon, 1998), 269–270. Mott prefaced his description of the purported Remington-Hearst exchange, writing that it was "said to have taken place." Mott, *American Journalism*, 529. Other authors have accepted the anecdote without reservation, including several who have written about the Spanish-American War. See, for example, Joseph E. Wisan, *The Cuban Crisis as Reflected in the New York Press (1895–1898)* (New York: Octagon Books reprint edition, 1965), 459; Charles H. Brown, *The Correspondents' War: Journalists in the Spanish-American War* (New York: Charles Scribner's Sons, 1967), 78; Lubow, *The Reporter Who Would Be King*, 137–142; and Douglas Allen, *Frederic Remington and the Spanish-American War* (New York: Crown Publishers, 1971), 11. See also Philip S. Foner, who referred in a footnote to "the famous telegram Frederick [*sic*] Remington sent to William Randolph Hearst from Havana." Foner, *The Spanish-Cuban-American War and the Birth of American Imperialism, 1895–1902*, vol. 1 (New York: Monthly Review Press, 1972), 163. Hearst's biographers also have tended to accept the anecdote at face value. See, notably, Ferdinand Lundberg, *Imperial Hearst: A Social Biography* (New York: Equinox Cooperative Press, 1936), 68–69; W. A. Swanberg, *Citizen Hearst* (New York: Charles Scribner's Sons, 1961), 107–108, and David Nassaw, *The Chief: The Life of William Randolph Hearst* (Boston: Houghton Mifflin Company, 2000), 127. One of Hearst's biographers of the late twentieth century, Ben Procter, sought to qualify the account by stating that Hearst "allegedly replied" to Remington with the vow to "furnish the war." See Procter, *William Randolph Hearst: The Early Years* (New York: Oxford University Press, 1998), 103. Judith Robinson, a biographer of Hearst's mother, Phoebe Apperson Hearst, recounts the anecdote without reservation. See Robinson, *The Hearsts: An American Dynasty* (Newark, DE: University of Delaware Press, 1991), 324.

12. The purported exchange was mentioned in the *Times* of London in 1907, which prompted Hearst to reply, calling the report "frankly false and . . . ingeniously idiotic." See W. R. Hearst, "Mr. W. R. Hearst on Anglo-American Relations," *Times* [London] (2 November 1907): 5. Hearst later was quoted by his son as denying the purported exchange. See William Randolph Hearst Jr. with Jack Casserly, *The Hearsts: Father and Son* (Niwot, CO: Roberts Rinehart, 1991), 38.

13. See Louis A. Pérez Jr., *Cuba Between Empires, 1878–1902* (Pittsburgh, PA: University of Pittsburgh Press, 1983), 43–52, and Louis A. Pérez Jr., *Cuba Between Reform and Revolution*, 2d ed. (New York: Oxford University Press, 1995), 157.

14. Cited in Pérez, *Cuba Between Empires*, 54.

15. Pérez, *Cuba Between Empires*, 55–56.

16. A favored tactic of the insurgents was to set fire to sugar cane fields, in keeping with their call for a moratorium on economic activity on the island. See Pérez, *Cuba Between Reform and Revolution*, 162–163.

17. Some were, however. For a discussion about erroneous and exaggerated reporting during the first two years of the Cuban insurrection, see Rea, *Facts and Fakes about Cuba* (New York: G. Munro's Sons, 1897).

18. Pérez, *Cuba Between Reform and Revolution*, 166.

19. Richard Harding Davis, letter to his family, 25 December 1896; Richard Harding Davis Collection, Alderman Library of American Literature, University of Virginia.

20. Davis, letter to his family, 2 January 1897; Davis Collection, Alderman Library.

21. Davis, letter to his family, 2 January 1897.

22. See, Davis letter to Rebecca Harding Davis, 9 January 1897; Davis Collection, Alderman Library.

23. Davis letter to Rebecca Harding Davis, 10 January 1897; Davis Collection, Alderman Library.

24. Arthur Lubow, a Davis biographer, wrote that the "dry pathos" of the dispatch "anticipates the work of Hemingway." See Lubow, *The Reporter Who Would be King*, 141.

25. Richard Harding Davis, "Davis and Remington Tell of Spanish Cruelty," *New York Journal* (2 February 1897): 1.

26. James Creelman, "The Real Mr. Hearst," *Pearson's* (September 1906): 259.

27. See, for example, Lundberg, *Imperial Hearst*, 68. In addition, Hiley H. Ward has written that Creelman "could have been present when" Remington "had the exchange with Hearst." See Ward, *Mainstreams of American Media History*, 279. The anecdote also has been recounted as Hearst's having sent a "famous message" to "his reporters in Cuba who, excluded from the putative theater of war by the Spanish military authorities, had wired their employer that there was 'no trouble here' and they wished to return." See Anthony Smith, *Goodbye Gutenberg: The Newspaper Revolution of the 1980's* (New York: Oxford University Press, 1980), 161–162. Another version is that Remington followed Davis to Cuba, "to convey visually what Davis had done with words." For that version, see Phillip Knightley, *The First Casualty: From the Crimea to Vietnam: The War Correspondent as Hero, Propagandist, and Myth Maker* (New York: Harcourt Brace Jovanovich, 1975), 55. Knightley said the anecdote about the Remington-Hearst exchange may be "apocryphal" but he recounted it nonetheless.

28. Joyce Milton wrote: "Creelman specialized in interviewing the greatest men and women of the day. And since he considered himself the conscience of the fourth estate, he normally did as much talking as listening." Milton, *The Yellow Kids*, 93. Creelman was not reluctant to recall for readers his past interviewing coups, either. In a report from Rome in February 1897, he said of Pope Leo XIII: "The Pope's voice ringing vigorously over the heads of the kneeling multitude in the Sistine chapel this morning was the best answer to the declaration that the august 'Prisoner of the Vatican' is dying. I watched him for an hour this morning . . . and his eye was as bright and his tones as clear and sonorous as when I interviewed him in the Throne room seven years ago." Creelman, "Leo Strong in Body and Mind," *New York Journal* (9 February 1897): 1.

29. James Creelman, "Cleveland Strikes Cuba A Secret Blow," *New York Journal* (1 January 1897): 1.

30. Creelman, "Cleveland Strikes Cuba A Secret Blow," 1.

31. James Creelman, "Will Europe Try to Coerce Us?" *New York Journal* (21 February 1897): 1.

32. See David F. Trask, *The War With Spain in 1898* (New York: Macmillan Publishing Company Inc., 1981), 474.

33. See Jeffery M. Dorwart, "James Creelman, the *New York World* and the Port Arthur Massacre," *Journalism Quarterly* 50, 4 (Winter 1973): 699.

34. "The Port Arthur 'Outrages,'" *New York Tribune* (20 December 1894): 6. The *Tribune*'s editorial also described the reports as "so untrue that to call them wild exaggerations would be gross flattery."

35. Dorwart, "James Creelman," 699–700.

36. Edwin Dun to Secretary of State W. Q. Gresham, "The Affair of Port Arthur Subsequent to the Capture of that Town by the Japanese Forces," 20 December 1894; *Despatches from U.S. Ministers to Japan*, vol. 68, Record Group 59, National Archives, College Park, MD.

37. Creelman, *On the Great Highway*, 109.

38. Creelman, "Famine and Flames: Spain May Destroy, but She Cannot Keep Cuba Even With an Army of 180,000," *New York World* (17 May 1896): 1.

39. Creelman misstated, and perhaps misunderstood, the nature of the Cuban insurrection. Notably, he overestimated the size of the rebel forces under Gómez who, he wrote, "has drilled more men than he has arms for. I am quite certain that with arms and ammunition enough the Cuban Republic can put 100,000 men in the field." Creelman, "Famine and Flames." The most generous estimates are that the Cuban rebels never numbered more than 40,000 and usually they "were deployed in small, mobile detachments engaging in hit-and-run operations." See Trask, *The War With Spain*, 6.

40. Creelman, *On the Great Highway*, 177.

41. Davis, letter to Rebecca Harding Davis, 19 December [1896]; Davis Collection, Alderman Library. He also wrote that "you may not hear from us for a month and we may not hear from you." Davis asked his mother not to worry about his going to Cuba, writing: "No one loves himself more than I do so you leave me to take care of myself."

42. Davis, letter to his family, 29 December [1896]; Davis Collection, Alderman Library.

43. Davis, letter to Rebecca Harding Davis, 10 January 1897; Davis Collection, Alderman Library.

44. Davis, letter to Rebecca Harding Davis, 4 January 1897; Davis Collection, Alderman Library.

45. Davis, letter to Rebecca Harding Davis, 15 January 1897; Davis Collection, Alderman Library.

46. Davis, letter to Rebecca Harding Davis, 15 January 1897; Davis Collection, Alderman Library. Davis also said in the letter: "I was very glad he went for he kept me back all the time and I can do twice as much in half the time. He always wanted to talk it over and that had to be done in the nearest or the most distant cafe, and it always took him fifteen minutes before he got his cocktails to suit him. He always did as I wanted [in] the end but I am not used to giving reasons or traveling in pairs."

47. Davis, undated letter to Gus [Thomas?] [20? January 1897]; Davis Collection, Alderman Library.

48. Davis, letter to Rebecca Harding Davis, 15 January 1897, Davis Collection, Alderman Library.

49. Augustus Thomas, "Recollections of Frederic Remington," *Century Magazine* 86, 3 (July 1913): 357. A Remington scholar, Allen P. Splete, also said that the artist, because of his heft, probably found the assignment to Cuba very demanding. Splete, interview with author, Washington, DC, June 1999.

50. Davis, undated letter to Rebecca Harding Davis, [January 1897]; Davis Collection, Alderman Library.

51. Davis, undated letter to Rebecca Harding Davis, [January 1897]; Davis Collection, Alderman Library.

52. Frederic Remington, "Frederic Remington Sketches Spanish Guerillas Bringing 'Pacificos' Into Camp," *New York Journal* (24 January 1897): 3.

53. Frederic Remington, "Frederic Remington Writes to the World about Scovel," *New York World* (21 February 1897): 1. Remington's letter was written to support the release of Sylvester Scovel, the *World* correspondent then in jail in Cuba. Remington's reference to "the woman-killing outfit" reflected the theme, common in the U.S. press, that Spanish authorities routinely mistreated Cuban women.

54. The war commanded the attention of Congress as Remington and Davis prepared to travel to Cuba in late 1896. The U.S. Senate was considering a resolution encouraging the lame duck Cleveland administration to "use its friendly offices with the government of Spain to bring to a close the war between Spain and Cuba." "The Cameron Cuban Resolution," *Public Opinion* 21, 26 (24 December 1896): 1.

55. Murat Halstead, a venerable newspaper editor who had traveled to Cuba for Hearst's *Journal* in 1896, wrote in 1897: "The Cubans are as thoroughly in a state of revolt against Spain as the Virginians were in the height of the war of the early sixties against our federal government." See Halstead, *The Story of Cuba: Her Struggles for Liberty, the Cause, Crisis and Destiny of the Pearl of the Antilles*, 5th ed. (Chicago: Henry Publishing Company, 1897), 457.

56. "Cuban War Illustrated by Frederic Remington," *New York Journal* (24 January 1897): 1.

57. See "A War of Extermination," *New York Sun* (8 January 1897): 1; "War of Extermination," *New York Sun* (12 January 1897): 1; "War of Extermination," *New York Sun* (21 April 1897): 1.

58. "Two Reports from Western Cuba," *New York Sun* (29 December 1896): 6.

59. "'No Surrender' in Cuba," *New York Tribune* (17 January 1897): 6. Comparisons between the Cuban war and the American Revolution were often invoked in the New York press. The *Sun*, for example, described the Cuban insurgents as "not less determined than were the long-enduring Americans in the days of Washington." See "The Unequalling Patriots of Cuba," *New York Sun* (6 May 1897): 6. See also, "A Man in a Hurry, *New York Sun* (17 January 1897): 6, and "1778 and 1897," *New York Sun* (30 January 1897): 6.

60. "The Cuban Problem To Be Solved by Statesmanship, Not Force of Arms," *New York Herald* (27 January 1897): 8.

61. Davis, letter to Rebecca Harding Davis, 15 January 1897; Davis Collection, Alderman Library.

62. Davis, letter to Rebecca Harding Davis, 16 January 1897; Davis Collection, Alderman Library.

63. Davis, *Cuba In War Time* (New York: R. H. Russell, 1897). Davis described Cuba as being "divided into two military camps, one situated within forts, and the other scattered over the fields and mountains outside of them" (13). A publisher's note to *Cuba in War Time* says that Remington's illustrations were "here reproduced through the courtesy of Mr. W. R. Hearst."

64. One editorial published in January 1897 can perhaps be described as faintly bellicose. It stated in part: "Americans everywhere . . . have long since reached the conclusion that it is our duty to intervene between the butchers and their victims, and have long regarded that duty as a privilege to be eagerly longed for and joyfully taken at the first opportunity." See "Evidence in Support of Sulzer," *New York Journal* (10 January 1897): 12. The following day, however, the *Journal* returned to the theme that Spain was unlikely to hold out in Cuba. In an editorial discussing reports that Madrid was prepared to offer autonomy to the insurgents, the *Journal* stated: "The fact that Spain is willing to grant so much is sufficient indication that she is no longer in condition to retain anything. The Cubans should hold out for complete independence and admitted sovereignty." See "Some Late Cuban News," *New York Journal* (11 January 1897): 8. The insurgents consistently rejected Spanish offers of autonomy, insisting instead on outright political independence.

65. "The State of Spain," *New York Journal* (4 January 1897): 6. Creelman had reported: "The most thoughtful men in Spain today say that Cuba is lost to the monarchy, and that [President] Cleveland and [Secretary of State Richard] Olney are simply prolonging a cruel and disastrous struggle. But for their pride they would be glad to see the end come at once. It is impossible to talk with representative Spaniards without realizing this fact." Creelman, "Cleveland Strikes Cuba A Secret Blow."

66. "Belated Wisdom of Spain," *New York Journal* (31 January 1897): 38.

67. John K. Winkler made this point in his biography of Hearst, *W. R. Hearst: An American Phenomenon* (New York: Simon and Schuster, 1928), 144. Mott, however, rejected Winkler's view as "absurd," but neither elaborated on nor explained his dismissive characterization. See Mott, *American Journalism: A History*, fn 12, 529.

68. Murat Halstead, "Our Cuban Neighbors and Their Struggle for Liberty," *Review of Reviews* 13, 4 (April 1896): 424. The rigors of Spanish censorship were cited from time to time by the trade journal *Fourth Estate*. The publication suggested in February 1897 that censorship in Havana was a fundamental explanation for exaggerated reports about Cuba published in the U.S. press. See "The Press and War," *Fourth Estate* (18 February 1897): 6, and "War and Prize Fighting," *Fourth Estate* (15 April 1897): 6.

69. Fitzhugh Lee to Secretary of State Richard Olney, 10 February 1897; Richard Olney Papers, Manuscript Division, Library of Congress, Washington, DC.

70. Milton, *The Yellow Kids*, 83.

71. See "War on Correspondents," *Fourth Estate* (20 May 1897): 2.

72. See "The Journal's Bold Move," *Fourth Estate* (26 November 1896): 1.

73. Creelman himself knew that Spanish authorities in Cuba had little tolerance for correspondents who flouted the censors. He was expelled in 1896 after filing a report for the *New York World* about Spanish atrocities in Cuba—a report

he made a point of sharing with Weyler. Creelman, *On the Great Highway*, 167–169. See also Milton, *Yellow Kids*, 97.

74. With typical hyperbole, Creelman described Weyler as "the most sinister figure of the nineteenth century" and "the most monstrous personality of modern times." Creelman, *On the Great Highway*, 158, 169.

75. A similar point is made by Ian Mugridge in *The View from Xanadu: William Randolph Hearst and United States Foreign Policy* (Montreal: McGill-Queen's University Press, 1995), 11.

76. Brown, *The Correspondents' War*, 8.

77. Brown, *The Correspondents' War*, 8.

78. Charles Michelson, *The Ghost Talks* (New York: G. P. Putnam's Sons, 1944), 86. Overall in 1896, nine correspondents and translators for U.S. newspapers were expelled and/or jailed by Spanish authorities in Cuba. See "Enclosures with Despatch No. 278," Cuban Consular Correspondence, 1895-1898, U.S. State Department, container 124, John Bassett Moore papers, Manuscript Division, Library of Congress, Washington, DC.

79. Brown, *The Correspondents' War*, 85.

80. Brown, *The Correspondents' War*, 86–87. See also, "The Imprisoned Newspaper Correspondent," *Fourth Estate* (4 March 1897): 2, and "Potentiality of President and the Press," *Fourth Estate* (18 March 1897): 7.

81. The telegraph may have been an unreliable means of communication as well. See Jorma Ahvenainen, *The History of the Caribbean Telegraphs Before the First World War* (Helsinki: Suomalainen Tiedeakatemia, 1996), 132. Ahvenainen wrote: "During the revolutionary events in Cuba after 1895, the telegraph service was rather irregular and messages were transmitted by train during breakdowns." Indeed, the insurgents disrupted telegraphic communication to such an extent that Weyler in 1896 was unable to notify subordinates that he had arrived in Cuba to take command of Spanish forces. The telegraph lines had been cut. See "Weyler in His Own Defence," *New York Herald* (25 October 1897): 9. There were more general complaints about the reliability of the telegraph in the 1890s. See Richard T. Ely, "Should the Government Control the Telegraph?" *Arena* (December 1895): 49–53. About the telegraph in the United States, Ely wrote, 50: "The service in this country is so defective and irregular that frequently the telegraph is not used when it would be a great convenience. It is impossible to send a telegram and to be sure that a prompt reply will be received."

82. William Randolph Hearst, trans-Atlantic cablegram to James Creelman, 19 February 1898; Ohio State University Library, Creelman Collection.

83. Hearst, trans-Atlantic cablegram to Creelman, 19 February 1898; Ohio State University Library, Creelman Collection.

84. Hearst, trans-Atlantic cablegram to Creelman, 23 February 1898; Ohio State University Library, Creelman Collection.

85. Hearst, trans-Atlantic cablegram to Creelman, 24 February 1898; Creelman Collection, Ohio State University Library.

86. Some accounts say that Remington obeyed Hearst and "stayed." See, for example, Ward, *Mainstreams of American Media History*, 280.

87. For a reference to this side of Hearst's character, see Procter, *William Randolph Hearst: The Early Years*, 77. See also, Swanberg, *Citizen Hearst*, 79.

88. Churchill, *Park Row*, 48. However, Willis Abbot, an editor at the *New York Journal*, wrote that Hearst never showed irritation or lost his temper. See Abbot, *Watching the World Go By*, 145. For a sympathetic assessment of Hearst's management technique, see "Mr. Hearst as an Employer," *Overland* 50 (December 1907): 53. The writer, identified only as "one of his employees," said Hearst was a kind-hearted employer who granted paid leaves of absence to writers suffering the effects of overwork. "In the treatment of his men," the author stated, "Mr. Hearst is the kindest and best of employers." Even so, insubordination on the scale that Remington committed, if Creelman's account is accurate, probably would have been difficult to excuse or overlook.

89. "Cuban War Sketches Gathered in the Field by Frederic Remington," *New York Journal* (24 January 1897): 31–33.

90. "Cuban War Sketches," 31.

91. "Frederic Remington Sketches A Familiar Incident of the Cuban War," *New York Journal* (29 January 1897): 2.

92. "The Spanish-American War," in Edmond D. Coblentz, ed., *William Randolph Hearst: A Portrait in His Own Words* (New York: Simon and Schuster, 1952), 58.

93. Frederic Remington, letter to Poultney Bigelow, 28 January 1897, in Allen P. Splete and Marilyn D. Splete, *Frederic Remington – Selected Letters* (New York: Abbeville Press, 1988), 219.

94. Frederic Remington, letter to [?] Harper, [16 September 1898?]; Frederic Remington Collection, Alderman Library of American Literature, University of Virginia.

95. Davis, letter to Rebecca Harding Davis, 16 January 1897. He wrote: "I got a grand lot of letters today which Otto my interpreter brought back from Havana after having conducted Remington there in safety."

96. See Davis, *Cuba In War Time*, 123. He wrote: "In order to leave Havana, it is first necessary to give notice of your wish to do so by sending your passport to the Captain General, who looks up your record, and, after twenty-four hours, if he is willing to let you go, visés your passport and so signifies that your request is granted."

97. Davis was vain and not easily liked. *Fourth Estate* said of him in 1895: "Richard Harding Davis has never been especially popular with newspaper men, because he knew enough to know his own worth and could not conceal his knowledge." See "Three Bright Newspaper Men," *Fourth Estate* (9 May 1895): 3.

98. See, Remington, letter to Bigelow, 28 January 1897, in Splete and Splete, *Frederic Remington – Selected Letters*, 218.

99. Richard Harding Davis, "Does Our Flag Shield Women?" *New York Journal* (12 February 1897): 1–2. Remington's illustration depicting the strip-search appeared on page two.

100. See "Tale of a Fair Exile: Senorita Arango's Own Story of the Olivette 'Search Outrage,'" *New York World* (15 February 1897): 1.

101. In their detailed biography of Remington, Peggy and Harold Samuels do not question whether Remington sent the telegram to Hearst. They repeat the anecdote. See Peggy and Harold Samuels, *Frederic Remington: A Biography* (Garden City, NY: Doubleday, 1982), 249. They also note: "Remington had been paid for a month in Cuba, and the month was up" (248).

102. Splete, interview with author, June 1999.

103. Davis, letter to Rebecca Harding Davis, 24 January 1897; Davis Collection, Alderman Library.

104. Davis, letter to Rebecca Harding Davis, 20 January 1897; Davis Collection, Alderman Library.

105. Davis, letter to James Creelman, 18 November [1901]; Ohio State University Library, Creelman Collection. The letter reads: "I have today received your volume of reminiscences and descriptions and I thank you for them most heartily. Already I have read most of them with great interest, and I find them most admirably selected, and entertaining, full of information, full of unconscious proofs of a life well spent in a profession that is it's [*sic*] own reward. I am very glad you thought well of putting these experiences into a book. They will help to stimulate and to encourage to a like energy and effort. I hope it will have the generous circulation it deserves. Thank you again for sending it [to] me. . . ."

106. Creelman, *On the Great Highway*, 177.

107. One review that did mention the purported exchange was "On the Great Highway," *The Independent* (27 February 1902): 516–517.

108. Hearst's *Journal* lavished attention on the book—but ignored the anecdote about the Remington-Hearst telegrams. The *Journal*'s literary supplement carried two pages of excerpts from *On the Great Highway* and described it as "the book of the week" in early November 1901. See "Book of the Week: 'On the Great Highway' by James Creelman," *New York Journal's Saturday Review* (2 November 1901): 402–403. *On the Great Highway* was favorably reviewed as "a book to read and re-read; a book to keep in the library; truthful, manly, thrilling, instructive, and, above all—what a book of this sort should be—honest." See Max O'Rell, "'On the Great Highway' By James Creelman," *New York Journal* (24 November 1901): 25. An editorial in the *Journal* also said the book "combines all the elements of popularity, of fiction and truth. Every chapter . . . would make the setting for a novel." See "The New Reading World," *New York Journal* (17 November 1901): 26. Yet none of the excerpts, reviews, or comments appearing in the *Journal* at the time mentioned or discussed the purported exchange of telegrams. Similarly, the *New York World*'s review ignored the anecdote about the telegrams. See "Mr. Creelman's Book," *New York World* (2 November 1901): 9.

109. Scores of newspaper obituaries are among Creelman's papers at Ohio State University. None of those reviewed refer to the purported Remington-Hearst exchange.

110. "The American Press," *Times* (London) (30 September 1907): 5. The magazine article mentioned in the *Times* account may have been Creelman's profile about Hearst which appeared in *Pearson's* in 1906.

111. Hearst, "Mr. W. R. Hearst on Anglo-American Relations," *Times*, 5.

112. Hearst, "Mr. W. R. Hearst on Anglo-American Relations," *Times*, 5.

113. "The Spanish-American War," in *William Randolph Hearst*, 58.

114. David Hackett Fischer, *Historians' Fallacies: Toward a Logic of Historical Thought* (New York: Harper and Row, 1970), 87.

The *Journal* touts the special correspondents it sent to Cuba—the artist Frederic Remington and the reporter Richard Harding Davis. It was an ill-fated assignment that became known for what almost certainly did not occur—the purported exchange of telegrams between Remington and William Randolph Hearst, in which Hearst supposedly vowed to "furnish the war" with Spain.

The sole original source for the anecdote about the Remington-Hearst telegraphic exchange was James Creelman, a war correspondent who reported for the *World* and, later, the *Journal*.

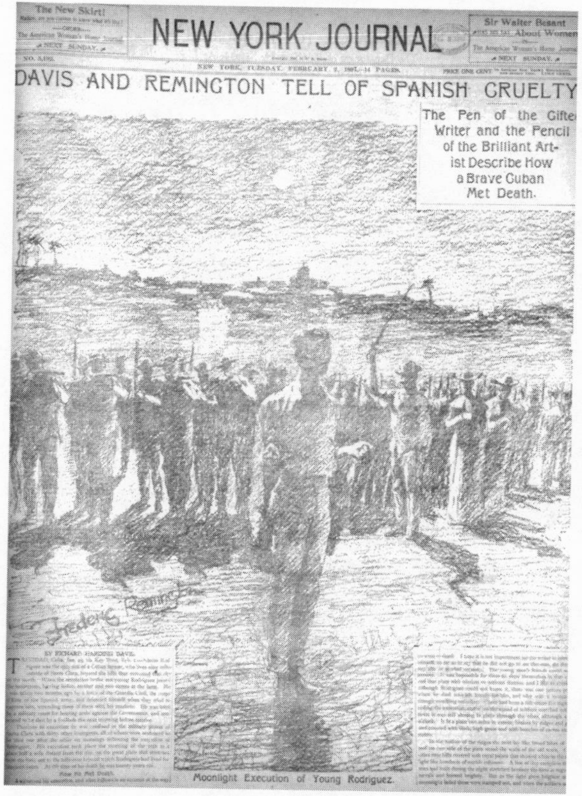

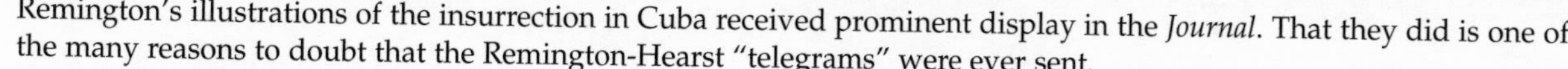

NEW YORK JOURNAL

DAVIS AND REMINGTON TELL OF SPANISH CRUELTY

The Pen of the Gifte Writer and the Pencil of the Brilliant Artist Describe How a Brave Cuban Met Death.

Moonlight Execution of Young Rodriguez.

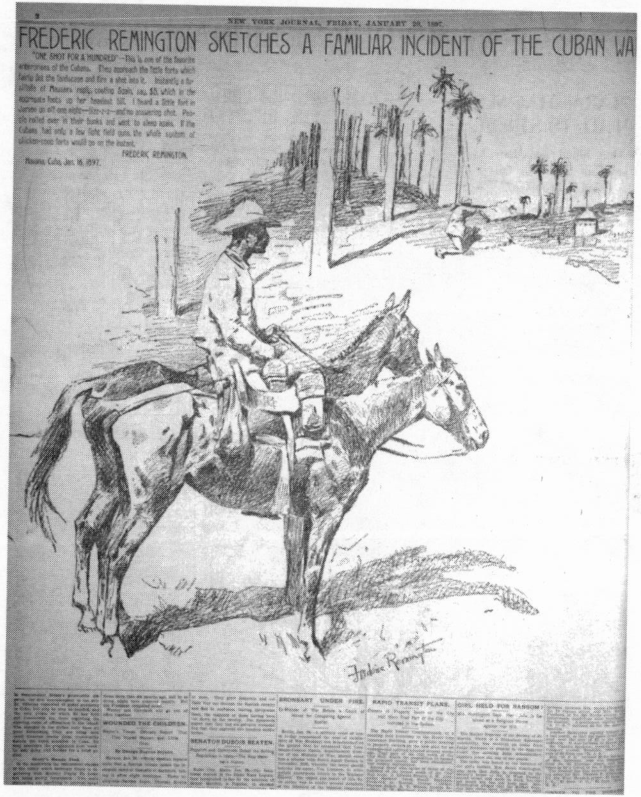

FREDERIC REMINGTON SKETCHES A FAMILIAR INCIDENT OF THE CUBAN WA

Remington's illustrations of the insurrection in Cuba received prominent display in the *Journal*. That they did is one of the many reasons to doubt that the Remington-Hearst "telegrams" were ever sent.

SPECIAL EASTER SUPPLEMENT.

NEW YORK JOURNAL

FREDERIC REMINGTON'S CUBAN SKETCHES.

SUNDAY, APRIL 11, 1897.

"PEACE ON EARTH, GOOD WILL TOWARD MEN," AS IT IS IN CUBA.

THE CUBAN SLAIN THROWN TO THE BUZZARDS.

Remington's gruesome illustration of slain Cuban insurgents was published in the *Journal* on Easter Sunday in 1897. That his work appeared in the *Journal* months after his brief assignment to Cuba suggested there were no hard feelings between the artist and Hearst—and further reason to doubt that the purported telegrams were ever exchanged.

NEW YORK JOURNAL

NEW YORK, SATURDAY, JANUARY 30, 1897.—16 PAGES.

THE NEW JOURNALISM AGAIN VINDICATED AND VICTORIOUS.

The Journal, Jan. 12, Said Cuba Was to Have Autonomy; the World, Jan. 12, Denied It; the Herald, Jan. 28, Confirmed It.

JOURNAL EXTRA

PREMIER CANOVAS AGREES TO OLNEY'S PLAN FOR AUTONOMY.

Minister De Lome Instructed to Inform the Secretary of State That Spain Will Definitely Accept the Proposition for Home Rule in Cuba.

This Means That That Island Will Be Allowed to Govern Herself, Collect Her Own Taxes, Spend Her Own Money and That Spain Must Keep Her Hands Off Revenues and Elections.

JAN 12

CLEVELAND-OLNEY DIPLOMACY HAS FAILED IN SPAIN.

Response from Canovas Ministry to Overtures in Behalf of Cuba Makes Mediation Seem Hopeless.

CLEVELAND TRIES IN VAIN TO HURRY CANOVAS

"NO FOREIGN POWER" MAY DICTATE TO HER.

THE WORLD JAN 12

AUTONOMY ACCORDED TO CUBA.

HERALD JAN 28

JOURNAL'S NEWS AGAIN CONFIRMED.

Weyler's Coming Deposition Is Known to Olney.

LIBERTY FOR AMERICANS.

Nearly All Now in Cuban Prisons Soon to Be Free.

Grand Jury Aroused to Indict the Broadway Cable Company for Maintaining a Nuisance at Dead Man's Curve.

EXTRA NEW YORK JOURNAL EXTRA

NEW YORK, MONDAY, FEBRUARY 22, 1897.—12 PAGES.

SHERMAN FOR WAR WITH SPAIN FOR MURDERING AMERICANS.

McKinley's Secretary of State Tells the Journal That We Cannot Stand Idly By While Our Citizens Are Being Butchered in Cuba.

Minister Taylor at Madrid Ordered by Olney to Demand an Immediate Investigation Into Dr. Ruiz's Death—All Now Waits Upon the Next Report from Lee.

"I ... THE ONLY WAY TO PUT AN END TO THE ATROCITIES IS TO DECLARE WAR ON SPAIN.

OLNEY SPAIN'S ALLY.

Creelman Makes Disclosure of a Secret Partnership.

LEE ANGRY.

Consul-General at Havana Finds Ruiz Was Killed.

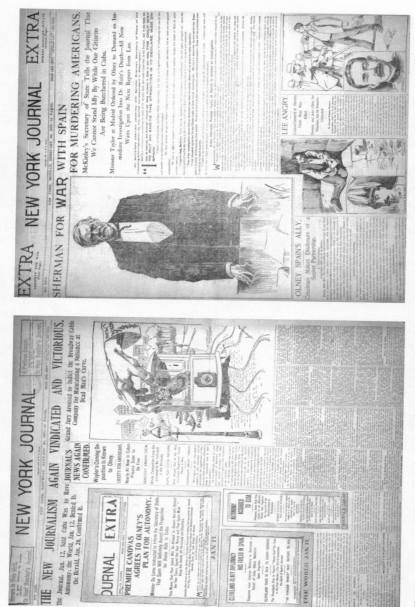

The *Journal*'s coverage of Cuba in the months before the Spanish-American War was marred by errors such as those that appeared on the front pages shown here. John Sherman, the U.S. secretary of state-designate, denied having spoken with the *Journal* reporter who quoted Sherman as calling for war with Spain in early 1897.

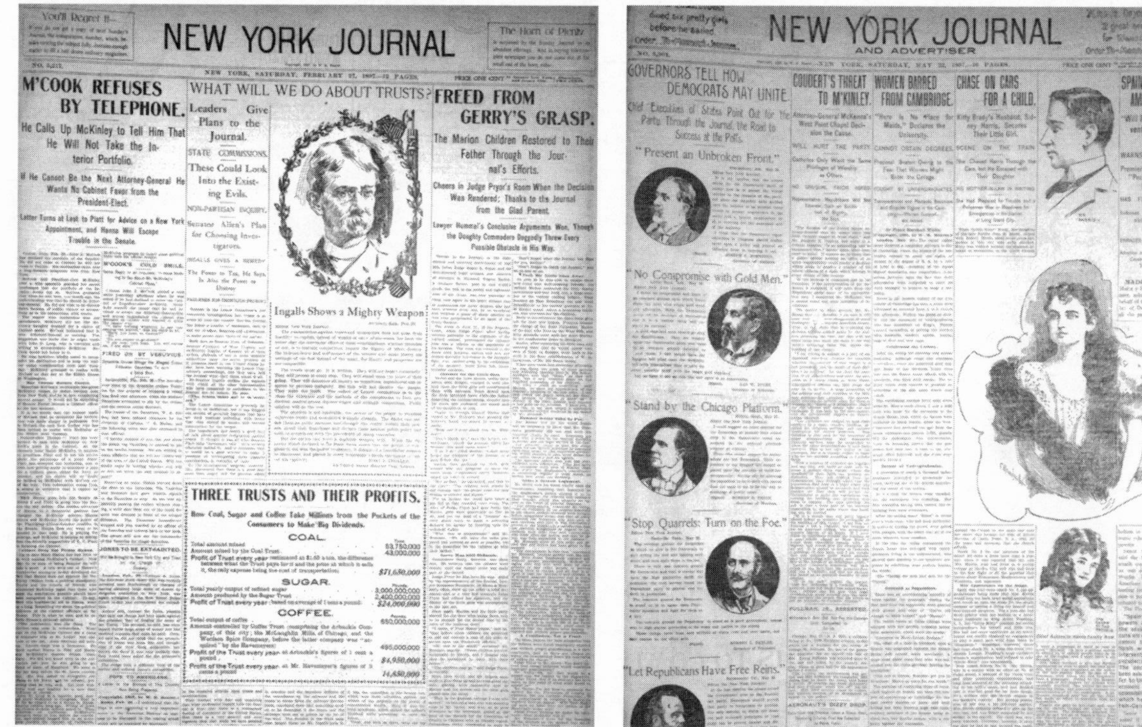

NEW YORK JOURNAL

NEW YORK, SATURDAY, FEBRUARY 27, 1897.—12 PAGES.

M'COOK REFUSES BY TELEPHONE.

He Calls Up McKinley to Tell Him That He Will Not Take the Interior Portfolio.

If He Cannot Be the Next Attorney-General He Wants No Cabinet Favor from the President-Elect.

Latter Turns at Last to Platt for Advice on a New York Appointment, and Hanna Will Escape Trouble in the Senate.

WHAT WILL WE DO ABOUT TRUSTS?

Leaders Give Plans to the Journal.

STATE COMMISSIONS.

These Could Look Into the Existing Evils.

NON-PARTISAN INQUIRY.

Senator Allen's Plan for Choosing Investigators.

FREED FROM GERRY'S GRASP.

The Marion Children Restored to Their Father Through the Journal's Efforts.

Cheers in Judge Pryor's Room When the Decision Was Rendered; Thanks to the Journal from the Glad Parent.

Lawyer Hummel's Conclusive Arguments Won, Though the Doughty Commodore Doggedly Threw Every Possible Obstacle in His Way.

Ingalls Shows a Mighty Weapon

THREE TRUSTS AND THEIR PROFITS.

How Coal, Sugar and Coffee Take Millions from the Pockets of the Consumers to Make Big Dividends.

COAL.	
Total amount mined	53,750,000
Amount mined by the Coal Trust	43,000,000
Profit of Trust every year (estimated at $1.65 a ton, the difference between what the Trust pays for it and the price at which it sells it, the only expense being the cost of transportation)	$71,650,000
SUGAR.	
Total yearly output of refined sugar	3,000,000,000
Amount produced by the Sugar Trust	2,400,000,000
Profit of Trust every year (based on average of 1 cent a pound)	$24,000,000
COFFEE.	
Total output of coffee	650,000,000
Amount controlled by Coffee Trust (comprising the Arbuckle Company, of this city; the McLaughlin Mills, of Chicago, and the Woolson Spice Company, before the latter company was "acquired" by the Havemeyers)	495,000,000
Profit of the Trust every year at Arbuckle's figures of 1 cent a pound	$4,950,000
Profit of the Trust every year at Mr. Havemeyer's figures of 3 cents a pound	14,850,000

NEW YORK JOURNAL AND ADVERTISER

NEW YORK, SATURDAY, MAY 22, 1897.—16 PAGES.

GOVERNORS TELL HOW DEMOCRATS MAY UNITE.

Chief Executives of States Point Out for the Party Through the Journal the Road to Success at the Polls.

"Present an Unbroken Front."

"No Compromise with Gold Men."

"Stand by the Chicago Platform."

"Stop Quarrels; Turn on the Foe."

"Let Republicans Have Free Reins."

COUDERT'S THREAT TO M'KINLEY.

WOMEN BARRED FROM CAMBRIDGE.

CHASE ON CARS FOR A CHILD.

SPAIN RESENTS AMERICAN ADVICE.

"Will Never Accept Intervention," Declares Canovas.

WARNS UNITED STATES.

The insurrection in Cuba was not an unending preoccupation for the yellow press. As suggested here, news about Cuba slipped off the front pages of the *Journal* for noticeable stretches during the months before the destruction of the battleship *Maine* in February 1898.

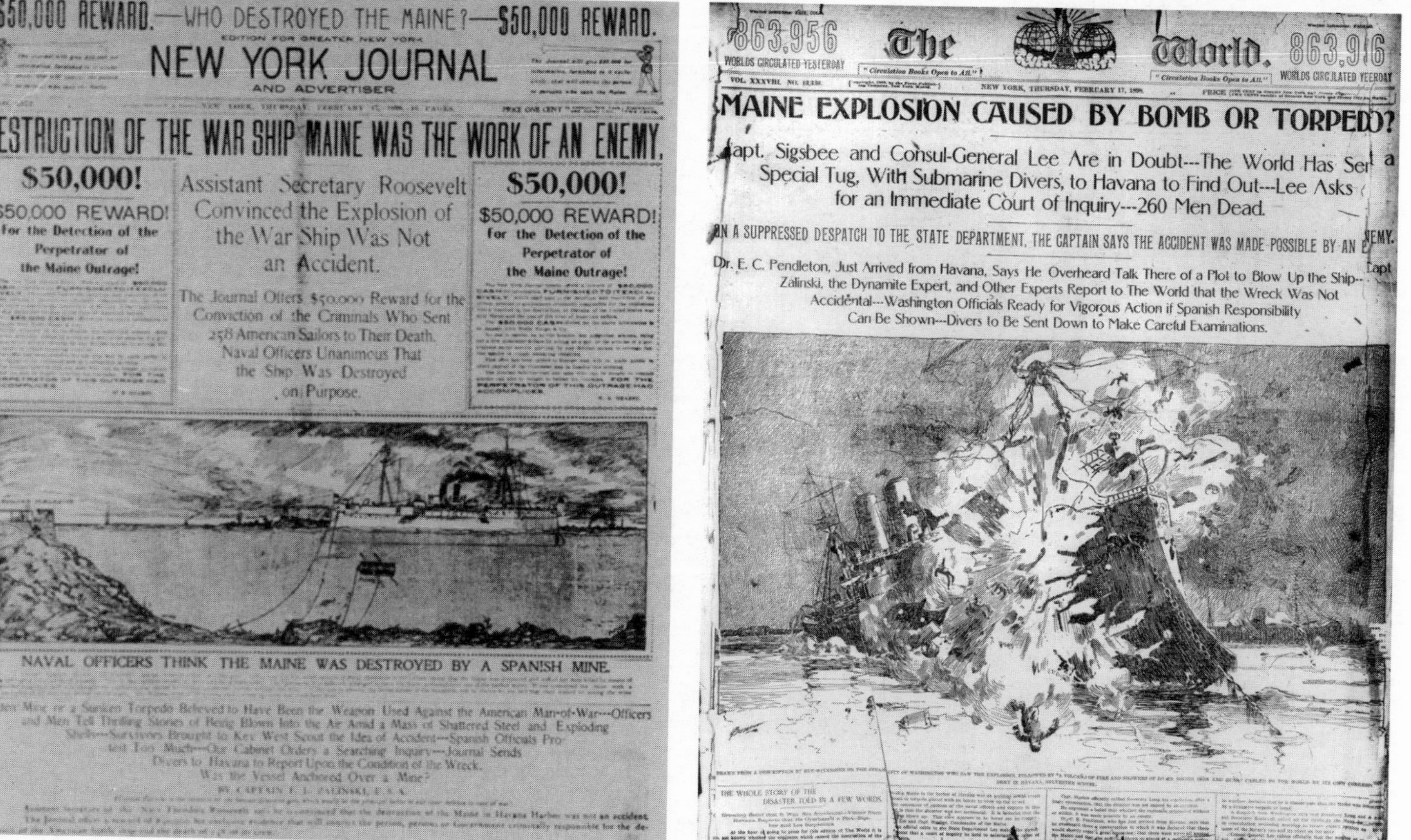

$50,000 REWARD.—WHO DESTROYED THE MAINE?—$50,000 REWARD.

EDITION FOR GREATER NEW YORK

NEW YORK JOURNAL

AND ADVERTISER

NEW YORK, THURSDAY, FEBRUARY 17, 1898.—16 PAGES.

PRICE ONE CENT

DESTRUCTION OF THE WAR SHIP MAINE WAS THE WORK OF AN ENEMY.

$50,000!

$50,000 REWARD!

For the Detection of the Perpetrator of the Maine Outrage!

Assistant Secretary Roosevelt Convinced the Explosion of the War Ship Was Not an Accident.

The Journal Offers $50,000 Reward for the Conviction of the Criminals Who Sent 258 American Sailors to Their Death. Naval Officers Unanimous That the Ship Was Destroyed on Purpose.

$50,000!

$50,000 REWARD!

For the Detection of the Perpetrator of the Maine Outrage!

NAVAL OFFICERS THINK THE MAINE WAS DESTROYED BY A SPANISH MINE.

Hidden Mine or a Sunken Torpedo Believed to Have Been the Weapon Used Against the American Man-of-War—Officers and Men Tell Thrilling Stories of Being Blown Into the Air Amid a Mass of Shattered Steel and Exploding Shells—Survivors Brought to Key West Scout the Idea of Accident—Spanish Officials Protest Too Much—Our Cabinet Orders a Searching Inquiry—Journal Sends Divers to Havana to Report Upon the Condition of the Wreck. Was the Vessel Anchored Over a Mine?

BY CAPTAIN E. L. ZALINSKI, U. S. A.

863,956

WORLDS CIRCULATED YESTERDAY

The World.

863,916

WORLDS CIRCULATED YESTERDAY

"Circulation Books Open to All."

VOL. XXXVIII. NO. 13,336.

NEW YORK, THURSDAY, FEBRUARY 17, 1898.

MAINE EXPLOSION CAUSED BY BOMB OR TORPEDO?

Capt. Sigsbee and Consul-General Lee Are in Doubt—The World Has Sent a Special Tug, With Submarine Divers, to Havana to Find Out—Lee Asks for an Immediate Court of Inquiry—260 Men Dead.

IN A SUPPRESSED DESPATCH TO THE STATE DEPARTMENT, THE CAPTAIN SAYS THE ACCIDENT WAS MADE POSSIBLE BY AN ENEMY.

Dr. E. C. Pendleton, Just Arrived from Havana, Says He Overheard Talk There of a Plot to Blow Up the Ship—Capt. Zalinski, the Dynamite Expert, and Other Experts Report to The World that the Wreck Was Not Accidental—Washington Officials Ready for Vigorous Action if Spanish Responsibility Can Be Shown—Divers to Be Sent Down to Make Careful Examinations.

THE WHOLE STORY OF THE DISASTER TOLD IN A FEW WORDS.

The triggering event of the Spanish-American War was the destruction of the *Maine*, depicted here in two of the most famous front pages of yellow journalism.

New Yorkers gather along Park Row in 1898 to read the latest news of the Spanish-American War, as displayed on newspaper bulletin boards. Reproduced from the Collections of the Library of Congress.

4

Not to Blame: The Yellow Press and the Spanish-American War

The yellow press is not to blame for the Spanish-American-War. It did not force—it could not have forced—the United States into hostilities with Spain over Cuba in 1898. The conflict was, rather, the result of a convergence of forces far beyond the control or direct influence of even the most aggressive of the yellow newspapers, William Randolph Hearst's *New York Journal*. Nevertheless, the notion that the yellow press *did* push the United States into the Spanish-American War is as powerful and enduring as it is inaccurate. This view has persisted among journalists and media historians[1] throughout the twentieth century.[2]

Proponents of this view argue that the yellow press inveighed extravagantly and often about the injustices in Spanish-ruled Cuba during a rebellion that began in 1895; that other U.S. newspapers picked up and reiterated the exaggerated reports of the yellow press, especially those published in the aftermath of the destruction of the U.S. battleship *Maine* in Havana harbor in February 1898; and that the American public and, ultimately, the administration of President William McKinley succumbed[3] to the pressure for war applied by the yellow press. "It was an unnecessary war," one of Hearst's most prominent biographers has written. "It was the newspapers' war. Above all, it was Hearst's war."[4] Such views seem to find support in the *Journal*'s swaggering claim, distilled in an epigram and published on the front page during the conflict's early days in May 1898: "How Do You Like the Journal's War?"[5]

The notion that the yellow press incited or fomented the Spanish-American War stands, moreover, as testimony to the supposedly powerful, even malevolent effects of the news media—that they can and sometimes do act in dangerous, devious, and manipulative ways.[6] The Spanish-American War was the example Philip Seib cited in describing the perverse effects of wayward news media: "If news organizations set aside their commitment to accuracy and objectivity, amplify their voices to a sustained roar, and pursue a policy goal with single-minded fervor, they may create a superficial 'reality' that captivates the public. The resulting public opinion can overwhelm all but the most resolute politicians. This does not happen often, but when it does, it offers convincing evidence of the influence of the news media on the making and implementing of policy."[7]

Such views, however, are exceedingly media-centric,[8] often rest on the selective use[9] of evidence, and tend to ignore more relevant and immediate factors that give rise to armed conflict.[10] In the case of the Spanish-American War, the policy objectives between the United States and Spain ultimately proved irreconcilable. Months of intricate diplomatic efforts ultimately failed to resolve what had become an intolerable state of affairs in Cuba, dramatized by the destruction of the *Maine* in a harbor under Spanish control and supervision. To indict the yellow press for causing the Spanish-American War is to misread the evidence and to ignore the intricacies of the diplomatic quandary that culminated in the spring of 1898 in an impasse that led to war.[11]

Evidence that the yellow press did not—could not—foment the war is extensive and persuasive, but is almost never compiled and assessed systematically, as this chapter undertakes. The evidence, drawn in part from the close reading of the *New York Journal*[12] and other newspapers during the months before the United States and Spain went to war in April 1898, can be summarized as follows:

- The abusive colonial policies of Spain *vis-à-vis* Cuba stirred outrage and condemnation in the United States. While the yellow press may have reported extensively on the consequences of Spain's failures and missteps, it did not create them. Spanish abuses included the harsh *reconcentración* policy which, beginning in February 1896, forced Cuban noncombatants into garrisons where they fell victim by the thousands to disease and starvation. Another Spanish blunder was the jailing of insurgent figures such as Evangelina Cosío y Cisneros, whose case became a *cause célèbre* in the *New York Journal*.

- The yellow press was not alone in calling attention to Spanish abuses in Cuba—or in reporting those accounts in a sensationalized manner. However, newspaper coverage of the insurrection tended to be cacophonous, inconsistent, and contradictory, due in part to the rigid censorship imposed on American journalists reporting from Cuba. In any case, the uneven nature of the reporting about the insurrection likely left readers bewildered, rather than eager and clamoring for war.

- As compelling as the Cuban insurrection was, it was not an unending preoccupation in the U.S. press. Cuba slipped off the *Journal*'s front page for noticeable stretches during the months before the destruction of the *Maine*.

- The *Journal* did not incessantly call for the United States to go to war with Spain but followed a more erratic editorial line. The newspaper's abiding call was Cuba's independence, not war between the United States and Spain. Moreover, the *Journal* was often in error in its editorial commentary about the course of events in Cuba. On several occasions in 1897, it mistakenly predicted the success of the Cuban insurgency.
- Whatever power the yellow press may have had to shape U.S. public opinion and U.S. policy toward Cuba, it was diluted by the fierce rivalry between the genre's leading exponents, the *Journal* and the *New York World*. The two newspapers were not in lockstep but sought instead to denigrate, undercut, or minimize the other's coverage during the months before and after the United States declared war on Spain.
- There is little evidence that the press beyond New York City, especially in small-town and rural America, was influenced by the content of the yellow journals, including their demands for war after the destruction of the *Maine*. A small but growing body of research indicates that the hinterland press was inclined to *condemn* the yellow newspapers for their exaggerated and fanciful reporting.
- There is almost no evidence that the demands of the yellow journals—especially during the critical weeks after the *Maine*'s destruction—penetrated the thinking of key White House officials, let alone influenced the Cuban policy of the McKinley administration. Notably, diary entries of White House officials disparage the yellow press as a nuisance but do not credit it as a factor in developing or shaping policy.

MEDIA EFFECTS DEBATED

Each of those points will be discussed in some detail. But first, it is important to recognize that the view the yellow press fomented the war took hold at the end of the nineteenth century and during the first years of the twentieth century in the face of a vigorous contemporaneous debate about the power of the press to shape public opinion and public policy. While little remembered, the debate was profound and at times sophisticated. In some respects, the debate anticipated the discussions about media effects that were to reverberate powerfully throughout the second half of the twentieth century.

What may be called the "powerful effects" school was an improbable coalition that included sociologists as well as practitioners and apologists for the yellow press, such as James Creelman. It also included bitter foes of yellow journalism, such as members of the clergy. The "powerful effects" advocates represented a dichotomy of views, describing the press both as a great educator in a rapidly changing American society *and* as a sinister, malevolent power. The press not only could promote literacy and reflection, it was a force for promoting democratic ideals. Other "powerful effects" advocates claimed the press possessed the deleterious capacity to corrupt and undermine values—a specter that encouraged the ill-fated effort in 1897 to boycott and marginalize the *Journal* and *World*.

The "limited effects" school, on the other hand, doubted the influences of the press, especially of metropolitan newspapers having large circulations like the yellow journals. The "limited effects" school argued that readers had become too sophisticated—and their lives too hurried—for them to be much influenced by newspaper content.

Powerful Effects Assumed

The powerful effects school tended to rely more on argument and assumption than on empirical evidence. The assumption was, rather simply, that the press in general[13] (and yellow journals in particular) was powerful and exerted influences, often to negative ends. The yellow press, moreover, was seen as representing a singular threat to democracy in America.[14] "They 'create' great men out of next to nothing," asserted a writer for the *American Journal of Sociology* in 1899, "and destroy the reputations of men truly fit for leadership. They decide questions of war and peace. They carry elections. They overawe and coerce politicians, rulers, and courts."[15]

A tenant central to the powerful effects school was that the masses were neither discerning nor particularly shrewd, and were therefore especially susceptible to the degrading allure of yellow journalism. "The people—the masses of the population of the country—are not given, as a rule, to doing their own thinking," asserted a writer for *Arena* magazine in 1897. "In matters of daily routine they believe what the newspapers tell them, not because they have implicit faith in the papers . . . but because they do not care to take the time to reason about what they read."[16]

The yellow press, moreover, was commonly seen as a vile and corrupting force. "The 'featuring' of suicides, murders, wrecks, fires, prize fights, scandals in business and society, is degrading because it is not elevating; it wastes time in unprofitable thrills and the indulgence of low forms of mental and sensational activity," said an article in *Bookman* in 1906.[17] The clergy was particularly emphatic about the virulence of yellow journalism, as suggested by characterizations such as these:

- The man who allows [the yellow press] in his family [home] opens a connection between the cradle and the sewer, the nursery and the swamp, and is inviting the germs of moral typhoid.[18]
- Great is the power of the American newspaper press. . . . [It] is a power which is rapidly poisoning the very fountain of American society, and that if not reformed will produce the most corrupt and godless civilization the world has ever known.[19]

- I arraign the new [yellow] journalism because it breeds crime. It is a noteworthy fact that child criminals are increasing in number, and the cause must be laid at the door of these papers which seek to picture youthful criminals and describe their doing in long accounts.[20]

Powerful Effects Doubted

The contrary or limited effects school was more nuanced, more empirical, and considerably less inclined to emotional appeals. It maintained—often with astonishment—that the press at the end of the nineteenth century was *losing* its power to shape and influence public opinion.[21] The influence of the editorial, in particular, was said to be in decline. A clear and sobering example came in 1897 when the U.S. Senate failed to ratify a treaty of arbitration reached the year before with Britain. The Senate's rejection was unexpected[22]—and widely interpreted as a rebuff to the press:

> The whole country ratified [the treaty] in advance. The press of the whole country, with few important exceptions, approved it. The Senate hesitated, and began to tamper with the treaty. The press remonstrated. The whole force, or nearly the whole force, of the most important and powerful papers throughout the United States was brought to bear on the Senate. It proved futile. The Senate gave no heed to the press, but went its own way, "amended" the life out of the treaty, wrecked it, left it a dead and empty thing. The Senate, in other words, either defied or entirely disregarded the press in a matter as to which the influence of the press might have been expected to be decisive.[23]

Another example came later in 1897, when most New York City daily newspapers supported Seth Low, a losing candidate in that year's mayoral election. (Hearst's *Journal*, however, backed the winner, Robert A. Van Wyck, and on the day after the vote printed a page full of congratulatory messages applauding the newspaper's efforts in the election.[24]) The election results prompted E. L. Godkin, perhaps the most eminent press critic of the time, to muse about the limited influences of the press: "A good deal of interest has been excited by the fact that although the larger and by far the better portion of the press was united, for the first time in the history of the city, on one side in a municipal election, that side was beaten badly, so far as numbers are concerned. Various inferences have been drawn from this, but the commonest one is that the influence of the press is overrated, that it does not mould opinion, and that it constitutes, in political contests at least, what the French call a 'quantité négligeable.' . . . That the influence of the press has undergone great diminution in all parts of the country there is no denying."[25]

Outcomes such as Low's defeat at the polls encouraged a revision in thinking about the masses of newspaper readers. Rather than being regarded as dull, uncaring, and indifferent (as the powerful effects school tended to argue), readers were seen instead as having become too sophisticated and too discerning to be much influenced by newspapers.[26] "The common people, if we may be allowed to use that expression, are better read and better educated than they were in the sixties and seventies," *Fourth Estate* said in an editorial in January 1900. "They now have ideas of their own on public topics . . . and they do not wish to be told by anybody how to think and what to do."[27] The American people in the 1890s were seen as unwilling to be led anywhere but "the way in which they want to go."[28] The public also was regarded as too hurried to devote much time to newspapers.[29] "We haven't the time to read it all if we wanted to," *Fourth Estate* said in 1899 about the content of daily newspapers. "In the morning the paper is scanned while going to business, and in the afternoon while going home. In this short space of time we can do little more than read the headlines, and take a sip here and there of the news that interests us individually."[30]

Moreover, large newspaper circulations were seen not as representative indicators of the capacity to shape opinion but, rather, as emblems of the *eroding* power of the press. Daniel T. Pierce, the editor of the weekly journal *Public Opinion*, argued at the turn of the century than the most influential newspapers were those published in *rural* America. The country newspapers, Pierce wrote, "are the truest reflectors of public opinion. Next to them come the papers published in cities of from ten to fifty thousand inhabitants. The country newspaper not only reflects public opinion—it anticipates it. Its editor is in close relations with his readers; he knows many of them personally and his interests are identical with theirs."[31] Editors of large metropolitan dailies, on the other hand, were too removed, too detached from their readers to gauge and thus reflect public opinion, Pierce argued. Their "attitude of superiority may be warranted," he wrote, "but it does not recommend our 'great newspapers' as echoes of the public voice."[32]

The press, according to Godkin, had also become trivialized—having indulged too often in too many sensations, a tendency that left the public more skeptical and wary than impressed or motivated. "People are so used to seeing the display headlines and big pictures employed to attract attention to all sorts of follies, falsehoods, and trivialities," he wrote in November 1897, "that they could hardly believe in the sincerity of an attempt to employ this same machinery on behalf of good government and good morals."[33] Similar observations appeared in the *Nation* and the *New York Times* in the weeks following the *Maine*'s destruction. "Nothing could be more curious," Godkin's *Nation* observed, "than the contrast between the wild aspect of the first pages of our [yellow journals] and the calm of the persons who are seen reading them. If half of what the 'scare' headlines reveal were true, the first impulse of the reader would be to remove his family to a place of safety, dispose of his property as best he could, and make arrangements to leave the country. A few years ago the mere sight of a newspaper got up in this extraordinary style, with headlines in bill-poster type reaching quite across the page, would have started a panic. . . . Now they are read with entire passivity, even although they declare war to be imminent, and indicate that a majority of the American people, including those of them who are in power, are either lunatics or maniacs. . . . The louder [the yellow press] shrieks, the less attention is paid to it."[34]

Similarly, the *New York Times* noted: "The grotesque inventions of the yellow journalist's fancy must still produce tumultuous excitement among stable boys and scullery women, but they now interest intelligent people only by their weird deformity."[35] The *Times* added:

> There are hysterical women of both sexes who continue to devour the unlikeliest untruths with the greatest avidity long after their rational neighbors have stopped reading them. During the first days of the epidemic the flood of mendacity had a great effect in promoting the sale of extras. But in the nature of things this is only a transient success. The more they lie the less they are believed, and, what is more to their purpose, the less they are bought. The sale of extras has been steadily dwindling now for many days.[36]

To be sure, such commentary carried a pronounced degree of self-interest. The *Nation* and the *New York Times* were, after all, decidedly conservative publications that deplored the tactics and the content of the yellow press. The *Nation* was hardly consistent, though, as it was soon to *blame* the yellow journals of New York for fomenting the war. But other anecdotal evidence suggests that the "shrieking" of the yellow press in the days and weeks after the loss of the *Maine* had effects akin to those of the proverbial boy who repeatedly cries wolf[37]—the cries soon were disbelieved and disregarded. *Fourth Estate* noted that the yellow press in New York City had in the wake of the *Maine*'s destruction "printed so many lying dispatches that people [were] beginning to mistrust any statement they make." The commentary further stated:

"A large proportion of the war news printed in the extras [published by the yellow press] is often founded on rumor, and the dispatches published under flaming headlines in one issue are contradicted in the next. The public is therefore unable to tell what is the truth in regard to the war situation."[38]

A "YELLOW" WAR

Despite the contemporaneous debate and widespread reservations about the power and influence of newspapers, the notion swiftly took hold that the yellow press was responsible for bringing on war with

Spain. Godkin, as noted, abandoned his doubts about the influence of the yellow journals and held them responsible for the conflict.[39] Regional newspapers in places as disparate as Kansas[40] and South Carolina also took up the cry of the "yellow war."[41]

Such claims only intensified after the hostilities. Creelman, an apologist for Hearst, asserted in his book of reminiscences in 1901, that the yellow press was responsible—"blood guilty"—for the conflict with Spain.[42] *Atlantic Monthly* claimed in 1902 that the *New York Journal* had "brought on a war which it is now known was not necessary to the freeing of Cuba, but was a great thing for the yellow journalism."[43] Studies published in the early 1930s about the press and the Spanish-American War—notably those by Marcus M. Wilkerson and Joseph E. Wisan—were influential in sustaining and deepening the view that the yellow press fomented the conflict.[44]

A succession of Hearst biographers, including Ferdinand Lundberg, W. A. Swanberg, and, more recently, Ben Procter,[45] reiterated the claims that the war was brought on by the yellow press of New York and by the *Journal* in particular.[46] (Although he offered little or no direct evidence, Lundberg even speculated that Hearst may have been responsible for the *Maine*'s destruction.)[47] Thomas Bailey's history of American diplomacy[48] and Gunther Barth's study of urban America in the nineteenth century[49] also argued the yellow press created the conditions that induced the U.S. public to clamor for war. By the end of the twentieth century, media history textbooks routinely invoked the claim that the yellow press forced the country into war.[50]

The indictment against the yellow journals,[51] which has varied surprisingly little over the years, maintains that the yellow press influenced the American public and policymakers by exposing them to a "steady drum roll"[52] of reports about Spanish atrocities and abuses—reports inspired not by any compelling interest about Cuba but by the cynical imperatives of a circulation war between Hearst's *Journal* and Pulitzer's *World*.[53] Gene Wiggins has written, for example: "Led by the *Journal* and the *World*, by Hearst and Pulitzer, the yellow press attained three highly sought after goals: higher circulation, increased profits, and war."[54] As we shall see, however, the higher circulations produced by the conflict *did not* boost newspaper profits.

Typically cited in the indictment of the yellow press is what Wilkerson called "a series of news events" in 1897 and early 1898, "for which the *Journal* was either wholly or partly responsible."[55] Those events were:

- the death in Spanish military custody in February 1897 of Dr. Ricardo Ruiz, a Cuban-born naturalized American dentist jailed on suspicion of links to the Cuban insurgents.

- the imprisonment of Evangelina Cisneros, whom the *Journal* rescued from jail and brought to New York City in October 1897.
- the publication in the *Journal* in February 1898[56] of an indiscreet private letter written a few months earlier by Enrique Dupuy de Lôme, Spain's chief diplomat in the United States. In the letter, de Lôme denigrated President McKinley as "weak" and "a low politician" who catered "to the rabble," and made other comments suggesting Spain's insincerity in seeking a negotiated end to the Cuban insurrection.[57]

Invariably, the final count in the indictment against the yellow press is that its decisive, final push to war came with the overheated and overwrought reporting about the *Maine*'s destruction. The *Journal*, in particular, accused Spain of complicity in the disaster[58] when the evidence was at best inconclusive. The cumulative effect of the coverage, Bailey wrote, was that the American people were "whipped to a white heat" and were "determined to have their war to free Cuba—and they got it."[59] Policymakers and Congress capitulated to demands for war pushed by the yellow press. Had public opinion been allowed to simmer in suspended judgment, war with Spain "might well have been averted."[60] But that was not to happen, not with the frenzy supposedly provoked by the yellow press. As Wisan stated in his often-cited work, *The Cuban Crisis as Reflected in the New York Press*:

> The newspaper reading public was subjected to a constantly increasing bombardment, the heaviest guns booming for 'Cuba Libre.' The effect was cumulative. The average reader, naturally sympathetic to the cause of freedom and critical of monarchies, became convinced that Spain was arrogant, insulting, vindictive, cruel. . . . Furthermore, the press had driven home the lesson that Spain was cowardly and weak, bankrupt, racked by internal dissension, friendless, and would prove no match for the magnificent forces of the United States. . . . Little wonder that the "average reader," indoctrinated with these opinions, called on his Government for War.[61]

While there certainly is factual basis for all the counts of the indictment, they do not add up to a persuasive or even very powerful case against the yellow press. The arguments tend, moreover, to rest on unsupported assumptions about the effects on readers in New York City and beyond, and on policymakers within the McKinley administration. Critics who blame the yellow press for bringing on the war fail to explain adequately or precisely how the often erroneous, and certainly exaggerated contents of the *Journal* and *World* were transformed into policy and military action. The newspapers' vast daily circulations are usually cited. But impressive circulation figures, after all, do not explain or correlate directly to political influence.

In reality, there was no steady drumbeat for war, no "constantly increasing bombardment" of calls in the yellow press for Cuba's independence. The principal exhibits in the case against the yellow press—the death of Ruiz, the rescue of Cisneros, and the disclosure of de Lôme's letter—were each separated by several months, during which time other events commanded wide attention and crowded Cuba off the front page. The months-long intervals tend to be ignored by those who invoke the three episodes in arguing the yellow press fomented the war. The episodes are sometimes described erroneously as "following closely," one after the other.[62]

But more important is that all three episodes were the direct consequence of Spain's harsh policies in Cuba: The yellow press did not place Ruiz in solitary confinement; the yellow press did not imprison Cisneros; the yellow press did not write or fabricate the de Lôme letter.[63] The *Journal* was the first to report all of those cases, and it exploited them relentlessly and extravagantly.[64] But they all were newsworthy—and they all were public-relations disasters of *Spain's* making.

As critics point out, the *Journal* and the *World* were undeniably extreme in their reporting, especially in the aftermath of the *Maine*'s destruction. But their excesses were not widely shared in the U.S. press; the excesses in fact were roundly deplored and even ridiculed. That they influenced many people, or whipped Americans "to a white heat" is doubtful: Several contemporaneous sources describe the sober calm with which the American public and many newspapers awaited the official U.S. report about the cause of the *Maine*'s destruction.[65]

Thus, as we shall see, the preponderance of evidence overwhelmingly supports the view that the yellow press did not cause, could not have caused, the war with Spain in 1898. An assessment of that evidence follows.

THE CONTRARY EVIDENCE

Spanish Policies *Were* Provocative

Spain's inept and clumsy policies *vis-à-vis* Cuba inevitably stirred outrage and condemnation in the United States. As such, the yellow press reflected, but did not cause, the consternation among Americans that resulted from the flawed colonial policies of Spain. That those policies were flawed had long been apparent. The rebellion that began in Cuba in 1895 represented the renewal of periodic challenges to Spanish rule.[66] In many respects, the Spanish reaction to the 1895 rebellion was exceptionally harsh.[67] In 1896, the Spanish governor-general in Cuba, Valeriano Weyler y Nicolau, imposed the first of his *reconcentración* orders under which as many as 400,000 Cuban noncombatants living in the countryside ultimately were compelled to move with their cattle and possessions inside fortified towns. The policy, intended to deprive the Cuban rebels of food, supplies, information, and logistical support,[68] was widely condemned in the United States for the starvation and disease it brought on. In fact, it has been argued that Weyler's policy toward Cuban civilians "did more to bring on the Spanish-American War than anything else the Spanish could have done."[69] In any case, *reconcentración* was emblematic of the severity of Spain's efforts to quell the rebellion.

Weyler, who frequently was described in the U.S. press as "the Butcher," also imposed a rigid censorship regime in Cuba, which led to clashes with the American reporters sent to cover the insurrection. Murat Halstead, a veteran and respected journalist who reported from Cuba for the *New York Journal* in early 1896, said Weyler was "disposed to regard correspondents of American newspapers as his foes."[70] Journalists frequently were harassed and those who spent time with the rebels risked jail sentences and expulsion. One of the most publicized cases of anti-press abuse was that of Sylvester Scovel, a correspondent for the *World* who was jailed for about a month in early 1897.[71] The *World* campaigned strenuously[72] for his release, even recruiting Richard Harding Davis to write an open letter of fulsome praise for Scovel, asserting hyperbolically that "Scovel may die [in prison] but if he does, his death will free Cuba."[73]

Their aggressive and ill-conceived policies exposed Weyler and Spanish authorities in Cuba and Madrid to withering attack in the U.S. press, by the yellow journals as well as conservative titles. The death in Spanish custody of Ricardo Ruiz, a naturalized American dentist suspected of helping insurgents derail a train in early 1897,[74] was such a blunder. Another was the jailing of Evangelina Cisneros, an insurgent figure's daughter. In both cases, Spain effectively handed the *Journal* stories that were easy to exploit—episodes that readily became metaphors for Spanish misrule of Cuba.

The Cisneros case won far more attention, in part because prominent American women, including Julia Ward Howe and the widow of Jefferson Davis, were enlisted in the *Journal*'s campaign for her release.[75] The Cisneros story also represented full development of a theme that appeared periodically in the yellow press, that of Spain's cruel treatment of Cuban women.[76]

Lundberg has argued that the Cisneros case "did much to intensify anti-Spanish opinion."[77] Another Hearst biographer, John K. Winkler, said the Cisneros episode was "Hearst's real opportunity to plough the war soil."[78] But in reality, Cisneros was far more important to a bellicose press had she remained in prison, as a female martyr for Cuban independence. By rescuing her from jail and bringing her in triumph to New York City,[79] the *Journal* was able to report an astonishing story, and to gloat that it had flouted Spanish law.[80] Freeing the young woman and spiriting her out of Cuba was "the greatest journalistic coup of this age," the *Journal* proclaimed.[81]

But at the same time, the *Journal* had removed a source of irritation between the United States and Spain—had removed the centerpiece of a captivating story that allowed the newspaper to point regularly to Spain's cruelty. Indeed, the Cisneros case faded from the newspapers[82] not long after her arrival in New York in October 1897.[83] As such, it is difficult to fathom how her jailing and rescue could have been at all decisive in propelling the United States to war six months later. Several newspapers in fact scoffed at the suggestion the Cisneros case held broad significance and implications.[84]

Disclosure of Dupuy de Lôme's intercepted letter, which the *Journal* published shortly before the destruction of the *Maine* in February 1898, undeniably exacerbated tensions between the United States and Spain. But de Lôme resigned shortly after the letter's contents were publicized,[85] thus excising a source of irritation and contention between the two countries.[86] Wilkerson has suggested that the *Journal* "could have relieved a tense situation by explaining that the communication was a private letter written to a private individual, the contents of which were disclosed by surreptitious means."[87] But such criticism misses the larger and more crucial point: de Lôme's letter was newsworthy for the insights it offered about the Spanish minister's duplicity, his insincerity, and his opinion of McKinley. The provenance of the letter was scarcely as important as its revealing contents.[88] In any event, some newspapers sought to dismiss the de Lôme affair as inconsequential. The *New York Evening Post* said de Lôme's letter revealed "no deliberate intention of affronting our government; the Minister was unluckily caught by some unknown pilferer of the mails—that is all."[89]

Wilkerson concluded that "the sensational press was largely responsible" for the three episodes—Ruiz's death, Cisneros' jailing and rescue, and disclosure of the de Lôme letter—and that those episodes "were agitated at a time when the relations between the United States and Spain were growing more strained each day."[90] In reality, however, other events appear to have been far more significant in the decision to go to war. The more decisive events—all of which came within weeks of one another in early 1898—made it clear to the McKinley administration that Spain could not quell the insurrection and restore its authority in Cuba.[91] The pivotal moments[92] were these:

- The rioting in Havana that greeted Spain's announcement of an ill-fated plan for limited political autonomy for Cuba. Spanish loyalists took to the streets in a spasm of violent protest on 12 January 1898; offices of three newspapers that favored autonomy were attacked and Spanish soldiers assigned to protect the offices were seen "fraternizing with [the] mob."[93] The

American consul-general in Havana, Fitzhugh Lee, reported, "Uncertainty exists whether [Spanish authorities] can control the situation."[94]

- The destruction of the *Maine* in Havana Harbor on 15 February 1898. The battleship's visit was precipitated by the riots in January.[95] Although no credible evidence ever was uncovered demonstrating that the *Maine* was destroyed on the order of Spanish authorities, those authorities did control the harbor.
- The speech 17 March 1898 by U.S. Senator Redfield Proctor, a conservative Republican from Vermont who had just returned from a visit to Cuba. In unemotional tones, Proctor described the appalling conditions, stemming from the *reconcentración* policies, that he found in Cuba.[96] Coming as it did (from a sober-minded friend of McKinley) and when it did (after the *Maine*'s destruction and before the release of the U.S. naval investigation report), Proctor's speech made a powerful impression[97] and probably helped galvanize public opinion about the plight of Cuba.[98]
- The report of the U.S. Naval Court of Inquiry, dated 21 March 1898, which said the *Maine* probably was destroyed by a submarine mine,[99] an act precipitated by person or persons unknown. The Court of Inquiry said it was "unable to obtain evidence fixing the responsibility for the destruction of the *Maine* upon any person or persons."[100] Nonetheless, the battleship had been destroyed in harbor guarded and administered by Spanish authorities; directly or indirectly, they were held responsible for the disaster.[101]

None of those episodes was the work of the yellow press; yet each of them was crucial to U.S. policymaking and, undoubtedly, to shaping public opinion in the weeks before the declaration of war in April 1898. As one historian of U.S. foreign policy has observed, "it is highly significant that . . . the public and Congress were not persuaded to take decisive action until convinced by reports [by Proctor and the Naval Court of Inquiry that were distinguished by] a sober, judicial nature."[102] Those reports, it has been perceptively noted, were persuasive not because they were sensational but because of their calm, *unemotional* quality.[103]

By April 1898, the United States and Spain faced a three-sided diplomatic impasse over Cuba: Spain was unwilling and probably unable, for reasons of domestic stability,[104] to grant Cuba independence. The insurgents in Cuba, unwavering in their inflexibility,[105] would accept nothing short of independence. And for political and economic reasons, the United States "could no longer tolerate the chronic turmoil" in Cuba.[106] Those were the fundamental factors that gave rise to the Spanish-American War.

Cuba Not an Unending Preoccupation

As powerful as the abuses of Spanish rule were, the insurrection in Cuba was not a ceaseless preoccupation in the U.S. press in 1895, 1896, and 1897. Contrary to claims that the yellow press "latched onto" [107] the rebellion and exploited it shamelessly for "three years of sensational, and often inaccurate, news stories" and "three years of banner headlines,"[108] Cuba was off the front pages for noticeable stretches during the months before the destruction of the *Maine*. Interest in the rebellion receded to such a modest level in April 1897 that the *New York Sun* decried how Cuba had been placed "on the shelf," eclipsed by other issues and domestic interests. It was difficult for the advocates of Cuba's independence, the *Sun* reported, "to hold the attention of Senators while pleading her cause in the Senate."[109]

Indeed, it is striking to review the issues of the *New York Journal* of 1897 and early 1898 and to note how often the Cuban rebellion had slipped off the front page:[110] In the ebb and flow of the news in 1897, reports about Cuba and Spain were absent, or failed to receive prominent treatment, in early March, most of April, the first half of May, much of June and July, the first part of September, early October, and most of November and December. Moreover, reports about Cuba and Spain seldom appeared on the front page in January 1898 until the rioting in Havana at mid-month. A variety of other events figured prominently on the *Journal*'s front page in the months before the Spanish-American War, including the brief but intensively covered[111] conflict between Greece and Turkey over Crete;[112] the inauguration in March 1897 of President McKinley; the heavyweight boxing championship match in Nevada between Robert Fitzsimmons and James Corbett; the Harvard-Yale-Cornell yacht race on the Hudson River; the headless torso murder mystery and the subsequent criminal trials in the case; the Klondike gold rush; the disrepair of New York's main streets; the city's mayoral election; a marathon indoor bicycle race,[113] and the *Journal*-sponsored New Year's Eve gala to celebrate the consolidation of the five boroughs of New York City.[114]

True to form, the *Journal* frequently and lustily injected itself into its coverage, calling attention unabashedly to its reporting exploits. It described in a front-page report how its "special inauguration train" had sped from Washington, D.C., to New York City in the record time of a little more than four hours, "bearing the artists and photographers who were to give the Journal's readers the true pictures of the scenes of [the inauguration]."[115] Even more dramatically, it touted its success in solving the headless, limbless torso murder mystery[116] by identifying the victim, William Guldensuppe, and then leading authorities to his killers.[117] "But for the Journal the arm of the law would have been palsied" in the murder case, the newspaper asserted.[118] The *Journal* also predicted the winner in the New York City mayoral election in 1897, a choice derived in part from its man-in-the-street surveys, an early if largely unscientific attempt to assess voter preferences.[119]

Thus, for the *Journal*, the insurrection in Cuba was among the many important, ongoing stories during 1897 and early 1898—much as it was for other U.S. dailies.[120] That changed with the destruction of the *Maine* in Havana harbor. As David F. Trask has observed, before the *Maine* blew up "the problem of Cuba constituted only one of a number of public issues to which the American people and their leaders gave attention." After the battleship's loss, however, "Cuban issues consumed the body politic, displacing all other concerns."[121]

An Erratic Editorial Line on Cuba

The *Journal*'s editorial line during the thirteen months before the destruction of the *Maine* was more erratic—and less routinely bellicose—than its critics typically acknowledge.[122] The *Journal* advocated Cuba's *independence*,[123] and did so far more routinely than it called for the United States to engage Spain in war.[124] Moreover, the *Journal* noted that American "intervention" in Cuba did not necessarily mean the introduction of military force, recalling how U.S. diplomatic pressure had forced France to retreat from Mexico in the late 1860s. "France under Napoleon III was a considerably more important power than Spain, and . . . we did not have war with France," the *Journal* observed in May 1897.[125] (The *Journal* offered contradictory opinions about whether the United States should annex Cuba.[126])

Not infrequently did the *Journal* betray frustration with its inability to move or influence the policy of the McKinley administration. Its annoyance became tinged with political partisanship, which was not surprising, given the *Journal*'s Democratic affiliation. However, exasperation about its limited influence can be seen in the following excerpts from the *Journal*'s editorials:

- "Congress has adjourned and the war in Cuba goes on. The sympathy for the patriots expressed in the Republican national platform was, it appears, campaign sympathy purely, and the pledge to take measures looking to the independence of the island of Cuba was not seriously meant. . . . Having the power, and the right, to issue a mandate for the cessation of this hideous war, we cannot escape moral responsibility for its blood and devastation"(26 July 1897).[127]
- "[W]hy should the bloodshed and starvation and misery in Cuba be allowed to go on, when we could stop it with a blow? The President does not even promise to end the war in a year"(7 December 1897).[128]
- "For the unutterable misery which afflicts the people of Cuba, for the destitution, starvation, torture, imprisonment and death which are their lot, the Republican party is responsible. . . . Its face is turned toward Madrid instead of to the rising sun of liberty on our Southern coast"(28 January 1898).[129]

- "The Republican party has accepted responsibility for the continuance of the status quo in Cuba, for the continuance of murder, starvation, rapine and theft. The responsibility will be brought home to it in [midterm elections in] November"(1 February 1898).[130]

In other editorials, and occasionally in news reports,[131] the *Journal* anticipated—quite incorrectly—the inevitable and even imminent success of the Cuban insurgency.[132] The newspaper could be characterized as never in doubt but often in error in its conjecture about Cuba. In any case, it is inconceivable that the newspaper's authority and influence would have been burnished by erroneous assessments such as these:

- "Whatever disposition Spain may now display, it will be belated wisdom. She has practically already lost her magnificent colony. . . . Cuba Libre will speedily cease to be a mirage if the Cubans continue loyal to their own honor and duty, and that but a little longer" (31 January 1897).[133]
- "In short, it can hardly be questioned that the insurrection, instead of being quelled, is to-day more formidable than ever, and enters upon a second year of its existence with decidedly improved prospects of successful results" (22 May 1897).[134]
- "In Cuba . . . revolution against Spanish rule [is] surging irresistibly toward success" (9 August 1897).[135]
- "Cuba's independence is in sight" (13 September 1897).[136]
- "The question is not whether the coming Spring [of 1898] will see the Cuban Republic among the Governments of the world, but whether it will see the Spanish monarchy there" (26 November 1897).[137]
- "The Spanish grip on Cuba is visibly loosening. Independence is certain, and it is needless for the patriots to try to hasten it by acts of barbarity" (20 December 1897).[138]

The *Journal*'s erratic editorial line reflected the shifting fortunes of the Cuban insurrection. But most certainly it did not "bombard" readers with unrelenting calls for war. If anything, the *Journal*'s uneven and inconsistent opinions would have left readers bewildered, rather than galvanized in a call for war.

Non-yellow Press Also Carried Erroneous Reports about Cuba

Although most assessments about the press and the causes of the Spanish-American War focus on the yellow journals, the Cuban insurrection was not, to be sure, exclusively covered by the *Journal* and the *World*. The rebellion was followed, at times quite closely, by many non-yellow newspapers, including the *New York Herald* and the *New York Sun*. Often their reporting was strikingly perceptive. The *Sun*, for example, revealed a keen understanding of the guerrilla tactics adopted by the outnumbered Cuban insurgents, noting their objective was "to wear out Spain, exhaust her resources, and compel her to give up the war as a failure."[139] The *Sun* also was known to issue editorial rebukes to correspondents who complained about the low-intensity warfare that characterized the insurgency.[140]

But more common than perceptive analysis were the conflicting, contradictory, and even wildly erroneous reports about the insurrection. *Fourth Estate* noted these inconsistencies in January 1896, stating that the "war in Cuba keeps all the papers guessing. There is no recent event that has led to such variously differing news reports. The papers are all on the alert for the truth—paying great sums for stories that have a Katy-did-Katy-didn't spirit."[141] Wisan's *Cuban Crisis* described how readers of New York City newspapers were in late 1896 and early 1897 "subjected to a bewildering barrage of conflicting reports emanating from both sides" of the conflict.[142] George Bronson Rea, a correspondent for the *New York Herald*, published in 1897 a well-documented catalog of the erroneous, exaggerated, and "faked" newspaper reports about the insurrection.[143] Rea drew many examples from the *New York Journal* and *New York World*, but reports published in their conservative rivals also figured in the book.[144]

The conservative press was even known to outdo the *Journal* in aggressive, intemperate commentary. The *Sun*, for example, declared Spanish forces in Cuba "guilty of deeds which no other modern army would perpetrate. If there be an American whose blood does not boil when he reads of them, or who would not take up arms to put a stop to them , his Americanism is bogus, and is manhood is a mockery of the word."[145] Spain, the *Sun* further asserted, "ought not be permitted to maintain a slaughter house this side [of] the sea. We should not permit her longer to carry on butchery in Cuba."[146]

Conservative newspapers also at times indulged in unrestrained and erroneous speculation, not unlike their yellow counterparts. The *New York Press*, for example, reported in late 1896 that "in case of war with Spain, the first move by our Navy would be the capture of Havana."[147] The *Press* and *Sun* both reported in early 1897 the rumors of Weyler's likely dismissal and departure from Cuba.[148] The *Sun* further speculated that Spain would soon give up the fight in Cuba.[149] Erroneous reports published in the Europe often found their way into American newspapers. The *New York Tribune*, citing a dispatch by the Paris correspondent of the London *Daily News*, reported in January 1897 that "the establishment of peace in Cuba is destined to be accomplished at no very distant date."[150] The *New York Times* inaccurately repeated reports circulating in

London that said Weyler faced punishment in Madrid following his recall from Cuba in late 1897.[151]

Such examples are by no means exhaustive. But they do indicate that the yellow press was not alone in publishing aggressive editorial comments and indulging in misguided speculation. The inconsistent and misleading reporting was attributable in part to the rigidity of Spanish censorship in Cuba. As Charles Brown wrote of the correspondents who covered the insurrection, "Spanish censorship and Cuban propaganda combined to make it difficult to find out the truth about even important events."[152] In any event, the insurrection was covered—at times wildly covered—by yellow newspapers and by their conservative rivals. Given the extent of the coverage, it is inconceivable that the reading public would somehow have sifted through the maze of often-contradictory reports and have allowed itself to be persuaded only by those accounts appearing in the yellow press. It is unreasonable, and indeed unfair, to single out the yellow journals for flawed and misleading reporting—and then to suggest that their reporting alone exerted special effects on public opinion.

Influence of Yellow Press Diluted by Rivalry

The power, if any, of the yellow press to shape public opinion was diluted by the fierce rivalry between the genre's leading two exponents—the *Journal* and the *World*. They were not in lockstep. They resisted their rivals' attempts to consider them a pair.[153] They sought often and eagerly to undercut each other's successes and to call attention to each other's flaws and missteps in coverage of the Cuban rebellion. [154]

A notable example was the strip-search report that appeared in the *Journal* in February 1897. The report, by Richard Harding Davis,[155] described how Spanish authorities boarded the U.S. passenger steamer the *Olivette* as it prepared to leave Havana and searched several passengers for contraband. Among the passengers was Clemencia Arango, a Cuban woman whose brother was an insurgent leader near Havana.[156] Davis' report began below the fold on the *Journal*'s front page and continued to the second page[157] where a provocative and (as it turned out) highly imaginary, illustration by Frederic Remington, was placed. Remington's drawing depicted the search aboard the *Olivette* as conducted by tall, leering Spanish male detectives.[158]

The *World* interviewed Arango in Tampa and promptly exposed Remington's illustration as fanciful.[159] She said no male detective had conducted the strip searches; they had been done in private by a matron, or "inspectress."[160] Davis, in a subsequent letter to the *World*, blamed Remington for drawing "an imaginary picture of the scene" and insisted his dispatch had not said that Arango was searched by men.[161]

The *World* soon had another occasion to ridicule and admonish the *Journal,* this time for the *Journal*'s "fraudulent,"[162] highly improbable, front-page report[163] that quoted John Sherman, the secretary of state-designate, as calling for war with Spain over the death in prison of Ricardo Ruiz.[164]

The cutthroat rivalry[165]—fueled by Hearst's stunning and demoralizing raids[166] of the *World*'s staff—also found expression in comparatively petty matters, as when the *World* asked municipal authorities to order the removal of an electric bulletin board on the *Journal* that provided scores of professional baseball games. The *World* claimed the popular scoreboard was a public nuisance, and the *Journal* won an injunction to block its removal. [167] The dispute prompted *Fourth Estate* to observe: "The fight between the New York *Journal* and *World* grows more bitter with every day of the struggle for supremacy. In both big and little ways, the war is waged."[168]

The *Journal* succeeded in embarrassing the *World* during the Spanish-American War. The *Evening Journal* published a contrived report about the supposed death in fighting near Santiago, Cuba, of an Austrian artillery officer, Colonel Reflipe W. Thenuz. The *World* promptly fell into the *Journal*'s trap. The next day it printed a nearly verbatim account describing the valor and death of Colonel R. W. Thenuz. The *World*'s account was copyrighted. The following day, the *Journal* exposed the hoax, rejoicing in the *World*'s blunder and explaining that "Reflipe W. Thenuz" was an anagram for "We pilfer the news."[169]

Those episodes were but a few of the many occasions in which the leading yellow journals sought to excoriate,[170] contradict, and undercut each other. [171] The broader effect of the rivalry[172] likely was to diminish the integrity and, in turn, the credibility and presumed influence of both newspapers. As *Fourth Estate* asserted in 1899, "the public has learned to disbelieve, generally, what one newspaper man may say about his rival; and [such criticism] leaves in the public mind a belittled idea of the press as a whole."[173] It was a recurring theme in the trade publication at the turn of the century.[174]

For the *Journal* and the *World,* the onset of war in 1898 was hardly a beneficial consequence of their rivalry. Critics have long argued that the yellow journals agitated shamelessly for war with Spain in order to boost their circulations.[175] Godkin, for example, declared in 1898: "The war increases their circulation immensely. They profit enormously by what inflicts sorrow and loss on the rest of the community."[176] But the war was *not profitable* for the yellow press. The conflict may have boosted their circulations,[177] but it also drove away advertisers who feared the war's potential to undercut recovery from hard economic times of the early 1890s. Newsprint costs soared,[178] and so did the expenditures on war coverage.

Fourth Estate noted that circulation gains failed to translate into profits.[179] "It is generally believed by the public that war is a good thing for the newspaper business," the trade journal said as the conflict began in the spring of 1898. "The assumption is that the largely increased circulation of the papers is extremely remunerative to the publishers. The contrary, however, is true."[180] Increased circulation, *Fourth Estate* noted as the war neared its end in the summer of 1898, "has not meant more advertising but on the contrary less. This was largely due of course to the fear that the business world would be demoralized by war, and then too the advertisers were forced to pay more than their share."[181] *Fourth Estate* also reported that many newspapers cut their staffs during the war "in order to save expenses."[182]

Covering the conflict was extraordinarily expensive. *Fourth Estate* estimated that the *Journal* spent $50,000 a week[183]—the equivalent 100 years later of $1 million—on cable tolls, reporters' salaries, and dispatch boats that ferried correspondents' reports from Cuba for transmission to New York. The additional expenses for the *World* were estimated at $30,000 a week.[184]

Cable traffic during the Spanish-American War was extraordinary. The volume of war-related dispatches significantly contributed to a nearly seven percent increase in all messages sent by Western Union during 1898.[185] Western Union traffic fell by one percent in 1899, another measure of the remarkable use of telegraph during the war.[186]

The *Journal* a few years later scoffed at claims that it fomented the war as part of a cynical scheme to build circulation and boost profits. "Would you like to know what effect the war had on the money-making feature of this particular newspaper? The wholesale price of paper was greatly increased. Advertising diminished, expenses increased enormously," the *Journal* said, adding that its expenses related to covering the conflict exceeded $750,000—the equivalent 100 years later of more than $20 million.[187]

No Newspaper "Outcry" after *Maine*'s Destruction

Historian John Tebbel has written that the voice of the *Journal* "was merely the loudest . . . in a journalistic outcry emanating from most of the nation's newspapers" in the aftermath of the loss of the *Maine*.[188] Wiggins has asserted that the *Journal*, the *New York World*, "and many other newspapers wanted a U.S. declaration of war."[189] Simon Michael Bessie wrote: "The louder the yellow press screamed the greater waxed its popularity and the stronger its grip grew upon American journalism."[190]

The evidence, however, is scant that the yellow press had such an effect, that it led or provoked an insistent, nationwide "outcry" for war after the *Maine*'s destruction. Press reaction in the days following the disaster was, instead, notably becalmed and restrained. *Fourth Estate* observed: "The frightful news from Havana, telling of the destruction of the . . . *Maine*, was treated here as a terrible calamity. The natural suspicion that Spanish methods of warfare had destroyed the ship moved men to cry for war, but the press as a whole published and reiterated the message from the [*Maine*'s] Captain, to 'suspend judgment.'"[191] The trade journal added: "Some of our papers, overheated with natural anger, have clamored for war, but the *great majority* have shown to the world that the press of the United States is in accord with the Government and is anxious for war only when it must be."[192]

The *New York Times* also commented about the calm reaction in the United States, stating in late February 1898: "No Latin race, we imagine, would have kept its head as well as the American people have kept theirs during the disturbing events of the past two weeks. In Spain or France or Italy there would have been tumultuous assemblages, much outcry in the streets, and incitements to riots. Outside of the reckless newspapers there has been no raving here."[193]

Yellow journals beyond New York City were also restrained. Notably, the *Boston Post* said that "the war scare" created by the *Maine*'s loss was unlikely to give rise to hostilities.[194] In what appears to have been a reference to yellow journals in New York, the *Post* deplored the "fantastic yarns that have been published as truth and the fanciful speculations which have been printed as fact."[195]

There is, quite simply, little evidence to support the claims that "a journalistic outcry" for war arose in the wake of the *Maine*'s destruction—and little evidence to uphold the view, offered by historian Philip S. Foner, that "most [U.S. newspapers] aped the 'yellow press' of New York."[196] A significant body of research indicates that newspapers in small-town and rural America scoffed at, condemned, and ignored the exaggerated and fanciful reports appearing in New York City's yellow journals before and after the *Maine*'s destruction. Rather than taking a lead from accounts published in the *Journal* and *World*, newspapers in the American heartland turned away from their excesses. The yellow press of New York in short lacked any extensive or generalized agenda-setting function in the runup to war.

To be sure, the yellow journals of New York *did* reach the hinterland. Some farm newspapers offered discounts in which a subscriber would receive the *Journal* or *World* along with the local daily or weekly newspaper.[197] But there was little evidence the yellow press was especially influential, given that the farm press attempted "to provide virtually all the reading a farmer or his family would require."[198]

The *World* noted that its out-of-town sales typically surged in the immediate aftermath of major events such as the *Maine*'s destruction. But such gains in circulation were fleeting because, the *World*'s managing editor observed, "the reader's interest subsides as quickly as the excitement; the event past, The World ceased to be the best general newspaper for the out-of-town reader."[199]

Moreover, studies of the heartland press in 1898 signal the limited influence of the Hearst and Pulitzer newspapers—and note that few local newspapers immediately and vigorously advocated war over the *Maine*.[200] Harold J. Sylwester, in his study of Kansas newspapers, said the state's press "hardly led the masses to clamor for war. Rather, they tended to follow a cautious course and generally came to endorse war only after McKinley had declared its necessity."[201] J. Stanley Lemons reported finding uneven and irregular press attention to the Cuban question in the Missouri press, noting that some newspapers "generally ignored" Cuba until the *Maine*'s destruction. [202]

Newspapers in Indiana tended to be "more moderate, more cautious, less imperialistic and less jingoistic than their eastern counterparts,"[203] and leading titles such as the *Indianapolis Journal* criticized the yellow press for having "'consistently lied about Cuba.'"[204] Few newspapers in Minnesota cited the Cuban reporting of the *Journal* or *World*.[205] Editors in Indiana "generally assumed a posture of caution and restraint" following the loss of the *Maine*[206] and their counterparts in Iowa swung overwhelmingly for war only after the Naval Court of Inquiry reported its findings on the battleship's destruction.[207] If editors of the Midwest were at all influential in shaping popular views about Cuba, it was not in sensational treatment of the insurrection but in focusing on more mundane matters, such as the fundamental economic interests of the United States in the Caribbean and Spain's challenges to those interests.[208]

War fever, moreover, was slow to take hold in North Carolina, where editors tended to deplore "the yellow sheets . . . which were spreading war germs," as George H. Gibson has written.[209] The effects of the Civil War and Reconstruction, Gibson stated, left little eagerness for hostilities with Spain.[210] In Texas, "journalists clearly did not follow the early sensationalist clamor for war," Marvin Olasky has reported. "Instead, that clamor may even have *impeded* the support of Texans for war against Spain by making them believe that the reasons given for war were without factual foundation."[211]

In New York City, the *Press* claimed thousands of new readers from those who had rejected the outlandish reporting of the yellow journals. It asserted as the conflict began that "the answer of the American people to Yellow Journalism is the growth of the New York Press, which relies for its success upon nothing but the news, the truth and the intelligence of American citizenship."[212]

To be sure, the discrete studies and examples cited here by no means represent a comprehensive survey of the American press during the weeks and months before the Spanish-American War. But the separate studies suggest undeniably that the aggressive tone of the yellow press was little echoed in the newspapers in the small cities and towns of the United States. The saber-rattling of the yellow journals in New York City was not at all "aped" — or much respected — in America's heartland press in 1898. Even generally friendly publications such as *Fourth Estate* criticized the yellow journals, likening their coverage as akin "to fouling one's own nest to create an unpleasant odor."[213]

No Evidence the Yellow Press Guided Policy

The claims that the yellow press fomented the Spanish-American War contain almost no discussion about how, specifically, that influence was brought to bear within the McKinley administration.[214] The reason for such a gap is straightforward: There is almost no evidence that the content of the yellow press, especially during the decisive weeks following the *Maine*'s destruction, shaped the thinking, influenced the policy formulation, or informed the conduct of key White House officials.

If the yellow press did foment the war, researchers should be able to find some hint of, some reference to, that influence in the personal papers and the reminiscences of policymakers of the time. But neither the diary entries of Cabinet officers nor the contemporaneous private exchanges among American diplomats indicate that the yellow newspapers exerted *any* influence at all. When it was discussed within the McKinley administration, the yellow press was dismissed as a nuisance or scoffed at as a complicating factor. It was regarded neither as a source of insight into popular thinking in the United States nor as a useful guide in pursuing the delicate and ultimately futile negotiations with Spain.

The administration's best known characterization of the yellow press was probably Theodore Roosevelt's withering dismissal in March 1898 of the *Journal*'s fabricated claim that Roosevelt had praised the newspaper's coverage. "I never, in public or private, commended the New York *Journal*," Roosevelt asserted.[215]

The comments of other, more senior and influential figures in the administration are, if anything, more revealing. Charles G. Dawes, the comptroller of the currency and a confidant of McKinley, wrote in mid-March 1898: "The sensational papers make more difficult the situation. If war comes it will be because the starvation and suffering in Cuba is such that the United States orders it stopped upon grounds of humanity and outraged justice, and that order of intervention is resisted by Spain."[216] John D. Long, the Navy secretary, complained in mid-January 1898 about what he termed the general tendency toward exaggeration and sensationalism in the press: "The whole situation, as incessantly happens now-a-days, is complicated by the press. With too many newspapers, there is an utter recklessness with regard to the statement of fact or the ascertainment of truth. The wildest rumors are gathered from the outside, or concocted in a reporter's brain, and are printed with headlines and pictures, as actual occurrences. The whole tendency is to sensationalism and the exploitation of the circulation of the newspaper."[217] Long's sentiments echoed those of Fitzhugh Lee, the U.S. consul-general in Cuba, who complained to Washington that "a great many" reports of the Havana riots in January 1898 "were untrue, much exaggerated and highly sensational."[218]

Perhaps the most valuable contemporaneous insights are those from the diary of George B. Cortelyou, the assistant secretary to McKinley. In that position, Cortelyou was the White House official who met most frequently with the press and with the president in 1897 and 1898.[219] Cortelyou, therefore, was uniquely positioned to assess the influence of the yellow press on the chief executive and administration policymakers.

As such, it is revealing to note how rarely Cortelyou commented about the yellow press. What infrequent reference he made tended to be disparaging and dismissive. As war loomed in mid-April 1898, Cortelyou wrote:

> The sensational newspapers publish daily accounts of conferences that never take place, of influences that are never felt, of purposes that are nothing but the products of the degenerate minds that spread them before a too-easily-led public. One of the most absurd lies that have [*sic*] found currency of late is the one to the effect that the President sees only the favorable side of the correspondence which comes to the Executive Mansion. . . . The President sees everything, whether in the shape of mail, telegrams or newspapers, that can indicate the drift of public sentiment.[220]

It is possible that such observations were self-serving and that those closest to power would scarcely acknowledge that newspapers exerted important influences in their deliberations and policies. But Cortelyou, while solicitous of McKinley,[221] was known to be candid and even generous in describing the accomplishments of the press. For example, he characterized as "remarkably accurate" the Associated Press report in late March 1898 that disclosed details of the Naval Court of Inquiry's report about the destruction of the *Maine*.[222]

In addition to the diaries of White House officials, the exchanges in early 1898 among U.S. diplomats in Madrid, Havana, and Washington are revealing for their silence about the influence of the yellow press. The diplomatic traffic suggested great frustration with an inability to move the Cuban question toward resolution short of war. Hopes were raised and dashed; various approaches considered and abandoned. But nowhere in the cables and correspondence is there evidence that the yellow press was exerting any influence whatsoever.

The diplomatic traffic—which contains reference to "great forbearance and self-restraint" among the American public during the tension-filled weeks after the destruction of the *Maine*—makes clear that events in Cuba, and not the coverage of those events, guided policymakers in Washington. On 20 March 1898, for example, William R. Day, an assistant secretary of state, wrote to Stewart L. Woodford, the chief U.S. diplomat in Madrid:

"Feeling in the United States is very acute. People have borne themselves with great forbearance and self-restraint last month. . . . *Maine* loss may be peacefully settled if full reparation is promptly made. . . . But there remains general conditions in Cuba which can not be longer endured, and which will demand action on our part, unless Spain restores honorable peace which will stop [the] starvation of people."[223]

In another message to Woodford in late March 1898, Day reiterated the administration's preoccupation with Spain's inability to end the abuses of *reconcentración* and to restore order in Cuba: "The concentration of men, women, and children in the fortified towns and permitting them to starve is unbearable to a Christian nation geographically so close as ours to Cuba. All this has shocked and inflamed the American mind, as it has the civilized world. . . . There is no hope for peace through arms. The Spanish Government seems unable to conquer the insurgents."[224]

Those and other exchanges during the critical weeks following the *Maine*'s destruction took place, as Wisan's study noted, [225] beyond the immediate notice of the press. The yellow journals not only exerted little influence on the administration's diplomacy, they "seemed imperfectly informed" about the details[226]—scarcely a combination for fomenting a war. The *Journal*'s reports, moreover, were often in error in the aftermath of the *Maine*'s destruction[227] and as such hardly qualified as a credible source. It is therefore inconceivable that the administration would have "succumbed" to the extravagant, distorted, and overwrought reports in the yellow press.

CONCLUSION

The evidence, then, is exceptionally thin that the yellow press was much of a factor in bringing on the Spanish-American War. The forces that culminated in the conflict were, as we have seen, far greater than the power of the yellow press to direct or notably influence. The newspapers of Hearst and Pulitzer may have mirrored, but they assuredly did not cause, the irreconcilable differences between the United States and Spain over Cuba.

So what, then, accounts for the enduring tendency to blame the yellow press (and Hearst in particular) for inciting the war? At least two factors appear to be at work. One is that blaming the *New York Journal* and *New York World* for the war has become a convenient way to excoriate yellow journalism, a ready way of summarizing its excesses and defining its malevolence. Blaming the yellow press for bringing about the Spanish-American War also represents an effective manner of signaling the presumed perils of an unrestrained press.

The other factor is that the *New York Journal* was, in a sense, hoist with its own petard. As many historians have noted, the *Journal* did suggest it was responsible for causing the war: It did place on its front page for three days in May 1898 the epigram, "How Do You Like the Journal's War?"[228]

But in so asserting, the *Journal* was mocking the claims of other newspapers, notably the *New York Evening Post* which had pointedly accused the yellow press of "fomenting" the war.[229] The timing and context of the *Journal*'s retort is significant—and is seldom considered by critics who argue the yellow press was responsible for the war.

The *Evening Post*'s "fomenting" editorial was published 30 April 1898. The next day, U.S. naval vessels engaged and destroyed a Spanish squadron in Manila Bay in the first major engagement of war. News of the naval battle appeared in U.S. newspapers 2 May 1898.[230] On its editorial page that day, the *Journal* published the portion of the *Evening Post*'s editorial that accused the yellow press of "fomenting" the war. That assertion was derided in a headline spread across the *Journal*'s editorial page. It read: "Some People Say the Journal Brought on This War. How Do You Like It as Far as It's Gone[?]"[231] That headline and the epigram on the *Journal*'s front page a few days later—"How Do You Like the Journal's War?"—were clearly intended to be ironic, cutting retorts to the *Evening Post* in the aftermath of a stunning U.S. naval victory. They were certainly not serious claims of responsibility for instigating the war. The *Journal*, moreover, was soon to express its exasperation about the conduct of the war, stating in late May 1898: "A whole month gone and nothing done! Nothing but the Manila victory, the great blaze of which now lights up the astounding lethargy of the Government. . . . Wake up, Mr. McKinley, wake up!"[232]

When it did specifically address the notion that it fomented the war, the *Journal* was much more oblique and ambiguous. For example, the *Journal* stated in early May 1898:

> This war has been called a war brought on by the New York Journal and the press which it leads. This is merely another way of saying that the war is the war of the American people, for it is only as a newspaper gives voice to the American spirit that it can be influential with the American masses. The Journal is powerful with the masses because it believes in them—because it believes that on issues of national policy, their judgment is always likely to be sounder than that of the objecting few.[233]

That statement scarcely qualifies as a ringing claim of responsibility. The *Journal* later returned to the theme of responsibility, with somewhat less ambiguity:

> The newspapers of the United States—those, that is, which speak for the people and not for private interests—were largely instrumental in bringing on this war. That is infinitely to their credit, for they gave voice to the manhood of the Republic, to its heart, conscience, courage and love of liberty. Had the American press, the real American press, been listened to in time the war would not have been necessary, since the recognition of the Cuban Republic, which it advised two years ago, would have armed the patriot forces of [Cuban insurgent leader Máximo Gómez] for victory without the intervention of the American Government.[234]

The editorial's logic is unpersuasive: It is improbable that recognizing a Cuban Republic in 1896 would have averted the Spanish-American War. Recognition might well have hastened the conflict. Moreover, the editorial may be read to suggest that the conflict represented the *failure* of the yellow journals, that if their demands had been heeded, war would have been unnecessary.[235]

But as to the specific causes of the Spanish-American War, the evidence undeniably points elsewhere—undeniably *away* from the yellow press. At most, the *Journal* and the *World* were irritants to policymakers in Washington and to Spanish authorities in Havana and Madrid. They were discordant and at times erratic voices amid the cacophony and confusion that characterized the making of policy and, ultimately, making of the war. The yellow journals, Lewis Gould, a political historian of the late nineteenth century, has correctly observed, "did not create the real differences between the United States and Spain."[236]

As discussed in this chapter, the hostilities were the consequence of a prolonged, three-sided impasse: Spain, for domestic political reasons, could not agree to grant independence for Cuba. The rebel movement in Cuba would accept nothing less.[237] The United States, for political and economic reasons, could tolerate no longer the disruption and the abuses so near to its mainland and so important to its strategic interests.[238]

To indict the yellow press for instigating the Spanish-American War is fundamentally to misread the evidence and thus do disservice to the broader understanding of a much-misunderstood conflict.[239] It does disservice as well to keener appreciation of the much-maligned genre of yellow journalism.

NOTES

1. Among them was Frank Luther Mott, who wrote in his widely cited textbook: "The 'ifs' of history are usually more amusing than profitable, but there seems to be great probability in the frequently reiterated statement that if Hearst

had not challenged [Joseph] Pulitzer to a circulation contest at the time of the Cuban insurrection [which began in 1895], there would have been no Spanish-American War." Mott, *American Journalism: A History: 1690–1960*, 3d ed. (New York: Macmillan, 1962), 527.

2. For claims made near the end of the twentieth century, see, among others, Harold Evans, "What a Century!" *Columbia Journalism Review* (January–February 1999): 28. He wrote that the Spanish-American War was "incited by the young Hearst and his feverish *Journal*, which accused Spain of blowing up the battleship *Maine* in Havana harbor." See also, Bruce W. Sanford, *Don't Shoot the Messenger: How Our Hatred of the Media Threatens Free Speech for All of Us* (New York: Free Press, 1999), 45. Sanford wrote: "When the yellows ran out of stories about beleaguered heiresses or gory murders, they turned to stunts like . . . starting the Spanish-American War. Readers were drawn like flies to cupcakes." See also, Michael Grunwald, "First Lady Meets the (N.Y.) Press," *Washington Post* (20 April 1999): A4. Grunwald wrote that "it was the vicious competition between William Hearst's New York Journal and Joseph Pulitzer's New York Sun [*sic*] that launched the Spanish-American War—and the phrase 'yellow journalism.'" Pulitzer's New York newspaper was, of course, the *World*. See also, Carl Nolte, "A Newspaper Empire: Hearst's Style Took Shape in the Examiner," *San Francisco Chronicle* (18 March 2000): A12. Nolte wrote: "Hearst and his main opposition, Joseph Pulitzer, defined yellow journalism and got the United States into the Spanish-American War."

3. See, among others, W. A. Swanberg, *Citizen Hearst: A Biography of William Randolph Hearst* (New York: Charles Scribner's Sons, 1961), 144. See also, Julian S. Rammelkamp, "Yellow journalism," in Kenneth T. Jackson, ed., *The Encyclopedia of New York City* (New Haven, CT: Yale University Press, 1995), 1281. The entry for "yellow journalism" says: "The militaristic sentiment provoked by the yellow press spread throughout the nation and persuaded President William McKinley to declare war on Spain."

4. Swanberg, *Citizen Hearst*, 144. For similar claims, see Gene Wiggins, "Sensationally Yellow!" in Lloyd Chiasson Jr., ed., *Three Centuries of American Media* (Englewood, CO: Morton Publishing Company, 1999): 161.

5. See *New York Journal*, 8, 9, and 10 May 1898.

6. See, for example, Clifford Krauss, "Remember Yellow Journalism," *New York Times* (15 February 1998): 4, 3. In a commentary published on the 100th anniversary of the destruction of the *Maine* and at a time when a sex-and-lies scandal was enveloping U.S. President Bill Clinton, Krauss wrote that the news reports about the president's misconduct were "tame, really, compared with the excesses of the coverage 100 years ago that incited the Spanish-American War." News coverage of the unfolding Clinton scandal evoked other comparisons to the yellow-press period. Historian Arthur Schlesinger Jr., for example, stated: "It's reminiscent perhaps of the 1890s, the beginning of yellow journalism. Everyone is trying to scoop everyone else, and therefore the accountability and the responsibility of the press becomes an immediate casualty." Cited in Joan Konner, "Publisher's Note: Of Clinton, the Constitution & the Press," *Columbia Journalism Review* (March/April 1999): 6.

7. Philip Seib, *Headline Diplomacy: How News Coverage Affects Foreign Policy* (Westport, CT: Praeger, 1997), 1.

8. For a discussion of this point, see Michael Schudson, "Toward a Trouble-shooting Manual for Journalism History," *Journalism and Mass Communication Quarterly* 74, 3 (Autumn 1997): 464–465.

9. A striking example of selectivity in citing evidence of the effects of the yellow press can be found in the often-quoted editorial published in the *New York Evening Post* a few days after the *Maine*'s destruction. The editorial deplores the *Journal* and *World* for their "disgraceful" reporting about the disaster. The portion of the editorial most often quoted reads: "Nothing so disgraceful as the behavior of two of these newspapers this week has ever been known in the history of American journalism." See, among others, Mott, *American Journalism*, 532; John Tebbel, *The Compact History of the American Newspaper* (New York: Hawthorn Books Inc., 1963), 203, and Walter Millis, *The Martial Spirit: A Study of Our War With Spain* (Cambridge, MA: Riverside Press, 1931), 110. Rarely if ever cited, however, is the remainder of the editorial, which *discounts* the notion that the yellow press exerted extensive influence on public opinion. The neglected portion of the editorial reads: "It speaks well for the good sense of the masses that *so little effect* has been produced by all this stuff. It is evident that *a large proportion of the public refuses to take the sensational newspapers seriously*, and reads them only from motives of curiosity. At the same time there is abundant evidence that thousands of people are affected by such announcements in print as 'War Sure' and that this sort of recklessness disturbs the public mind unnecessarily. It is a crying shame that men should work such mischief in order to sell more papers, and the first impulse of every right-minded person is to wish that journalism of this sort might be suppressed by the hand of the law." Untitled editorial page comment, *New York Evening Post* (19 February 1898): 4. Emphasis added.

10. Occasionally, the claim the yellow press fomented the Spanish-American War is based almost entirely on secondary sources. Bartholomew H. Sparrow, for example, directly cites neither the *New York Journal* nor the *New York World*—nor any other newspaper—in asserting the yellow press "succeeded in initiating the war with Spain." See Sparrow, "Strategic Adjustment and the U.S. Navy: the Spanish-American War, the Yellow Press, and the 1990s," in Peter Trubowitz, Emily O. Goldman, and Edward Rhodes, eds., *The Politics of Strategic Adjustment: Ideas, Institutions, and Interests* (New York: Columbia University Press, 1999): 139–175.

11. For detailed discussions about the diplomatic efforts that failed to avert the war, see, among others, Lewis L. Gould, *The Spanish-American War and President McKinley* (Lawrence, KS: University Press of Kansas, 1982), 19–53; John L. Offner, *An Unwanted War: The Diplomacy of the United States and Spain Over Cuba, 1895–1898* (Chapel Hill, NC: University of North Carolina Press, 1992), 225–236; and Ivan Musicant, *Empire by Default: The Spanish-American War and the Dawn of the American Century* (New York: Henry Holt and Company, 1998), 78–190.

12. The *Journal* in particular was read closely in this study, a decision inspired by the many claims that Hearst's was the prime mover in fomenting the war. See Swanberg, *Citizen Hearst*, 144. See also John K. Winkler, who asserted in his treatment of Hearst: "The Spanish-American War came as close to being a 'one man war' as any conflict in history." Winkler, *W. R. Hearst: An American Phenomenon* (New York: Simon and Schuster, 1928), 146.

13. John P. Ferré, a media historian who has studied the claims of media influences at the end of the nineteenth century, has noted, perceptively: "Reading

press criticism at the turn of the [twentieth] century is much like reading early popular notions of the effect of television: there seemed to be little that the medium could not do." Ferré, "The Dubious Heritage of Media Ethics: Cause-and-Effect Criticism in the 1890s," *American Journalism* 5, 4 (1988): 196.

14. "Topics of the Times: A Danger to American Democracy," *Century Magazine* 72, 2 (June 1906): 317–318.

15. V. S. Yarros, "The Press and Public Opinion," *American Journal of Sociology* 5 (November 1899): 372.

16. John Henderson Garnsey, "The Demand for Sensational Journals," *Arena* (November 1897): 684. He added: "We do not want sensational journals; we are only made to think that we do" (686). See also, Sydney Brooks, "The American Yellow Press," *Fortnightly Review* 96 (December 1911): 1137. A contrary argument —that the yellow press reflected but did not create the superficiality—was proposed by an apologist for the genre, Lydia Kingsmill Commander, who wrote: "For the shortcomings of the yellow press we must blame the American people. As a whole we are interested in crime, scandal, prize-fights and horseracing. If we were not, the yellow journals would not be the most popular newspapers in the country." Commander, "The Significance of Yellow Journalism," *Arena* 34 (August 1905): 151

17. John A. Macy, "Our Chromatic Journalism," *Bookman* 24 (October 1906): 128. The writer also suggested an elaboration on the metaphor of the "yellow" press to "blue" or chronically despondent and "censorious" journalism; "black" or ill-informed, usually small-town journalism; and "white" or "pure and honest" journalism.

18. The Rev. Dr. W.H.P. Faunce, quoted in "New Journalism and Vice," *New York Times* (3 March 1897): 2.

19. The Rev. J. B. Hawthorne of Nashville, quoted in "Sensationalism: Its 'Yellow' Advocates Roundly Scored," *Fourth Estate* (28 April 1898): 4.

20. The Rev. E. S. Tipple, quoted in "New Journalism Attacked," *New York Times* (8 March 1897): 3.

21. The limited effects argument, if anything, became more sophisticated and nuanced during the first years of the twentieth century. A sociologist at Columbia University wrote in 1912: "What is actually known, for example, concerning the net stimulus to public opinion given by the 25,000 daily papers of this country? Practically nothing. . . . Nobody . . . knows in exact terms even such a simple quantitative fact as the relative proportion of attention paid by the newspapers of the country as a whole to matters of cultural interest compared with the amount of attention paid to topics of a political or business nature." Alvan A. Tenney, "The Scientific Analysis of the Press," *The Independent* 73 (17 October 1912): 895.

22. The *New York World* had confidently but erroneously predicted that the Senate "cannot afford to disregard" the expressions in newspapers and elsewhere of broad public support for the treaty. The *World* also said: "It is an impeachment of the Senate to doubt the ratification of the treaty." See "Public Opinion and the Treaty," *New York World* (19 January 1897): 6.

23. George W. Smalley, "Notes on Journalism," *Harper's New Monthly Magazine* 67 (July 1898): 220. Smalley also wrote: "If the editor of one or another of those journals which confuse circulation and influence would ask any of the representative men with whom he comes in contact what they think about the

power of the press, he would probably be astonished by their answers. They will tell him, or many of them will, that they have ceased to pay much attention to what his paper says."

24. "Democracy's National Leaders Praise the Journal's Work," *New York Journal* (3 November 1897): 3.

25. E. L. Godkin, "The Influence of the Press," *The Nation* 65 (25 November 1897): 410. The results of the New York City mayoral election 1909 gave rise to a similar interpretation: "After the last ballot had been cast and counted . . . the successful candidate paid his respects to the newspapers which had opposed him. This is equivalent to saying that he paid them to the whole metropolitan press; for every great daily except one had done its best to defeat him, and that one had given him only a left-handed support." Francis E. Leupp, "The Waning Power of the Press," *Atlantic Monthly* (February 1910): 145.

26. See, for example, A. Maurice Low, "The Modern Newspaper As It Is," *Yale Review* 2 (1912): 101. Low wrote: "Circulation is not necessarily influence; although the circulation of newspapers today is larger than at any time since a modern press existed, the newspaper has become less a leader than a follower of public opinion. Nor is this surprising. The more a people think for themselves and the more they understand the complexity of motives, the less they will be inclined to believe in the sincerity of a mission whose success depends upon its profits."

27. "The Influence of the Editorial Column," *Fourth Estate* (27 January 1900): 6. The editorial also suggested that readers sought brevity in newspaper reports, stating: "The paragraph is read, while the long editorial is skipped by the average citizen for the reason that he has no time to wade through it. Brief discussions of live topics are what the people want, and it is a waste of effort to give them anything else."

28. John A. Cockerill, "Some Phases of Contemporary Journalism," *Cosmopolitan* 13 (October 1892): 698.

29. See Leupp, "The Waning Power," 146. The view that the public had little time to devote to newspapers prompted Leupp to speculate: "Does the ordinary man of affairs show so scant regard for his newspaper because he no longer believes half of what it tells him, or only because his mind is so absorbed in matters closer at hand, and directly affecting his livelihood? Have the newspapers perverted the public taste with sensational surprises till it can no longer appreciate normal information normally conveyed?"

30. "On the Newspaper Habit," *Fourth Estate* (19 October 1899): 4. Interestingly, the amount of time people say they spend reading or scanning newspapers remained fairly stable, at 15 to 25 minutes, throughout the twentieth century. See Felicity Barringer, "As Data About Readers Grows, Newspapers Ask: Now What?" *New York Times* (20 December 1999): C41.

31. Daniel T. Pierce, "Does the Press Reflect Public Opinion?" *Gunton's Magazine* (November 1900): 421.

32. Pierce, "Does the Press Reflect Public Opinion?" 421. Pierce cited what he described as the limited discussion in the large-circulation metropolitan newspapers to the implications of the United States' defeat of Spanish forces in the Philippines in 1898, at the outset of the Spanish-American War. "I venture the statement," Pierce wrote, "that not ten 'great' city journals had at any time for a moment considered the annexation of the Philippines or any of the ques-

tions now grouped under the head of 'imperialism.' . . . But the country papers of the West quickly took up the discussion, and a majority of them were ardent expansionists. The idea of a Greater America pleased them mightily" (423).

33. Godkin, "The Influence of the Press," 411.

34. "The Week," *The Nation* 66 (3 March 1898): 157.

35. "Spanish Alliances," *New York Times* (1 March 1898): 6.

36. "Lies and War," *New York Times* (1 March 1898): 6. The *New York Press* asserted in the aftermath of the *Maine*'s destruction "that even habitual readers of Yellow Journals . . . know that they can be trusted in serious matters no matter in those that are trivial. When the Yellow readers, therefore, want news and the whole truth about momentous questions they seek them in other papers than the . . . maniacal Yellow Journals." Untitled editorial page comment, *New York Press* (22 February 1898): 6.

37. The dangers of crying wolf were noted in an article in *Munsey's Magazine* in 1900, which described how large headlines that told of the deadly hurricane in Galveston, Texas, at first "made no impression. The readers dismissed them as the familiar exaggeration, and there was no increased sale. They thought of the old cry of 'Wolf!' 'Yellow journals' are beginning to understand that it doesn't pay to put head lines on unimportant news, and that means change." Hartley Davis, "The Journalism of New York," *Munsey's Magazine* 24 (November 1900): 233. The diminished impact of large headlines appears to be a recurring problem for newspapers. As the British newsmagazine the *Economist* observed in 1998: "Over-use has so devalued banner headlines that editors on both sides of the Atlantic now find it hard to differentiate a truly sensational story, such as the bombing of the World Trade Centre, from, say, revelations about changes in the cast of a television soap." See "Behind the Headlines," *Economist* (7 February 1998): 86.

38. "Unreliable War News," *Fourth Estate* (19 May 1898): 6.

39. See *Nation* 66 (5 May 1898): 336, cited in Willard Grosvenor Bleyer, *Main Currents in the History of American Journalism* (Boston: Houghton Mifflin Company, 1927), 285.

40. The *Atchison Globe*, for example, asserted when war was declared: "'Yellow Journalism' Having Won a Great Victory, Yellow Fever is Now to Be Given a Fair Chance." See Harold J. Sylwester, "The Kansas Press and the Coming of the Spanish-American War," *Historian* 31 (1969): 261–262.

41. "A Yellow War," *Charleston News and Courier* (22 April 1898).

42. James Creelman, *On the Great Highway: The Wanderings and Adventures of a Special Correspondent* (Boston: Lothrop Publishing Co., 1901), 175–176. Creelman wrote: "And yet no true history of the war . . . can be written without an acknowledgement that whatever of justice and freedom and progress was accomplished by the Spanish-American War was due to the enterprise and tenacity of 'yellow journalists.'"

43. Brooke Fisher, "The Newspaper Industry," *Atlantic Monthly* 89 (June 1902): 751.

44. For an example of a media history textbook that draws heavily on Wisan and Wilkerson, see Michael Emery and Edwin Emery with Nancy L. Roberts, *The Press and America: An Interpretative History of the Mass Media*, 8th ed. (Boston: Allyn and Bacon, 1996), 201. The writers stated: "Those who have sought to explain the causes of this unwarranted war have often centered the

blame on William Randolph Hearst in particular and the newspapers of the country in general." Bartholomew Sparrow likewise makes extensive use of Wisan and Wilkerson. See Sparrow, "Strategic Adjustment and the U.S. Navy." For further discussion about the broader influence of the works of Wilkerson and Wisan, see Mark M. Welter, "The 1895-98 Cuban Crisis in Minnesota Newspapers: Testing the 'Yellow Journalism' Theory," *Journalism Quarterly* (Winter 1970): 723-724.

45. Procter seems inclined to spread responsibility for the conflict, writing, "With the *Journal* and *World* clamoring for war, with a jingoistic Congress reflecting the popular will, President McKinley was unable to withstand such public pressure." But elsewhere, in recounting the purported Remington-Hearst telegrams, Procter writes: "Hearst allegedly replied, 'Please remain. You furnish the pictures and I'll furnish the war.' And that was exactly what Hearst did." See Procter, *William Randolph Hearst: The Early Years, 1863–1910* (New York: Oxford University Press, 1998), 103, 118.

46. A biography of Hearst published in 2000 expresses doubt that the yellow press fomented the war. See David Nassaw, *The Chief: The Life of William Randolph Hearst* (Boston: Houghton Mifflin Company, 2000), 132–133.

47. Ferdinand Lundberg, *Imperial Hearst: A Social Biography* (New York: Equinox Cooperative Press, 1936), 74, 81. He wrote: "Studies of probable causes [of the *Maine*'s destruction] have erred, in my opinion, by not considering the Hearst organization, its character and its biases. The man most interested in plunging the country into war was William Randolph Hearst" (74). See also, Allen Churchill, *Park Row* (New York: Rinehart & Company Inc., 1958), 112. Joyce Milton dismisses such speculation, stating: "The best argument against the existence of any Hearst connection is that it is impossible to imagine that other correspondents in Havana would not have heard of it. . . . It is inconceivable that rumors of *Journal* involvement in such a plot would not have reached the ears of representatives of other papers, and equally inconceivable that they would have kept quiet about them." See Milton, *The Yellow Kids: Foreign Correspondents in the Heyday of Yellow Journalism* (New York: Harper & Row, 1989), 232–234.

48. Thomas A. Bailey, *A Diplomatic History of the American People*, 8th ed. (New York: Appleton-Century-Crofts, 1969), 463–464.

49. Gunther Barth, *City People: The Rise of Modern City Culture in Nineteenth-Century America* (New York: Oxford University Press, 1980), 101.

50. See, among others, Donald A. Ritchie, *American Journalists: Getting the Story* (New York: Oxford University Press, 1997), 142. A study published in 1984 found that U.S. history textbooks used in high school classes typically included references to the yellow press as a factor in the Spanish-American War. See Dan B. Fleming, "Benjamin Franklin to Watergate: The Press in U.S. History Textbooks," *Journalism Quarterly* 61 (Winter 1984): 887.

51. See, for example, Gene Wiggins, "Journey to Cuba: The Yellow Crisis," in Lloyd Chiasson Jr., ed., *The Press in Times of Crisis* (Westport, CT: Greenwood Press, 1995): 105. Wiggins wrote: "If the press was guilty of being the primary instigator of a major war, then the two publishers generally credited with doing most of the instigating were Hearst, owner of the New York *Journal*, and Joseph Pulitzer, owner of the New York *World*, with the former getting the lion's share of the credit."

52. Procter, *William Randolph Hearst: The Early Years*, 104.

53. See, notably, Joseph E. Wisan, *The Cuban Crisis as Reflected in the New York Press (1895–1898)*, (New York: Octagon Books reprint edition, 1965), 458. Wisan wrote: "In the opinion of the writer, the Spanish-American War would not have occurred had not the appearance of Hearst in New York journalism precipitated a bitter battle for newspaper circulation. The Cuban insurrection and its attendant horrors furnished a unique opportunity to the proprietors of the sensational press to prove their enterprise and provide the type of news that sold papers. Even the conservative journals, irritated by the emphasis the 'new journalists' placed upon Cuba, were compelled by that very emphasis to devote considerably more space to Cuban affairs than they otherwise would have done. In their treatment of Cuban affairs, none of the papers seemed primarily concerned with Cuba *per se*, with the possible exception of the *Sun* . . . and the less important *Times*." Wisan's arguments, while intriguing, rest more on assertion than evidence. He offered no evidence to support his claim that conservative newspapers were "compelled" by the yellow press to bolster their reporting about Cuba. Nor did Wisan present a persuasive case that the *Journal* and *World* "simply used Cuba to achieve their prime purpose—an increase in circulation" (459). His references to source material beyond newspaper accounts are notably few.

54. Wiggins, "Journey to Cuba," 117.

55. Marcus M. Wilkerson, *Public Opinion and the Spanish-American War: A Study in War Propaganda*. (Baton Rouge, LA: Louisiana State University Press, 1932), 83. Mott also discussed those events at some length, as did Sidney Kobre. See Mott, *American Journalism*, 529–531, and Kobre, *The Yellow Press and Gilded Age Journalism* (Tallahassee, FL: Florida State University Press, 1964), 284–288.

56. "The Worst Insult to the United States in its History: Spain's Minister Calls President McKinley a 'Low Politician, Catering to the Rabble,'" *New York Journal* (9 February 1898): 1.

57. See "Political and General: The Spanish Minister's Letter," *Public Opinion*, 24, 7 (17 February 1898). See also, "Fac-Simile of Letter Written by the Spanish Minister, In Which He Insults the President, Calling Him 'A Low Politician,'" *New York Journal* (9 February 1898): 1.

58. See, for example, "Destruction of the War Ship Maine was the Work of an Enemy," *New York Journal* (17 February 1898): 1. See also, "How a Spanish Submarine Mine May Have Destroyed the Maine and Many of Her Crew," *New York Journal* (17 February 1898): 2. The *Journal* argued that blowing up the *Maine* would not have been an irrational act for Spain or rogue Spanish officers: "What if the men who committed the deed cherished the belief, rampant in Havana and prevalent in the highest official circles in Spain, that war was already inevitable? Would it not be desirable then to reduce the naval superiority of the United States as far as possible before hostilities began? . . . The chances of destroying the Maine in battle would be extremely slim. To take an opportunity that would never come again of disposing of one enemy warship in advance would be deviltry, but anything but lunacy." See "Our Relations With Spain," *New York Journal* (18 February 1898): 10.

59. Bailey, *Diplomatic History*, 463–464.

60. Seib, *Headline Diplomacy*, 13.

61. Wisan, *The Cuban Crisis*, 460. But rather than touting the "magnificent forces of the United States," the *New York Journal* on occasion faulted America's

preparations for a conflict. See, for example, "Are We Going to Fight?" *New York Journal* (9 September 1897): 6, and "Why We Should Act at Once," *New York Journal* (13 February 1898): 50. The editorial titled "Are We Going to Fight?" stated: "We may be at war within a month. And yet, while Spain is feverishly drilling troops, building ships, negotiating for others already built, arming fortifications and borrowing money, we are apparently making no preparations for trouble. Congress has been allowed to adjourn without authorizing the enlistment of an additional man by land or sea, and without providing for any new ships." Fifteen days later, however, the *Journal* stated in an editorial: "Nobody of sense, of course, wants a war with Spain, but should a conflict come our navy would make short work of that of Spain." See "Quite Ready for Spain," *New York Journal* (24 September 1897): 6. The editorials are also instructive in revealing the conflicting, erratic, and contradictory nature of the *Journal*'s editorial positions. Moreover, its prediction of "war within a month" was an example of the *Journal*'s not infrequent errors in editorial assessments about the insurrection and about U.S. policy toward Cuba.

62. See, notably, Wilkerson, *Public Opinion and the Spanish-American War*, 97, who was in error in writing: "The publication of the De Lome letter, following closely the Ruiz case and the Cisneros rescue, furnished additional fuel to feed the flame of American indignation toward Spain."

63. This point also was made by John L. Offner in his study of events leading to the war. "Hearst published the de Lôme letter, but he did not make it up. . . . Had there been no sensational press, only responsible editors, the American public nevertheless would have learned about the terrible conditions in Cuba [and] would have wanted Spain to leave." See Offner, *An Unwanted War*, 229–230.

64. For example, the *Journal* characterized the de Lôme letter "the worst insult to the United States in its history." See "The Worst Insult to the United States in its History," *New York Journal*.

65. The *New York Evening Post*, among others, commented upon the calm reaction in the days after the *Maine*'s destruction. "The country," it said, "has received the news of the Maine explosion like men; but two of our newspapers here [the *Journal* and the *World*] have received it as if we were all ten-year-olds." Untitled editorial page comment, *New York Evening Post* (17 February 1898): 6.

66. An insurrection begun in 1868 lasted ten years and ended with Spain's agreement, never fulfilled, to grant autonomous rule to Cuba.

67. The harshness of Spanish rule was lost on some commentators at the end of the twentieth century. See, for example, Jonathan Yardley, "The Making of a Mogul," *Washington Post* (26 April 1998): X3. Yardley wrote in reviewing *William Randolph Hearst: The Early Years, 1863–1910*: "There was in fact nothing especially tyrannical about Spanish rule in Cuba; it just provided an excuse for a war—a circulation war, as it sometimes was called." For a dismissive account about the Cuban insurgency, see Churchill, *Park Row*. Churchill wrote that the Cuban people were "too sunk in lassitude to care whether they lived under Spanish rule or not. A few firebrands worked hard to stir them up, with small visible success" (104).

68. See Offner, *An Unwanted War*, 13, and David F. Trask, *The War with Spain in 1898* (New York: Macmillan Publishing Co., 1981), 7–8.

69. Musicant, *Empire by Default*, 69.

70. Murat Halstead, "General Weyler Face to Face: A Character Sketch," *New York Herald* (28 November 1897): 5, 2.

71. Scovel's assignment to Cuba may have had a diplomatic objective as well. Joyce Milton has written that Scovel explored the prospects for a negotiated settlement among the Spanish, Cuban insurgents, and the Americans. See Milton, *The Yellow Kids*, 142–145.

72. Fifty-two newspapers joined in calling on Spanish authorities to free Scovel, and Congress and fourteen state legislatures passed resolutions urging the State Department to press for the journalist's release. Charles H. Brown, *The Correspondents' War: Journalists in the Spanish-American War* (New York: Charles Scribner's Sons, 1967), 86.

73. Richard Harding Davis, "Richard Harding Davis Writes of the World's Correspondent," *New York World* (18 February 1897): 1. Davis had just returned from an assignment to Cuba for the *New York Journal*. See Chapter Three.

74. See Offner, *An Unwanted War*, 34–35.

75. See Julius Chambers, "Women's Noble Appeal for Miss Cisneros," *New York Journal* (19 August 1897): 1, and James Creelman, "American Womanhood Roused," *New York Journal* (20 August 1897): 3. The circumstances that led to Cisneros' jailing were disputed. She said she was arrested after resisting the advances of a Spanish military officer. The officer claimed she had attempted to lure him into a trap. See, among others, George Clarke Musgrave, *Under Three Flags in Cuba* (Boston: Little, Brown and Company, 1899), 96–98.

76. See, for example, George Eugene Bryson, "Weyler Throws Nuns Into Prison: Butcher Wages Brutal Warfare on Helpless Women," *New York Journal* (17 January 1897): 1. See also, "Persecutes Women Now: Beast Weyler, Baffled by Men, Attacks Patriots' Wives, Sisters, Mothers," *New York World* (8 February 1897): 7.

77. Lundberg, *Imperial Hearst*, 71. Some sources have downplayed the rescue of Cisneros, alleging that her escape was facilitated by bribes. See Willis J. Abbot, *Watching the World Go By* (Boston: Little, Brown, 1933), 215–216. Detractors, however, do not attempt to explain why Spanish authorities would have countenanced or consented to such an embarrassing turn of events, which came during Weyler's final weeks as governor-general. It is inconceivable that Weyler would have allowed the *Journal* to score such a coup at the end of his controversial tenure in Cuba.

78. Winkler, *W. R. Hearst: An American Phenomenon*, 147. John Tebbel likened the Cisneros rescue to "an incident straight out of a bad movie." Tebbel said, erroneously, that the jailbreak came during the early days of the Spanish-American War. See Tebbel, *Compact History of the American Newspaper*, 204.

79. See "The People Unite With the Journal to Welcome Miss Cisneros to Freedom," *New York Journal* (17 October 1897): 45. Accounts in other newspapers were considerably more restrained and some avoided mentioning the *Journal*'s role in her release. See, for example, "Fair Refugee Here," *New York Herald* (14 October 1897): 11. The *Herald*'s report said simply that "her rescue was effected by two American reporters."

80. The *Journal* acknowledged having "flouted Spanish law in breaking into the foul jail . . . and helping the martyr prisoner out. It is happy in the knowledge. It would like to violate some more Spanish law of the same sort. When right and wrong are turned upside down . . . there is a savage satisfaction in

striking a smashing blow at a legal system that has become an organized crime." See "Beyond Weyler's Reach," *New York Journal* (12 October 1897): 6.

81. "Evangelina Cisneros Rescued by the Journal," *New York Journal* (10 October 1897): 1. The report read: "Evangelina Cossio [*sic*] y Cisneros is at liberty and the Journal can place to its credit the greatest journalistic coup of this age. It is an illustration of the methods of new journalism, and it will find an indorsement in the heart of every woman who has read of the horrible sufferings of the poor girl who has been confined for fifteen long months in Recojidas Prison" in Havana. *Fourth Estate* also lauded the *Journal* and Karl Decker, the correspondent who spirited Cisneros from jail, stating: "They have smashed journalistic records." See "New York Newspaper's International Triumph," *Fourth Estate* (21 October 1897): 6.

82. The rescue of Cisneros was reported across several pages of issues of the *Journal* in mid-October, but the frenzy was largely spent by the closing days of the month. By then, the *Journal*'s attention had turned to the death of Charles A. Dana, venerable editor of the *New York Sun*, and to the New York City mayoral campaign. The *Journal* had feuded with Dana and the *Sun* but demonstrated in tributes to the editor that it could be charitable toward foes. "Charles A. Dana was a brilliant journalist," the *Journal* said in an editorial. "He was one of the last of the old-time 'great editors'—a type which seems passing in journalism. . . . [It] is doubtful whether even his enemies will remember their grievances against him when they reflect how great and vigorous was the intellect which death has thus obliterated." See "Charles Anderson Dana," *New York Journal* (18 October 1897): 6.

83. The *Journal* reported periodically about her life after the rescue. See, for example, "Miss Cisneros Will Wed After the War," *New York Journal* (21 May 1898): 8, and "Evangelina Cisneros is a Happy Mother," *New York Journal* (24 May 1899): 3. She was married in June 1898 to Carlos Carbonnel, one of the men who helped in her jailbreak.

84. The *New York Mail and Express*, for example, doubted the Cisneros case, audacious as it was, would have lasting consequence, stating: "It is necessary . . . to question whether this adventure will end with nothing more serious than a broken window bar, a hurried flight, and the appearance of the fugitive among friends in New York. It is to be hoped that the government at Madrid may be content to ignore a subject so fraught with possible complications." The *Chicago Times-Herald* said the episode "shows that the time is rapidly approaching when it will be necessary to lay the hand of the law not too gently on the yellow journalist." Both comments cited in "Jail-breaking Journalism: The Escape of Miss Evangelina Cossio [*sic*] y Cisneros," *Public Opinion* 23, 17 (21 October 1897): 520.

85. For the *Journal*, Dupuy de Lôme's departure offered another occasion to indulge in self-congratulation. See "Journal's Letter Frees Country from De Lome," *New York Journal* (11 February 1898): 1.

86. Dupuy de Lôme had generated controversy eleven months before the disclosure of his indiscreet letter. At that time, New York newspapers reported on the contents of his book, *Madrid á Madrid*, which contained critical comments about the United States and unflattering observations about American women. See "Senor De Lome and His Book," *New York Sun* (10 March 1897): 6.

87. Wilkerson, *Public Opinion and the Spanish-American War*, 97.

88. The *Journal* received the letter from Horatio S. Rubens, a Cuban exile and active member of the anti-Spanish Cuban junta then based in New York City. Rubens accurately noted that the letter "showed McKinley what the Spanish official closest to him at Washington really thought of him." Rubens, *Liberty: The Story of Cuba* (New York: AMS Press, 1970), 291. According to Rubens, de Lôme's letter, addressed to a Spanish politician and newspaper editor then visiting Havana, was stolen by a junta agent who brought it to New York. Rubens said he offered the letter first to the *New York Herald*, which demurred, and then took it to the *Journal*. If not for the *Herald*'s reluctance or hesitation, the *Journal* likely would not have broken the story.

89. Untitled editorial page comment, *New York Evening Post* (11 February 1898): 4.

90. Wilkerson, *Public Opinion and the Spanish-American War*, 97.

91. See Charles Campbell, *The Transformation of American Foreign Relations 1865–1900* (New York: Harper and Row, 1976), 250. Charles Campbell is no relation to this author.

92. For a discussion of these episodes, see Campbell, *The Transformation of American Foreign Relations*, 250–257. See also Offner, *An Unwanted War*, 225–236.

93. Fitzhugh Lee to William R. Day, 13 January 1898, *Papers Relating to the Foreign Relations of the United States, 1898* (Washington, DC: Government Printing Office, 1901), 1025.

94. Lee to Day, 13 January 1898, *Papers Relating to the Foreign Relations of the United States, 1898*, 1025. By January 1898, Weyler had been replaced as Cuban governor-general by the more moderate but ineffectual Ramón Blanco.

95. Lee, the American consul-general in Havana, had written as the rioting subsided, "Presence of ships may be necessary later, but not now." Lee to Day, 13 January 1898, *Papers Relating to the Foreign Relations of the United States, 1898*, 1025. Lee was informed 24 January 1898 that "the *Maine* will call at the port of Havana in a day or two." William R. Day to Fitzhugh Lee, 24 January 1898, *Papers Relating to the Foreign Relations of the United States, 1898*, 1025. Lee suggested that the *Maine*'s visit "be postponed six or seven days." Lee to Day, 24 January 1898, *Papers Relating to the Foreign Relations of the United States, 1898*, 1026. The battleship arrived in Havana 25 January 1898. By 4 February 1898, Lee was resisting moves to recall the *Maine* because of health and sanitary concerns in Havana. "Do not think [there is the] slightest sanitary danger to officers or crew until April or even May. Ship or ships should be kept here all the time now. . . . Americans would depart with their families in haste if no vessel [were] in harbor." Lee to Day, 4 February 1898, *Papers Relating to the Foreign Relations of the United States, 1898*, 1027.

96. Proctor's speech effectively corroborated the many reports of abuse in Cuba that had appeared in the U.S. press, in yellow journals as well as conservative titles, since the insurrection began in 1895. "I went to Cuba," he said, "with the strong conviction that the picture had been overdrawn; that a few cases of starvation and suffering had inspired and stimulated the press correspondents, and they had given free play to a strong, natural, and highly cultivated imagination. . . . It must be seen with one's own eyes to be realized." See "Political and General: Senator Proctor on Cuba," *Public Opinion* 24, 12 (24 March 1898): 358.

97. Spanish sources were among those who noted the effect of Proctor's speech. Dupuy de Lôme's successor as Spanish minister to the United States said

in a telegram to the foreign minister in Madrid that the speech "produced great effect because of [the senator's] temperate stand." Luis Polo de Bernabé to Pío Gullón y Iglesias, 19 March 1898, in *Spanish Diplomatic Correspondence and Documents, 1896–1900* (Washington, DC: Government Printing Office, 1905), 93.

98. The *Boston Globe* observed that Proctor corroborated "almost every word that has been said by American newspaper correspondents as to Cuban horrors," which meant "that every possible pretext for disbelief that such savage cruelties has been demolished." Similarly, the *New York Journal* asserted: "It has been the custom of the advocates of peace with dishonor to dismiss all accounts of the heartrending condition of the people of Cuba . . . as inventions of the 'lying correspondents' of 'sensational newspapers.' Mr. Proctor is thrillingly sensational, because the facts he has to present do not allow him to be anything else, but he is not a 'lying correspondent.' He is one of the leaders of the senate . . . and a close friend of President McKinley." Both comments cited in "Press Comment," *Public Opinion* 24, 12 (24 March 1898): 359. Proctor's speech drew far more attention than the more predictable reports of the three U.S. senators and two congressmen whom the *Journal* sent to Cuba in early 1898. Even advocates of the view the yellow press instigated the Spanish-American War decline to assign much significance to the *Journal*'s congressional delegation. Wisan, for example, devotes just two sentences to the delegation—and six pages to Proctor's speech. See Wisan, *The Cuban Crisis*, 402–403, 412–417.

99. The Naval Court of Inquiry's finding was supported by a separate official U.S. investigation conducted in 1911 but challenged in a study by Rickover in 1976. See H. G. Rickover, *How the Battleship Maine Was Destroyed* (Washington, DC: Government Printing Office, 1976). However, Rickover's conclusion was questioned in a study commissioned by *National Geographic* magazine and published in 1998. That study, conducted by Advanced Marine Enterprises, concluded that "it appears more probable than was previously concluded that a mine caused the inward bent bottom structure" and the resulting explosion that sank the *Maine*. See Thomas B. Allen, ed. "Special Report: What Really Sank the Maine," *Naval History* (March/April 1998): 38–39.

100. Cited in "Political and General: Our Relations With Spain, The Maine Report," *Public Opinion* 24, 13 (31 March 1898): 390. The Court of Inquiry's principal evidence for concluding the *Maine* was destroyed by a submarine mine was that the battleship's keel had been thrust inward, in the shape of an inverted "V." The U.S. investigators concluded: "In the opinion of the court, this effect could have been produced only by the explosion of a mine situated under the bottom of the ship." See "Political and General: Our Relations With Spain, The Maine Report," *Public Opinion*, 390. Fitzhugh Lee, while ruling out the complicity of Spanish authorities, speculated that "some subordinate [Spanish] officers, or some bribed mechanical experts or other outside parties might have" destroyed the *Maine*. Lee to William R. Day, 1 March 1898, *Personal Correspondence: General Lee to the Secretary of State: Havana, 1897 and 1898*, in container 124, John Bassett Moore papers, Manuscript Division, Library of Congress, Washington, DC.

101. That the *Maine* was destroyed in a harbor under Spanish control figured often in U.S. newspaper comment about the Naval Court of Inquiry's findings. The *Philadelphia Inquirer*, for example, remarked: "A submarine mine blew up the *Maine*. It was a massacre, and for that massacre Spain is responsible—not, perhaps, as an active conspirator, but in her failure to control her subjects." The

Providence [RI] *Journal* said of Spanish authorities: "If they did not explode the mine themselves, it must at any rate be admitted that it was exploded through their connivance or neglect." The *Age-Herald* of Birmingham, Alabama, argued: "The vessel was moored in a friendly harbor at the exact spot selected by the Spanish authorities. At that spot she is destroyed by a powerful explosion. . . . Every reasonable presumption is against the Spanish people, if not the Spanish nation; every reasonable presumption is against the exercise on the part of the Spanish authorities of 'due diligence' in the protection of a friendly ship in a friendly harbor." And the *Denver Republican* stated: "Spain should be held to strict responsibility for remissness if it can not be punished for direct complicity." All comments cited in "Political and General: Our Relations With Spain, The Maine Report," *Public Opinion* 24, 14 (7 April 1898): 419–421.

102. Campbell, *The Transformation of American Foreign Relations*, 244.

103. Campbell, *The Transformation of American Foreign Relations*, 257. See also, Musicant, *Empire by Default*, 165. Musicant noted that Proctor's speech "legitimized intervention for those groups hitherto opposed," notably business interests.

104. Offner, in his study of the diplomacy of Spain and the United States before the Spanish-American War, suggested that by retreating from Cuba in the face of American pressure, Spain's civilian governments would have risked domestic political upheaval "and perhaps even a military coup." See Offner, *An Unwanted War*, 69.

105. Offner, *An Unwanted War*, 226–227.

106. Campbell, *The Transformation of American Foreign Relations*, 257.

107. Wiggins, "Journey to Cuba," 106.

108. Wiggins, "Journey to Cuba," 106. Wiggins also wrote: "Daily, the American public was treated to fresh sensations" about the rebellion in Cuba (108). See also Sparrow, "Strategic Adjustment and the U.S. Navy," 158.

109. "Cuba on the Shelf," *New York Sun* (27 April 1897): 6. The report also mentioned the "inexorable enemies of Cuban independence in both houses of Congress. They are opposed to the granting of any rights whatever to the revolutionists; they would maintain the Spanish despotism there; they care nothing for Spain's violation of the laws of war or for the success of freedom, or for the rights of American citizens in Cuba; they would not even enter a protest against Spain's butchery of the world of the native population of the island." The destructive tactics pursued by the insurgents, which included putting fields of sugar cane to the torch, antagonized American property owners, many of whom had "direct access to the White House and congressional offices." See Louis A. Pérez Jr., *Cuba Between Empires, 1878–1902* (Pittsburgh, PA: University of Pittsburgh Press, 1983), 131.

110. The *Journal* was inclined to play down clearly exaggerated reports, such as the rumor in March 1897 that Spain had decided to seek an end to the war and sell Cuba to the insurgents. The *Journal* reported: "Those in authority laughed at the story, and treated it as a huge joke." See "Cuban War Not Ending," *New York Journal* (12 March 1897): 7. The report suggests that the *Journal* was not necessarily given to publishing extravagant or fanciful reports from Cuba.

111. No fewer than five correspondents reported the conflict for the *Journal*, including Imogene Carter, who in one brief, decidedly unrevealing dispatch

(described as being "from the front") wrote: "The soldiers were amazed at the presence of a woman during the fighting." Imogene Carter, "Imogene Carter's Pen Picture of the Fighting at Velestino," *New York Journal* (10 May 1897): 3. The *Journal* said of its reporting corps assigned to the war: "Such an array of alert, experienced, courageous correspondents in the service of one newspaper is unparalleled in the history of journalism, not only in the United States but in the world." The intense coverage anticipated that of the Spanish-American War a year later. See "The Journal's War Correspondence," *New York Journal* (30 April 1897): 8.

112. James Creelman was among the correspondents who covered aspects of the conflict. His inclination to hyperbolic treatment was evident in the report of his interview with King George of Greece. Creelman wrote: "It was like encountering a Crusader of old to meet this slender, hard-eyed Dane, who has picked the cross of Christ from under the bloody feet of Islamism and held it aloft like a king. He has put Europe to shame by his courage and humanity." James Creelman, "King George of Greece Talks for the Journal about Crete," *New York Journal* (5 March 1897): 14.

113. See "Miller Wins, Breaking All Six-Day Records," *New York Journal* (12 December 1897): 1.

114. "To Greet a City Gloriously," *New York Journal* (30 December 1897): 1.

115. "From Washington to New York in 4 Hours!" *New York Journal* (5 March 1897): 1. Four inside pages were devoted to coverage of the inauguration.

116. See "Beheaded, Cast Into the River," *New York Journal* (27 June 1897): 1, and "More of the Headless Body Is Found," *New York Journal* (28 June 1897): 1.

117. "Journal Fixes Guilt On Nack and Thorn," *New York Journal* (6 September 1897): 1.

118. "The Journal and the Nack Case," *New York Journal* (11 November 1897): 8.

119. The *Journal* was not the first newspaper to undertake public opinion polling. In her study of polling in the nineteenth century, Kathleen A. Frankovic noted that the *Chicago Record* "conducted a large, sophisticated and apparently non-partisan newspaper poll" in 1896, mailing postcard ballots to all registered voters in Chicago. "The results," Frankovic wrote, "were extremely accurate within Chicago." See Frankovic, "Public Opinion and Polling," in Doris Graber, Denis McQuail, and Pippa Norris, eds., *The Politics of News, The News of Politics* (Washington, DC: Congressional Quarterly Press, 1998): 152.

120. The variety of newspaper reporting and editorial comment excerpted and published during that period in the weekly *Public Opinion* journal suggests as much. The insurrection in Cuba was but one of many issues commanding press attention and comment.

121. Trask, *The War with Spain*, 28–29.

122. Seib, for example, maintained that throughout that period, "Hearst's purpose remained constant: to see the United States go to war with Spain." Seib, *Headline Diplomacy*, 5.

123. See, for example, "Let Us End the Strain," *New York Journal* (6 November 1897): 6. The editorial stated: "There is only one reform that will really be worth anything, and that is independence." See also, "Recognize Cuba's Independence," *New York Journal* (15 November 1897): 6. It stated: "What the Ameri-

can people expect from their representatives is the full recognition of the Cuban Republic, and with less they will not be satisfied."

124. Only in the first weeks of 1898 did the *Journal*'s editorials about Cuba become routinely bellicose. There were, however, occasions in 1897 when the newspaper did call for war. The aftermath of Ruiz's death in prison in Cuba was such a time. The *Journal* asserted: "If it is true that the Spaniards murdered Ruiz in his Cuban prison national self-respect as well as national honor demands that the United States declare war with Spain. . . . War is a dreadful thing; but there are other things more dreadful than even war, and one of them is dishonor." See "Must We Have War With Spain?" *New York Journal* (22 February 1897): 6. The call for war was not sustained, however. An official U.S. inquiry into the circumstances of Ruiz's death was inconclusive, reporting that the wound on the top of the victim's head either could have been self-inflicted or caused by a club. See W. J. Calhoun, "Report of W. J. Calhoun, Special Commissioner to Cuba to investigate the death of Dr. Ricardo Ruiz" (10 June 1897), National Archives, College Park, MD.

125. See "Light for Cuba," *New York Journal* (23 May 1897): 8. The *Journal*'s editorial said: "For those of you who insist that our peremptory intervention to end the Cuban anarchy would necessarily mean war with Spain we may recall the facts that France under Napoleon III was a considerably more important power than Spain, and that we did not have war with France."

126. For editorials favoring the annexation of Cuba, see "Hawaii, Cuba and Annexation," *New York Journal* (10 April 1897): 6, and "Very Short-Sighted Patriots," *New York Journal* (13 May 1897): 8. The latter editorial enumerated four reasons why "Cuba should belong to the United States," including, "it is a land of rich natural resources and would by immigration speedily be transformed into a prosperous American state." The *Journal* later backed away from annexation. See "Spaniards for Annexation," *New York Journal* (19 October 1897): 8. That editorial stated: "But until the Cubans themselves apply for annexation, the movement in that direction will meet with no encouragement from the American people. . . . We do not want Cuba. We might take it, but with reluctance, if it were freely offered by the Cubans themselves; we certainly should never take it against their will."

127. "And Now, What of Cuba?" *New York Journal* (26 July 1897): 6. McKinley won election in 1896 on a platform that said "the Government of the United States should actively use its influence and good offices to restore peace and give independence to the island." Cited in *Public Opinion* 20, 26 (25 June 1896): 806.

128. "The President and His Promises," *New York Journal* (7 December 1897): 6.

129. "The Democratic Struggle for Cuba," *New York Journal* (20 January 1898): 8.

130. "The Republicans and Cuba," *New York Journal* (1 February 1898): 8.

131. See, for example, "Spain Ready to Back Down," *New York Journal* (17 March 1897): 7, and "Spain Is Ready to Back Down," *New York Journal* (2 April 1897): 2. The latter report appeared under a Washington, DC, dateline and stated, without attribution that "Spain has decided at least to cease offensive military operations in Cuba at the beginning of the wet season, now only a few weeks away. She is preparing to withdraw all her active forces from the interior

and to send back to Spain and the Philippines a large share of her troops. . . . This is the downfall of Spain in Cuba."

132. The *World* also anticipated the collapse of Spain's military effort in Cuba. See, for example, "Spain's Failure in Cuba," *New York World* (23 March 1897): 6. The editorial stated: "The Spanish are virtually whipped already. Their campaign of 1896–97 is now at its close, and is admitted to be a disastrous failure. It leaves them bankrupt and disheartened, with the Cubans in possession of nearly the entire island. Before the fall campaign can be opened the Cubans will have greatly strengthened themselves, while Spain will be ever more disheartened and more bankrupt than ever."

133. "Belated Wisdom of Spain," *New York Journal* (31 January 1897): 38.

134. "Light for Cuba," *New York Journal* (22 May 1897).

135. "The Assassination of Canovas," *New York Journal* (9 August 1897): 6.

136. "Cuba's Hardest Strike for Liberty," *New York Journal* (13 September 1897): 6.

137. "Spain's Grip Breaking," *New York Journal* (26 November 1897): 6.

138. "A Crime and a Blunder," *New York Journal* (20 December 1897): 6. The editorial reproached Cuban insurgents for executing a Spanish colonel who had entered their camp as a messenger of the Spanish captain-general, Ramón Blanco.

139. "In Cuba—The State of Things There at the Opening of April," *New York Sun* (4 April 1897): 6. Such insight contradicts the claims of Gerald Linderman, who wrote the U.S. press failed to recognize or understand the nature of the guerrilla warfare that characterized the Cuban insurrection. See Linderman, *The Mirror of War: American Society and the Spanish-American War*. (Ann Arbor, MI: University of Michigan Press, 1974), 132–137. See also, Brown, *The Correspondents' War*, 25: "Most of the correspondents did not understand the kind of war [the insurgents were] waging. To them, war was battles and there were none except those they invented or heard of from insurgent sources." Among the correspondents who clearly *did* recognize the insurgents' guerrilla tactics were Sylvester Scovel of the *New York World* and Murat Halstead, who went to Cuba in 1896 for the *Journal*. Scovel wrote: "The Cuban policy is not to fight. They are winning the war by running away." See Sylvester Scovel, "All Cuba Aflame, Scovel Says," *New York World* (10 February 1897): 2. Halstead referred to the fighting in Cuba as "an endless system of skirmishes in ambuscades." See Halstead, *The Story of Cuba: Her Struggles for Liberty, the Cause, Crisis and Destiny of the Pearl of the Antilles*, 5th ed. (Chicago: Henry Publishing Company, 1897), 308.

140. See "A Man in a Hurry," *New York Sun* (17 January 1897): 6. The editorial stated: "It is the complaint of a correspondent that 'the Cuban war drags.' He would like to see the revolutionists fight a grand battle, whip the enemy, and drive Spain out of their country. He is in a hurry. That is not the way we broke the power of England at the time of our Revolution. It was a long war that our ancestors had to fight before they gained their purpose; and the war often dragged. . . . Our correspondent desires that the Cuban revolution shall be pushed along more quickly than the Cubans are able to push it. Let him understand that the Cubans are doing their best, against an army five or six times greater than their own."

141. "Note and Comment," *Fourth Estate* (23 January 1896): 6. The commentary also stated: "In fact the press is in a position somewhat similar to that of the

man who bought a seat every night for four weeks to see the same melodrama. When asked how he could stand it mentally or financially, he replied: 'Some night the hero will be too late, and I'll be here to save the girl and smash the villain.'"

142. Wisan, *The Cuban Crisis*, 217.

143. See George Bronson Rea, *Facts and Fakes about Cuba* (New York: G. Munro's Sons, 1897), 152–200.

144. Among the examples was an erroneous report by the Associated Press in January 1896 that Havana had fallen to the insurgents. See Rea, *Facts and Fakes About Cuba*, 152–154.

145. "The Men Who Seek to Fight for Cuba," *New York Sun* (20 December 1896): 6. The *Sun* later defended jingoism, declaring: "The American in whose veins no drop of jingo blood is flowing, in whose soul no jingo sentiment is felt, is a poor creature indeed." Untitled editorial page comment, *New York Sun* (28 January 1897): 6.

146. "Three Spanish Despatches," *New York Sun* (8 December 1896): 6.

147. "Havana's Forts: What Our Ships Could Do In Case of War," *New York Press* (6 December 1896): 1.

148. See "Weyler May Intend to Quit Cuba," *New York Press* (2 March 1897): 1, and "Weyler May Go Home," *New York Sun* (14 March 1897): 1.

149. See "Spain Will Give It Up," *New York Sun* (10 March 1897): 1, and "Spain About to Give Up?" *New York Sun* (15 March 1897): 1.

150. "Is Peace At Hand for Cuba?" *New York Tribune* (14 January 1897): 1. Similarly, the *Tribune* cited the *Times* of London in reporting that Antonio Maceo, an insurgent general, had survived the grievous wounds received in a firefight in December 1896. Maceo had in fact been killed in action. See "Is Maceo Alive After All?" *New York Tribune* (14 January 1897): 9. For an account of the death of Maceo, perhaps the insurgents' most skilled commander, see Musicant, *Empire by Default*, 74–75.

151. "Weyler May Be Impeached," *New York Times* (5 November 1897): 1.

152. Brown, *The Correspondents' War*, 9. Supporters of the Cuban rebellion, members of what was called the *junta*, courted journalists in New York City, Tampa, and Key West.

153. The *World*, for example, protested that it had "nothing in common" with the *Journal*, declaring: "The Journal's attempted rivalry of The World has not been the flattery of imitation, but the vulgarity of caricature." See "A Continuous But Futile Conspiracy," *New York World* (20 March 1897): 6.

154. Wisan made passing reference to this aspect of the *Journal-World* rivalry, but did not explore how it undercut the authority or influence of the yellow press. See Wisan, *The Cuban Crisis*, 459.

155. Richard Harding Davis, "Does Our Flag Shield Women?" *New York Journal* (12 February 1897): 1–2. Davis' report mistakenly challenged Spain's authority to conduct searches abroad a U.S. flagged vessel. Spain's rebuttal was published the next day across the top of the *Journal*'s front page—an unusual and seldom-noted instance of the response receiving greater prominence than the original report. See "Minister De Lome's Retort," *New York Journal* (13 February 1897): 1.

156. "Tale of a Fair Exile: Senorita Arango's Own Story of the Olivette 'Search Outrage,'" *New York World* (15 February 1897): 1. See also, Arthur

Lubow, *The Reporter Who Would Be King: A Biography of Richard Harding Davis* (New York: Charles Scribner's Sons, 1992), 142.

157. Some sources erroneously assert that Remington's illustration appeared on the front page. See, for example, David Traxel, *1898: The Birth of the American Century* (New York: Vintage Books, 1998), 86.

158. Remington, who accompanied Davis on assignment to Cuba, had returned separately and was in New York when the search took place. He drew the illustration based on Davis' report, which was ambiguous about whether male detectives were present during the search.

159. As Charles Brown noted, "the opportunity to score off the *Journal* was not one the *World* would miss." See Brown, *The Correspondents' War*, 82.

160. "Tale of a Fair Exile," *New York World*. Arango stated in the *World*'s report: "At neither search was I ill-treated, except the humiliation of being stripped by a strange woman. She was not rough but treated the matter quite indifferently. I suppose she had performed the same task many times before." Arango was unequivocal in stating that "no men were admitted into the rooms nor could they have seen into them."

161. See Richard Harding Davis, "Mr. Davis Explains: The 'Olivette Search Outrage' Is Now Made Clear," *New York World* (17 February 1897): 2. However, a biographer of Davis, noting the ambiguity of the report about the strip-search, stated: "Remington's eye-opening sketch plausibly illustrated Davis's text." See Lubow, *Reporter Who Would Be King*, 144. The *New York Times*, in an editorial the day after the *World* exploded the strip-search story, said "the artist went much further than his text warranted." See "'Beats' and 'Fakes,'" *New York Times* (16 February 1897): 6.

162. See "Two Kinds of Journalism," *New York World* (23 February 1897): 1.

163. Sherman was at the time drifting toward senility and conceivably could have made the statement but soon forgotten that he had. Sherman's biographer wrote that by the time the secretary of state resigned in April 1898, at the start of the Spanish-American War, he "had become forgetful, and in many important matters of detail this lack of memory threatened complications in relations with the ambassadors of other nations. So complete was his failure of memory that he sometimes failed to recognize old acquaintances." Theodore E. Burton, *John Sherman* (Boston: Houghton, Mifflin and Company, 1906), 414. Moreover, the repudiation of controversial statements given to newspaper reporters was not uncommon at the time. See "The Repudiated Interview," *Fourth Estate* (27 April 1899): 6. Such disavowals, the trade journal said, were most likely "when the views expressed are not of a creditable character or contain opinions which, for political or social reasons, ought not to have been made public. . . . Members of Congress, holders of municipal offices, prominent leaders of the bar, and even clergymen have been known to repudiate remarks they have made to journalists in order to 'set themselves right' with their supporters."

164. "Sherman for War With Spain for Murdering American," *New York Journal* (22 February 1897): 1. Sherman was quoted as saying "the only way to put an end to Spanish atrocities is to declare war on Spain." The *Journal* did not retract from the report, insisting instead that Sherman "is cursed with a most convenient or inconvenient forgetfulness. It will be well for the country if, in charge of its State affairs, Mr. Sherman remembers more accurately." See "Where Is the Lie?," *New York Journal* (3 March 1897): 6.

165. The *Journal* and *World* were bitter foes—but their rivalry was not so implacable as to prevent their representatives from exploring a joint agreement in 1899 to raise prices, establish a shared delivery system, and end editorial attacks against each other. Discussions to those ends became quite detailed but ultimately collapsed, due in part to mutual suspicion. For reports about the *Journal-World* negotiations, see Don C. Seitz, "Memo on Line of Argument with Los on Geranium-Genuine Agreement," undated memorandum, 1896 file, *New York World* Papers, Butler Library, Columbia University, New York. See also, Seitz, "Memo on the Evening Edition," 17 November 1899, 1899 file, *New York World* Papers, Columbia University. Seitz's memoranda routinely invoked Pulitzer's codenames for the *World* (Genuine) and the *Journal* (Geranium).

166. For an insider's account about the effect of Hearst's hiring many of the *World*'s leading editors and reporters, see Don C. Seitz, *Joseph Pulitzer: His Life and Letters* (New York: Simon and Schuster, 1924), 211–212, 216.

167. "Papers at War," *Fourth Estate* (22 July 1897): 1.

168. "Papers at War," *Fourth Estate*, 1.

169. "Hearst Hits Hard," *Fourth Estate* (16 June 1898): 1. The trade journal's account stated: "Mr. Hearst keeps the public and the professional newspaper men guessing just what he will do next, and his surprises are met with approval." See also, Brown, *The Correspondents' War*, 268–269.

170. The *Journal* likened itself to "the rod which Providence has used for the chastening of Mr. Pulitzer, and what is his loss is our gain." See "A Plea for Mr. Pulitzer," *New York Journal* (5 April 1897): 6.

171. Other newspapers noted this tendency, referring to it as "bane and antidote." See "'Beats' and 'Fakes,'" *New York Times*. The *Times* said, tongue-in-cheek: "We remark with interest the rivalry of our esteemed freak contemporaries, and especially the keen interest they manifest in exposing each other's 'beats.' . . . If [the reader] remarks a 'beat' in one of his favorite journals which is not mercilessly exposed as a 'fake' in the other, he may in most cases conclude that it is really a piece of news. . . . By investing his two centers in the two papers, his bane and antidote, the antidote twenty-four hours behind the bane, are both before him. . . . Whether he can long continue to stand the wear and tear of intellect and moral character is his affair."

172. The *Journal-World* rivalry continued well after the Spanish-American War. In 1901, for example, the *Journal* accused the *World* of slavish imitation, stating: "The Journal adopts a peculiar kind of type, aiming at distinctiveness. Promptly the World copies that type. The Journal issues with its Sunday newspaper a magazine, printed in colors. Immediately the World imitates that. The Sunday Journal issues an 'Editorial Section,' containing the writings of the ablest men available. The World imitates that and issues an 'Editorial Forum,' containing writings trashily imitative of the Journal's features." See "Who Edits the New York World?," *New York Journal* (4 January 1901): 4. See also, "Stealing and Lying," *New York Journal* (30 January 1902): 14. That editorial said: "Every day, every hour, every inch of every step it takes, this newspaper is followed and imitated by a foolish and slobbering idiot. That idiot, as you know, is the NEW YORK WORLD."

173. "Speak Up, Mr. Yerkes," *Fourth Estate* (31 August 1899): 4. The trade journal also stated: "No man who believes in lofty journalistic ideals can fail to deplore the freedom with which many editors 'befoul their own nest,' as it were,

by endeavoring to persuade the public that their contemporaries are fools or knaves, or both."

174. See "An Improper Basis of Newspaper Rivalry," *Fourth Estate* (27 April 1901): 8. The editorial stated: "There is entirely too great a tendency among rival newspapers to arraign themselves on opposite sides of a question for the sole purpose of belittling the efforts of rival forces, and in order to gain some little temporary advantage. . . . Unquestionably, the influence of the press can be greatly increased by unity of action, whether it be in support of a good cause or the condemnation of a bad one. It most certainly cannot be increased by indulgence in petty spites, and by attempting to drag the public into them."

175. See Wisan, *The Cuban Crisis*, 458–459. He wrote: "The *Journal* and *World* simply used Cuba to achieve their prime purpose—an increase in circulation." That argument has proved quite resilient. At the time the Hearst Corporation completed its acquisition of the *San Francisco Chronicle*, the newspaper noted: "As a corporation, Hearst bears little resemblance to the company that helped ignite the Spanish-American War to sell papers." Carolyn Said, "An Evolving Empire," *San Francisco Chronicle* (29 July 2000): D1.

176. *The Nation* 66 (5 May 1898), cited in Bleyer, *Main Currents*, 285.

177. Arthur Brisbane, "The Modern Newspaper in War Time," *Cosmopolitan* 25, 5 (September 1898): 553. Brisbane noted that during the war the *Evening Journal* once printed 1,068,000 copies and "fell short of the advance demand by more than two hundred thousand copies."

178. Demand for newsprint was acute, given that the yellow press in New York produced as many as forty "extra" editions a day during the war. Brisbane, "The Modern Newspaper in War Time," 547.

179. For a brief reference to the *World*'s losing money in 1898, see W. A. Swanberg, *Pulitzer* (New York: Charles Scribner's Sons, 1967), 253. Mott noted, "Few newspapers increased profits during the Spanish-American War, and many found their net incomes dwindling or disappearing." Mott, *American Journalism*, 537.

180. "War and the Newspapers," *Fourth Estate* (5 May 1898): 6.

181. "Cost of the War Service," *Fourth Estate* (21 July 1898): 4.

182. "A Favorable Outlook," *Fourth Estate* (25 August 1898): 4.

183. "The Year's Record," *Fourth Estate* (12 January 1899): 2.

184. "War Reporting," *Fourth Estate* (28 April 1898): 1.

185. See *Annual Report of the President of the Western Union Telegraph Company to the Stockholders, Made at Their Meeting October 12th, 1898* (New York: Kempster Printing, 1898): 6–7.

186. See *Annual Report of the President of the Western Union Telegraph Company to the Stockholders, Made at Their Meeting October 11th, 1899* (New York: Kempster Printing, 1899): 6–7.

187. "Just One Small Fact," *New York Journal* (21 January 1902): 14.

188. Tebbel, *Compact History of the American Newspaper*, 202. See also, Sparrow, "Strategic Adjustment and the U.S. Navy," 154.

189. Wiggins, "Journey to Cuba," 113.

190. Simon Michael Bessie, *Jazz Journalism: The Story of the Tabloid Newspapers* (New York: E. P. Dutton and Company, 1938), 58.

191. "Conservative and Careful," *Fourth Estate* (24 February 1898): 6. One yellow newspaper outside New York, the *Boston Post*, similarly noted: "The gen-

eral sentiment—so general, indeed, that it may be called unanimous—is that judgement should be suspended until the exact facts of the lamentable disaster in Havana Harbor are established, and that then such action shall be taken as the facts warrant." See "Responsibility for War," *Boston Post* (27 February 1898): 14. The same day, however, the *Boston Post* published a checkerboard on which its readers were invited to play a "war game" using cutout markers that represented U.S. and Spanish vessels in waters near coastal cities of Cuba, Spain, and the United States. The game was over "when one sides loses all of its ships." See "Directions for Playing the Sunday Post War Game," *Boston Post* (27 February 1898): 23.

192. "Conservative and Careful," *Fourth Estate* (24 February 1898): 6. Emphasis added.

193. "The President," *New York Times* (23 February 1898): 6. For another reference to the calm in the immediate aftermath of the *Maine*'s destruction, see "On the Tip of the Tongue: Calm Americans," *New York Press* (27 February 1898): 6.

194. "The Lesson of the War Scare," *Boston Post* (25 February 1898): 4. The newspaper did say that the lesson to be taken from the scare was "the country should make better preparations for war. . . . Our coast, while not naked of defence, is largely unprotected."

195. "Real News and 'Fake' News," *Boston Post* (19 February 1898): 4. It added: "Do people who read newspapers enjoy such stuff? We do not believe they do. We have a greater respect for the intelligence of the American public."

196. Philip S. Foner, *The Spanish-Cuban-American War and the Birth of American Imperialism, 1895–1902*, vol. 1 (New York: Monthly Review Press, 1972), 238.

197. Dane Claussen and Richard Shafer, "American Imperialist Zeal in the Periphery: The Rural Press Covers the Spanish-American War and the Annexation of the Philippines," paper presented at the annual conference of the Association for Education in Journalism and Mass Communication, Baltimore, MD, August 1998: 7.

198. Claussen and Shafer, "American Imperialist Zeal in the Periphery," 22.

199. Bradford Merrill, undated memorandum, *New York World* papers, 1899 file, Butler Library, Columbia University, New York. Merrill's memorandum specifically cited the *Maine* among the major events that produced noticeable but fleeting out-of-town circulation gains.

200. There was, however, saber rattling among the yellow press of the Midwest. The *Cincinnati Enquirer*, for example, declared in March 1898: "Now let there be no more hesitation. The country is almost breathless for the report of the [naval] court of inquiry; but whatever that report may be let us remember that we have abundant cause for interference to stop the cruel war on the island of Cuba and guarantee that rich island a place among the republics of the western world. Spain's domination of that island, even in peace, has been against nature and international morals. . . . Now is the time to strike off the shackles." Cited in "Political and General: Our Relations With Spain," *Public Opinion* 24, 11 (17 March 1898): 25.

201. Sylwester, "The Kansas Press," 266.

202. See J. Stanley Lemons, "The Cuban Crisis of 1895–1898: Newspapers and Nativism," *Missouri Historical Review* 60, 1 (October 1965): 72. Lemons examined Missouri newspapers that were divided in their support for the gold and

silver standards. He wrote: "The problem of Cuba was generally ignored by the gold papers until the sinking of the *Maine* and then counseled moderation. . . . [T]he silver press was more insistent and more shrill on the issue all along. However, they considered the Cuban question only part of a larger campaign against alien elements in the bloodstream of America."

203. Morton M. Rosenberg and Thomas P. Ruff, *Indiana and the Coming of the Spanish-American War* (Muncie, IN: Ball State University, 1976), 21.

204. Cited in Rosenberg and Ruff, *Indiana and the Coming of the Spanish-American War*, 25.

205. Welter, "The 1895-98 Cuban Crisis in Minnesota Newspapers," 723. Welter also found: "The failure of the [Minnesota] press to imitate [the yellow journals] was virtually complete. . . . The Minnesota press was either disinterested in the rebellion, or it turned to more objective sources to cover the struggle."

206. Rosenberg and Ruff, *Indiana and the Coming of the Spanish-American War*, 25.

207. Robert C. Hilderbrand, *Power and the People: Executive Management of Public Opinion in Foreign Affairs, 1897–1921* (Chapel Hill, NC: University of North Carolina Press, 1981), 22–27.

208. George W. Auxier, "Middle Western Newspapers and the Spanish-American War, 1895–1898" *Mississippi Valley Historical Review* (1940): 524.

209. George H. Gibson, "Attitudes in North Carolina Regarding the Independence of Cuba, 1868–1898," *North Carolina Historical Review* 43, 1 (1996): 64.

210. Gibson, "Attitudes in North Carolina," 65. He wrote: "Indeed during the last half of the nineteenth century, North Carolinians showed no symptoms of spoiling for a fight or of having any but a casual interest in the affairs of Cuba and Spain. Civil war and reconstruction had inoculated North Carolina from another conflict, and the effects of this immunization had but slightly worn off by 1898."

211. Marvin N. Olasky, "Hawks or Doves? Texas Press and Spanish-American War," *Journalism Quarterly* 64 (Spring 1987): 208. Olasky also wrote: "It appears that the more the 'yellow journals' clamored for war during [the] first month following the sinking of the *Maine*, the more suspicious Texas journalists became."

212. "The Press First of All," *New York Press* (24 April 1898): 6.

213. "Patriotism and the Press," *Fourth Estate* (31 March 1898): 4. The trade journal was reacting to criticism of President McKinley that appeared in the *New York Evening Journal* and *New York Evening World*.

214. It has been suggested that "deliberately misleading reporting made it next to impossible for the United States and Spain to negotiate a peaceful settlement." Michael Richman, "A 'Splendid Little War' Built America's Empire, *Washington Post* (8 April 1998): H1. But the issues that contributed to the diplomatic impasse over Cuba in 1898 were complex and cannot be attributed simply to misguided or erroneous newspaper reports.

215. See "Journalism," *New York Evening Post* (21 March 1898): 7. Roosevelt was assistant secretary of the navy and he issued his statement to deny that he had granted an interview to a *Journal* reporter in which he had complimented the newspaper. The comment attributed to Roosevelt was: "It is cheering to find

a newspaper of the great influence of the Journal tell the facts as they exist. . . ." Cited in Bleyer, *Main Currents*, 376.

216. Charles G. Dawes, diary entry, 19 March 1898, cited in Bascom N. Timmons, ed., *A Journal of the McKinley Years by Charles G. Dawes* (Chicago: Lakeside Press, 1950): 147.

217. John D. Long, diary entry, 14 January 1898, cited in Margaret Long, ed., *The Journal of John D. Long* (Rindge, NH: Richard R. Smith Publisher, 1956): 213.

218. Fitzhugh Lee to William R. Day, 21 January 1898, *Personal Correspondence: General Lee to the Secretary of State: Havana, 1897 and 1898*, container 124, John Bassett Moore papers, Library of Congress. Lee conceded that he did not know what could be done about such reporting, "unless the proprietors of some of these papers could be reached by a friendly request from your department to ask that they caution their correspondent to keep within bounds and 'tell the truth and nothing but the truth.'" Given the reporting of Cuba-related events during the weeks that followed Lee's correspondence, it appears unlikely that his suggestion to approach U.S. newspaper owners received any serious consideration in Washington.

219. Margaret Leech, a McKinley biographer, referred to Cortelyou as "the President's right hand." Leech, *In the Days of McKinley* (New York: Harper and Brothers, 1959), 128.

220. George B. Cortelyou, diary entry, 16 April 1898: 7–8; container 52, Cortelyou Papers, Manuscript Division, Library of Congress, Washington, DC.

221. Cortelyou said of McKinley as war neared: "In the midst of it all the President is firm, dignified and endears himself to those of us near him by his thoughtfulness and gentleness. He looks very worn and haggard. I see him many times a day. I have taken pains to give him opinions of the messages as they have come in—both sides. There are not many of the critical kind notwithstanding statements made by members of Congress and others." Cortelyou, diary entry, 12 April 1898; container 52, Cortelyou Papers, Library of Congress.

222. Cortelyou, diary entry, 28 March 1898; container 52, Cortelyou Papers, Library of Congress.

223. William R. Day to Stewart L. Woodford, 20 March 1898, in *Papers Relating to the Foreign Relations of the United States 1898*, 692.

224. Day to Woodford, 26 March 1898, in *Papers Relating to the Foreign Relations of the United States 1898*, 704.

225. Wisan, *The Cuban Crisis*, 417–420.

226. Wisan, *The Cuban Crisis*, 417.

227. See, for example, "Spain in Revolt—Weyler May Be Dictator," *New York Journal* (4 May 1898): 3.

228. The epigram appeared on the front page, on either side of the newspaper's masthead. See *New York Journal*, 8, 9, and 10 May 1898. As John D. Stevens perceptively noted: "Because it fit the picture of Hearst as an evil genius, [the epigram] is about the only Hearst boast that historians ever believed." See Stevens, *Sensationalism and the New York Press* (New York: Columbia University Press, 1991), 97.

229. "The New Political Force," *New York Evening Post* (30 April 1898): 4. The editorial, which was long on argument and short on evidence, declared: "As a strange fate would it have it . . . the subject on which the very worst portion of

the press exerts most influence is war. The fomenting of war and the publication of mendacious accounts of war have, in fact, become almost a special function of the press which is known as 'yellow journals.'" The editorial referred to Hearst as "a blackguard boy with several millions of dollars at his disposal [who] has more influence on the use a great nation may make of its credit, of its army and navy, of is name and traditions, than all the statesmen and philosophers and professors in the country."

230. See, for example, "Victory Complete! Glorious! Spanish Fleet in the Philippines Destroyed," *New York Journal* (2 May 1898): 1.

231. "Some People Say the Journal Brought on This War. How Do You Like It as Far as It's Gone[?]," *New York Journal* (2 May 1898): 10.

232. "Is Commander M'Kinley Asleep?" *New York Journal* (20 May 1898): 10. See also, "Who Is Muddling This War?" *New York Journal* (22 May 1898): 32.

233. "The American Newspaper," *New York Journal* (6 May 1898): 10.

234. "An Editorial for American Editors," *New York Journal* (18 May 1898): 10. The editorial also stated: "When the conservatism of the country, selfish and unselfish, intelligent and unintelligent, came up in 1898 to where the American press stood in 1896 it was too late for diplomacy, too late for peace with honor."

235. As noted in Chapter Three, Hearst scoffed after the war at the notion he and his newspapers fomented the conflict. He stated in 1907 that "the one cause of the Spanish war was Spain." See W. R. Hearst, "Mr. W. R. Hearst on Anglo-American Relations," *Times* [London] (2 November 1907): 5. Moreover, it is important to keep in mind that claims such as "How Do You Like the Journal's War?" were very much in keeping with the newspaper's well-developed tendency to take credit for all sorts of decisions and developments. The *Journal*'s self-congratulatory impulse at times may have been justified; at others, it was clearly overwrought. For example, the *Journal* claimed in 1897 to have found the key to settling a coal strike in Ohio—which turned out to be a rather obvious suggestion that both sides submit to arbitration. See "Journal's Plea to Arbitrate Heeded," *New York Journal* (4 September 1897): 1.

236. Gould, *The Spanish-American War and President McKinley*, 24.

237. As Offner noted, "Cuban nationalism and Spanish colonialism were irreconcilable forces allowing for no compromise." Offner, *An Unwanted War*, ix.

238. A humanitarian impulse probably was a contributing factor in the U.S. entry into the war. Trask, for example, has argued that Americans in 1898 "went to war convinced that they had embarked upon an entirely selfless mission for humanity." See Trask, *The War with Spain*, 58.

239. See, for example, Gould's attempt to address the persistent allegations of McKinley's weakness and vacillation. Gould, *The Spanish-American War and President McKinley*, 51–53.

Part Two

Defining the Legacies

5

How Yellow Journalism Lives On: An Analysis of Newspaper Content

Woven subtly into the literature of American journalism is the thread of an argument that yellow journalism lives on, that the defining features of the genre endure through adoption and adaptation. Among the historians who called attention to the long-term contributions of yellow journalism was Frank Luther Mott. While deploring the genre's excesses, Mott conceded that "the yellow papers contributed something—notably banner heads, free use of pictures, and the Sunday supplement—to modern journalism."[1] Similarly, a study of newspaper design in the late 1940s noted that "several of the methods introduced" by the yellow journals, notably banner headlines, "have had a lasting effect on the American press."[2] A 1990s handbook for newspaper designers featured the famous issue of the *New York Journal* that depicted the destruction of the battleship *Maine* in Havana harbor in 1898, and remarked: "By about 1900, newspapers began looking more like—well, like *newspapers*. Headlines grew bigger, bolder and wider."[3]

Other analysts have been even more sweeping. Writing in the late 1960s in *Journalism Quarterly*, Meredith and David Berg declared that William Randolph Hearst's turn-of-the-century *New York Journal*—the quintessential yellow journal—established widely imitated standards in newspaper page design. "In fact," they wrote, "the *Journal* of over a half century ago is almost identical in appearance to many of today's leading newspapers."[4] The competition between Hearst's *Journal* and Joseph Pulitzer's *New York World* established the contours of what in 1897 came to be called yellow journalism; Pulitzer's grandson claimed 100 years later: "[T]oday's journalism has *adapted*—maybe the better word is 'adopted' what Joseph Pulitzer did."[5]

The view that non-yellow newspapers borrowed characteristic features of the yellow press began to take hold at the turn of the twentieth century. An editorial in the *Independent* magazine in 1900 claimed that "those very journals which have hitherto most bitterly attacked [the yellow press] are now quietly adopting many of the most successful yellow methods."[6] The press critic Will Irwin asserted in 1911: "The life has passed out of pure yellow journalism. Its spirit remains, however, in the universal influence which it had on the profession at large. Generally, the good that it did lived after it: the evil is becoming interred with its bones."[7]

The literature, however, reveals no systematic attempt to test such claims, to assess whether, or to what extent, the salient features of yellow journalism have been incorporated into, and live on in, the content and appearance of American newspapers. This chapter presents such a study, a systematic content analysis of the front pages of seven leading U.S. newspapers, examined at ten-year intervals from 1899 to 1999. All seven newspapers were published throughout that period and, in most cases, were under stable ownership regimes.

The study was specifically designed to test whether, when, and to what extent, the principal typographic and content elements associated with the yellow press became embedded in American journalism during the twentieth century. As such, the study stands as a test of the claims of Mott, Irwin, the Bergs, Pulitzer's grandson, and others.

The newspapers in the study included four that were decidedly non-yellow, or "conservative,"[8] titles in 1899: The *Los Angeles Times*, the *New York Times*, the *Raleigh News and Observer*, and the *Washington Post*. Two titles in the study were recognized as exhibiting many of the features and qualities of the yellow press at the end of the nineteenth century: The *Denver Post* and the *San Francisco Examiner*.[9] One newspaper in the study, the *St. Louis Post-Dispatch*, exhibited a variety of yellow and conservative features in 1899 and is classified as "mixed."

To allow for benchmarks, the *New York Journal* and *New York World* were included in the study for 1899, a peak year in yellow journalism,[10] and in 1909,[11] when the genre was in declining popularity. In all, more than 1,130 front pages were analyzed and more than 11,300 coding decisions were made. In brief, the study found:

- Some typographic features characteristic of the yellow press indeed live on—notably the appearance of multicolumn headlines, of multicolumn illustrations, and of multiple front-page illustrations. But, contrary to the views of Mott and others, banner headlines, which were centrally associated with yellow journalism, have not become standard or routinely used in the newspapers examined. In addition, the study found that elements closely associated with the *content* of the yellow press—in particular, the keen taste for self-promotion, and the tendency to assign prominence to reports about sports and society events—have not been adapted by leading U.S. newspapers. Even the titles that ranked among the yellow journals of the late nineteenth century rarely during the twentieth century indulged in the most flamboyant features of yellow journalism.

- Newspapers that were the most conservative in 1899 were the least likely during the twentieth century to adapt salient features of yellow journalism. The *New York Times* was a notable in this respect: In 1899, the *Times* exhibited the fewest characteristics of yellow journalism of any newspaper examined. While it gradually adopted such features as multicolumn headlines and multiple front-page photographs and illustrations, the *Times* routinely eschewed the more ostentatious features of yellow journalism, especially banner headlines and self-promotion.
- Conversely, the newspapers recognized as representative of the yellow press at the end of the nineteenth century tended to retain some of those features throughout the twentieth century. This tendency was particularly pronounced for the *Denver Post*. It was evident, although to a lesser extent, in the *San Francisco Examiner*. None of the seven newspapers in the study swung dramatically between decidedly conservative and near-yellow, with the occasional exception of the *Post-Dispatch*.
- The striking disparity in the appearance and content of U.S. newspapers at the end of the nineteenth century lessened dramatically. While differences certainly can be detected among what were conservative newspapers and yellow journals, the dissimilarities are far less marked than they were 100 years ago. This may suggest that a predictable homogeneity has come to characterize leading U.S. daily newspapers.

METHOD

The study rests on the analysis of what were the salient features of yellow journalism, as determined from close reading of the *New York Journal* and the *New York World* during the first half of 1897, when the phrase "yellow journalism" began to appear in print. The salient features of yellow journalism included aspects of typography, of graphic illustrations, and of content. The following elements were specifically examined and categorized in this study (copies of the coding sheets and coding instructions used in the study appear as appendices):

Typography

- **Multicolumn headlines**. Yellow newspapers were almost immediately distinguishable from their conservative counterparts by the appearance of front-page headlines that spanned two columns or more.
- **Two or more multicolumn headlines**. Front pages of yellow newspapers were further characterized by the not infrequent appearance of more than one multicolumn headline.

- **Banner headlines**. While not necessarily an innovation of yellow journalism, banner headlines came to define the genre.[12] They tended to appear somewhat more frequently in the *Journal* than in the *World*, however.

Graphics and Illustrations

- **Multicolumn illustrations**. Another readily apparent feature of the yellow press was the use of illustrations—sketches or photographs—that were displayed across two or more columns.
- **Three or more illustrations**. Mott correctly described the yellow press as inclined to the "lavish use" of illustrations.[13] The *Journal* and *World* experimented often with front-page layouts that incorporated multiple illustrations.

Content

- **Use of newspaper's name in a headline**. New York's yellow journals were eager to tout their reporting exploits. Unabashed self-promotion was commonplace and the newspaper's name not infrequently appeared in headlines on the front page.[14]
- **Use of anonymous sources in a staff-produced article**. The yellow press was often eager to present reports without disclosing the sources. James Creelman, who reported for the *Journal* and the *World* and was an apologist for the yellow press, often cited anonymous sources in his reports, for example.
- **Prominence to reports about sports**. Sporting events from heavyweight boxing matches[15] to collegiate football[16] to Ivy League yacht races were prominently covered[17] in the *Journal* and *World*, and often above the fold on the front page.
- **Prominence to reports about society events**. Similarly, the *Journal* and *World* gave prominent coverage to charity balls and other society events, and to reports about the wealthy[18] and the well-to-do.[19]
- **Topic of main story**. The subject of the lead story on the front page also was categorized.

Except for the benchmark yellow journals, the *Journal* and the *World*, the newspapers examined were published without extended interruption throughout the study period. Moreover, ownership of the respective newspapers was largely unchanged throughout the period, thus reducing the possibility that changes in corporate control would pose confounding variables in the study. For all or most of the twentieth century, family-controlled media companies published the *Los Angeles Times*, the *New York Times*, the *St. Louis Post-Dispatch*, the *San Francisco Examiner*, and the *Washington Post*.[20] The *Raleigh News and Observer* was owned and published by Josephus Daniels and his heirs from 1894 until 1995, when the newspaper was sold to the McClatchy Company. Alone among the newspapers examined in this study, the *Denver Post* experienced several ownership changes during the twentieth century.[21]

The seven newspapers were chosen for several reasons. They represented in 1899 yellow as well as conservative titles. They include leading national and regional titles.[22] In addition, they offer a geographic distribution of East, South, Midwest, and West.

The study comprised a systematic content analysis of the front page (or the first news page) of each newspaper for a period of two constructed weeks at ten-year intervals, beginning in 1899 and continuing through 1999. Following the constructed-week method, the front page of each newspaper in the study was examined at intervals of eight days until a total of fourteen days for each year had been reviewed and analyzed. The starting point for each period was the first Monday in March, a day of the week chosen randomly. The period examined for each year in the study began, therefore, in early March and continued until mid-June.

The constructed-week method was adopted because of its effectiveness in allowing researchers to examine representative samples of content and to do so efficiently, without oversampling.[23] Moreover, the constructed-week method by design avoids the distorting effects that may come with random sampling. Such effects include the possibility of oversampling days of the week when news content tends to be particularly extensive (as with Sunday issues) or particularly thin (as with issues of Monday and Saturday).[24]

While each period in the study was marked by notable news events—from the war in the Philippines in 1899 to the aerial attacks in the Balkans in 1999—none of the events was epochal or so monumental as to impose a distorting effect throughout a period of two constructed weeks. None of the events rank among the most momentous and dramatic of the twentieth century, such as the use of atomic weapons in August 1945, the first manned lunar landing in July 1969, or the assassinations of U.S. presidents in September 1901 and November 1963.[25]

A check-coder who analyzed forty-five front pages that had been selected at random agreed with the author's coding decisions 87 percent of the time (N=390).

LIMITATIONS

While the salient features of yellow journalism were most conspicuous on the front page—in the banner headlines, in the self-congratulation accorded to reporting accomplishments, and in the generous use of illustrations—this study's focus on the front page represents a limitation, if a modest one. The study design does not incorporate other distinguishing features of the yellow press—notably, the Sunday supplement and the color comics. While important, those were once-a-week rather than daily features of yellow journalism. In addition, many conservative metropolitan newspapers in the late nineteenth century offered readers Sunday supplements and even comics, meaning that those features did not necessarily define yellow journalism. Their omission from the study was not, therefore, a significant shortcoming.

Another modest limitation may lie in the decision to analyze the newspapers at ten-year intervals. That means the study can characterize content at a point in time but not for an entire decade. However, the study's central objective was to detect and illuminate the broader *trends* in adopting and adapting the signature features of yellow journalism. That objective seemed well served by the constructed-week method. It is theoretically possible that sampling content at ten-year intervals may have failed to detect and illuminate a sudden and short-lived adoption of features of the yellow press. But the results of this study suggest that such flirtation was unlikely. Rather, the results indicate a more gradual, selective, and even diffident embrace of some of the salient features of yellow journalism. Systematic sampling at ten-year intervals thus appears to have been adequate.

A more significant limitation is that the study did not assess the use of color, a vivid, salient feature of yellow journalism. The limitation, while important, was inescapable: Nearly all the 1,130 front pages examined and analyzed were available as black-and-white images on microfilm. The conservative titles in 1899—including the *New York Times* and the *Washington Post*—were, by 1999, routinely displaying color photographs and graphic illustrations on their front pages.[26] Thus measuring the adoption and use of color on the front page fell beyond the reach of this study.

For the most part, the front pages examined were those available on microfilm at the newspaper and periodicals reading room of the Library of Congress in Washington, D.C.[27] In the few cases where microfilmed records allowed a choice between or among versions of the front page, as with the *Los Angeles Times* in 1969, the edition identified as "final" was consistently selected for analysis.[28] In instances when an issue was not available for analysis, the issue on the following day was examined and the coding pattern was thereafter resumed. For example, the *St. Louis Post-Dispatch* was not published 31 May 1969, the Memorial Day holiday that year. So the following day, 1 June 1969, was analyzed instead. Additionally, Saturday issues of the *Post-Dispatch* in 1999 appeared in tabloid form. Those issues were ignored and the following day, a Sunday, was analyzed.[29] The coding pattern was thereafter resumed.[30]

Another anomaly was that the *Raleigh News and Observer* did not publish Monday editions during the late nineteenth century and the early twentieth century. Therefore, Tuesdays were substituted for the

Monday issues of the *News and Observer* in 1899 and 1909. The coding pattern was otherwise followed for those years.

FINDINGS

The study produced several important findings, notably that the salient features of yellow journalism were gradually—but selectively—adopted and adapted during the twentieth century by the conservative newspapers. The adaptation tended to be more of features of typography than elements of content. Specifically, the newspapers that were conservative in 1899 had, by mid-century, abandoned their gray format of single-column headlines and their inclination to use few (if any) illustrations. By the late twentieth century, all were routinely displaying multicolumn headlines and multiple illustrations on their front pages.

However, the more flamboyant features associated with yellow journalism—the eagerness to tout the newspaper's achievements in front-page headlines, and the prominence often given to news of society and sporting events—were largely eschewed. Moreover, the bolder typographic features (notably, the banner headlines) never became routine features of the front pages. The ostentatious characteristics most often associated with the yellow press never were incorporated or adapted.

A partial explanation for the general absence of society and sports stories from the front pages was a general tendency—conspicuous by the late twentieth century—to place fewer articles on page one. The *Denver Post* displayed as few as two articles on its front page in some issues in 1999 and the *St. Louis Post-Dispatch* carried as few as three.[31] This tendency, of course, resulted in fewer opportunities for reports about sports or society events to command prominent placement.[32]

Although the flamboyant elements most closely associated with yellow journalism were generally eschewed, some distinctions remained among the newspapers in the study. Notably, the two newspapers that ranked among the yellow journals in 1899 tended to score consistently higher than their conservative counterparts in an index of yellow journalism that was compiled from the study's results. The "yellow index," which serves to clarify the variations among the newspapers in the study, was derived by assigning values to the specific components examined in the study. The values varied according to their comparative distinctiveness. Thus, a banner headline was assigned a higher value than a mere multicolumn headline.

The values were:

- 4 points for any front page in which the newspaper's name appeared in a front-page headline over a news story.

- 3 points for any front page having a banner headline.
- 2 points for any front page having two or more multicolumn headlines.
- 2 points for any front page having three or more illustrations.
- 2 points for any front page in which a report about a sporting event or sports figure was displayed above the fold.
- 2 points for any front page in which a report about a society event was displayed above the fold.
- 1 point for any front page having a multicolumn headline.
- 1 point for any front-page illustration across more than one column.
- 1 point for any staff-written report on the front page that cited an anonymous source.

The score for each newspaper at each interval is shown in Table 5.1. The table illustrates the gradual but steady progression toward adaptation of features of the yellow press, but only to a point. The peak scores for most newspapers, including all of those that were classified in 1899 as non-yellow or mixed, came late in the twentieth century. But their scores fell decidedly short of the levels achieved in 1899, at the height of the yellow press period, by the *Journal* and the *World*. Indeed, the *Journal*'s score of 1899 was matched only by another yellow newspaper, the *Denver Post* in 1929. The Hearst-owned *San Francisco Examiner* typically scored higher than the non-yellow and mixed titles, but it never approached the level of the *Journal* reached in 1899.

At the other extreme, the conservative titles that scored lowest on the yellow index in 1899—the *New York Times* and the *Washington Post*—were the least inclined overall to adapt yellow characteristics. Their mean scores were the lowest among the newspapers in the study. The *New York Times*' peak on the yellow index, reached in 1979, was the lowest such score for any title.

The yellow index, moreover, depicts the progressive narrowing of differences among leading U.S. daily newspapers: The variations in appearance and content that divided yellow titles from their conservative counterparts were dramatic in 1899. They were considerably less so by 1999, lending confirmation to earlier observations about "a trend toward standardization . . . in all segments of the press" in the United States.[33]

Table 5.1 also underscores the idiosyncratic quality of newspaper design. The leading yellow newspapers of the late nineteenth century modified or toned down the most prominent features of the genre in the ensuing years. The falloff for the *Journal* from 1899 to 1909 was due largely to a reduced tendency to use banner headlines and to publish self-congratulatory, front-page headlines. The *World*, which was less inclined than the *Journal* to display banners, was less likely in 1909 to

Table 5.1
Yellow index, 1899-1999
Peak scores and mean scores are in bold.

	1899	1909	1919	1929	1939	1949	1959	1969	1979	1989	1999	Mean
New York Journal	**145**	101										**123**
New York World	**122**	78										**100**
Denver Post	91	90	114	**145**	116	132	103	90	90	92	109	**107**
San Francisco Examiner	101	95	103	68	85	65	80	98	**119**	95	113	**92.9**
Los Angeles Times	25	81	75	77	81	67	65	68	**105**	89	101	**75.8**
New York Times	12	41	63	71	49	59	78	86	**95**	88	84	**66**
Raleigh News&Observer	29	55	40	87	68	75	88	99	100	98	**103**	**76.6**
Washington Post	22	24	35	79	81	74	**104**	**104**	99	98	103	**74.8**
St. Louis Post-Dispatch	46	99	45	74	58	82	66	87	**105**	101	97	**78.2**

make use of multicolumn headlines and to indulge in self-promotion.

Moreover, the table also captures the effects of a "graphics explosion" [34] that embraced American journalism during the 1970s. It was a time when many newspapers in the United States "took a significant step . . . into the visual age," [35] in part by elevating the status of graphics designers[36] and emphasizing the importance of horizontal layouts. For four newspapers in this study, the peak year on the yellow index was 1979, amid a "graphics explosion."

The specific tendencies of each newspaper in the study will be considered next.

THE YELLOW PRESS

New York Journal and *New York World*

The typographic exuberance of yellow journalism in New York City reached a peak in the late nineteenth century. The *Journal*, notably, became a far tamer newspaper, in appearance and even in some measures of content, by 1909 (by which time it had been renamed the *American*). In 1899, 43 percent (*N*=6) of the issues examined displayed banner headlines on the front page. By 1909, just 7 percent (*N*=1) carried a banner. The *World* displayed a front-page banner headline in one issue in 1899 and none in 1909. The *Journal* made frequent use of illustrations and photographs in 1899, a tendency that also was markedly curbed by 1909, as Table 5.2 shows.

Table 5.2
Three or more illustrations on front page

	1899	1909
New York Journal	57 percent (N=8)	35 percent (N =5)
New York World	35 percent (N =5)	43 percent (N =6)

However, both newspapers were by 1909 more inclined to assign prominence to stories about society events and figures than they had been in 1899, which suggests that aspect of yellow journalism briefly gained prominence during the relatively becalmed years of the twentieth century's opening decade. Table 5.3 shows the percentage of issues in which society stories appeared above the fold on the front page.

Table 5.3
Prominence to society stories

	1899	1909
New York Journal	29 percent (N =4)	71 percent (N =10)
New York World	29 percent (N =4)	43 percent (N =6)

The tendency toward tamer, somewhat more sedate typography—which was especially noticeable for the *Journal*—confirms the qualitative observations by Will Irvin and others of the early twentieth century, that the yellow press (at least in New York City) had faded from its late nineteenth century peak. Irwin, writing in 1911, stated: "Compare to-day's New York 'Journal' with the corresponding date in 1905 or, better, in 1903; you will find this but the dim tint of that."[37]

As yellow journalism aged, the more conservative it became, at least for the genre's archetypes in New York City. Pulitzer, after all, had instructed editors of the *World* to tone down the newspaper, typographically, after the Spanish-American War.[38] By 1901, Mott wrote, the *World* "showed . . . a remarkable change by dropping some of the more objectionable features of the yellow program."[39] Hearst, meanwhile, had turned his attention to pursuing a political career, winning election to Congress in 1902 and 1904, and making an ill-fated run for the Democratic presidential nomination in 1904.

In any event, the clear decline of the most flamboyant features of yellow journalism from 1899 to 1909 confirms the genre's idiosyncratic aspect: The manifestation of the genre was dictated more by publishers' choice and initiative than by the weight of such factors as demographic variables.

Denver Post and *San Francisco Examiner*

The *Denver Post*—the "Rocky Mountain outcropping of Hearst"[40] in the late nineteenth century—was the title that most consistently exhibited yellow features during the period of this study. The *Denver Post* in 1929 matched the *Journal*'s peak score on the yellow index (see Table 5.1). Reaching that threshold reflected the *Denver Post*'s embrace of the most flamboyant aspects of yellow journalism, notably the tendency toward self-promotion. The *Post*'s name appeared in front-page headlines fairly often in 1909 (N =6), in 1919 (N =4) and in 1929 (N =5). That practice was abandoned by the mid and late twentieth century, however.

The *Denver Post* also belatedly acquired a taste for banner headlines, displaying them most of the time in 1919 and 1929, after having used them only infrequently in 1899 and 1909. By the end of the twentieth century, the *Denver Post* and the *San Francisco Examiner* were the newspapers in this study most likely to use banners, as Table 5.4 suggests—a further indication that the yellow journals of 1899 tended to retain at least some of the genre's characteristic features throughout the twentieth century.

Indeed, the *Denver Post* and the *San Francisco Examiner* ranked highest on the yellow index in 1999. Moreover, their scores that year exceeded the peak total achieved by *any* of the conservative newspapers at anytime during the period examined. In addition, the overall mean scores for the *Denver Post* and the *Examiner* were the highest among the seven newspapers examined.

Table 5.4
Banner headlines on front page (1999)

Newspaper	Frequency
Denver Post	50 percent (*N*=7)
San Francisco Examiner	50 percent (*N*=7)
News and Observer	36 percent (*N*=5)
Washington Post	21 percent (*N*=3)
Post-Dispatch	21 percent (*N*=3)
New York Times	7 percent (*N*=1)
Los Angeles Times	None (*N*=0)

Interestingly, however, this study demonstrates that the Hearst-owned *Examiner* was not necessarily a West Coast facsimile of Hearst's *New York Journal*. While the *Examiner* in 1899 exhibited far more signature features of yellow journalism than its conservative contemporaries, the newspaper was less ostentatious than the *Journal*. Self-promotion was the notable difference: The *Examiner* was less inclined than the *Journal* to call attention to its accomplishments and to insert its name in self-congratulatory, front-page headlines.

For many years during the first half of the twentieth century, the *Examiner* limited its front page to one or two photographs or illustrations; sometimes during those years, the front page carried none at all. It was only after the *Examiner* restored photographs and illustrations to its front page that it reached a peak in the yellow index, in 1979. The *Examiner*'s front page afterward was notable for its generally lavish use of photographs and illustrations.

THE CONSERVATIVE PRESS

Los Angeles Times

The conservative newspapers of 1899 ultimately, if gradually, adopted many of the typographic elements that characterized yellow journalism—and the *Los Angeles Times* is a case in point. By the late twentieth century, the newspaper's front page was alive with multiple illustrations and photographs, in vivid contrast to the years early in the century when page one was staid, gray, and usually without illustrations.

While the newspaper had begun frequent use of multicolumn headlines by the 1930s, it never consistently adopted the use of banner headlines. The *Los Angeles Times* flirted with banner headlines in 1979, its peak year in the yellow index. The flirtation was not renewed in later periods, however. It was the only paper in the study to eschew banner headlines in issues examined for 1999 (see Table 5.4).

Alone among the conservative newspapers, the *Los Angeles Times* gave prominence to society news fairly routinely during the first part of the twentieth century, a time corresponding to Hollywood's emergence as an entertainment center. More than half (*N* =8) of the front pages examined in 1909 and a substantial number in 1929 (*N* =4) and 1939 (*N* =6) included prominently displayed reports about society news stories. Thereafter, however, that tendency became less pronounced.

New York Times

In many respects, the *New York Times* was the *antithesis* of yellow journalism at the end of the nineteenth century and remained as much throughout the twentieth century. It consistently eschewed the most flamboyant elements associated with the yellow press, infrequently displaying banner headlines and almost never indulging in self-promotion.

Underscoring its status as antithetical to yellow journalism, the *Times* was slow to place multiple illustrations on its front page, doing so consistently only after mid-century. Peak use for multiple illustrations on the front page came in 1979 (*N*=14).

The *Times* was, however, the newspaper most consistently inclined to use anonymous sources. Perhaps because of the newspaper's consistent and extensive coverage of federal politics and international affairs, anonymous sources have been fixtures on its front pages since at least 1909.

Raleigh News and Observer

The only title in the study to reach its peak score on the yellow index in 1999 was the *Raleigh News and Observer*—which also was the first year in the study when the newspaper was produced by the McClatchy chain. Notably, more than one third (*N*=5) of the *News and Observer*'s front pages examined in 1999 carried banner headlines—a culmination of a pattern that was noticeable by 1969 (*N* =4) and 1979 (*N* =4), long before the newspaper was sold.

Moreover, the *News and Observer*'s peak in 1999 was not significantly greater than its scores for 1969, 1979, and 1989, suggesting that the newspaper had reached a plateau and that the sale to McClatchy did not necessarily ignite a sudden passion for typographic features associated with yellow journalism.

Rarely was the *News and Observer*'s name in front-page headlines. However, it did appear in several issues (*N* =4) in 1909, during a promotion in which the *News and Observer* sought to build its circulation. But otherwise, self-promotion was almost as uncommon in the *News and Observer* as it was in the *New York Times*.

Washington Post

The *Post* was second to the *New York Times* as having the lowest overall score in the yellow index, a ranking largely due to its decidedly gray front-page layout during the first years of the study. The *Post* seldom placed multicolumn headlines on its front page before the 1930s. It did not consistently use multiple illustrations until the 1960s.

The *Post*'s peak scores on the yellow index came in 1959 and 1969, before its conservative counterparts. The *Post* in subsequent years eased only slightly from the peak scores, nearly returning to that level in 1999.

MIXED

St. Louis Post-Dispatch

The *Post-Dispatch* exhibited the sharpest swings of the seven newspapers in the study. It was by no means a duplicate of Pulitzer's *New York World*, however, despite the common ownership. The *Post-Dispatch* ranked above its more conservative counterparts in the yellow index in 1899, notably in use of multiple front-page illustrations. Even so, its score that year was well below those of the yellow journals. Consequently, the *Post-Dispatch* was described in this study as exhibiting "mixed" characteristics.

In 1909, the *Post-Dispatch* ranked higher than the *World* and rivaled the Hearst's *New York American* in yellow characteristics. At that time, multicolumn headlines appeared regularly (*N*=14) on the *Post-Dispatch*'s front page. By 1919, however, the *Post-Dispatch* had retreated from frequent use of multicolumn headlines (*N*=5) and its overall score on the yellow index fell. Its scores stabilized late in the twentieth century, by which time the *Post-Dispatch* routinely placed multiple illustrations on its front pages (*N*=14 in 1989, *N*=13 in 1999).

DISCUSSION AND CONCLUSION

Cries of "yellow journalism" were much in the air in early 1998, amid the intense news coverage of the unfolding sex-and-lies scandal that engulfed the administration of U.S. President Bill Clinton and led to his impeachment. "Remember Yellow Journalism," read a headline above an account in the *New York Times* that said: "With reports about suspected oral sex in the White House and possible Presidential semen stains on an intern's dress, even the most respectable newspapers and TV news programs seem over the top these days. But such reports are tame, really, compared to the coverage of 100 years ago that incited the Spanish-American War."[41] The *San Francisco Examiner* suggested the news media's rush to assess the severity of Clinton's misconduct had perhaps reached "lengths not seen since the yellow journalism of a century ago."[42] The *Hartford Courant* in Connecticut, in an editorial headlined "'Yellow Journalism' Revisited," mused: "The more things change, the more they remain the same."[43]

While the scandal's revelations were sensational, the news media assuredly were *not* indulging in yellow journalism, not making use of the flamboyant techniques practiced in the late nineteenth century by Hearst's *Journal* and Pulitzer's *World*. The results of this study do not support the notion—suggested by the Bergs, among others—that leading U.S. daily newspapers have imitated closely or slavishly the salient features of yellow journalism. After all, banner headlines on the front page did not necessarily become daily features of the newspapers examined in this study. Self-promotion was even more uncommon, emerging most conspicuously to commemorate milestone anniversaries[44] or to announce major awards won.[45]

Although the newspapers that exhibited many features of yellow journalism in 1899 were more inclined to retain, or return to, typographically bold page layouts, the differences that characterized the newspapers in 1899 have narrowed markedly. The results of this study suggest that American newspapers have become more uniform in content and appearance. They have become more graphically vivid while generally eschewing the most flamboyant content variables associated with yellow journalism.

The narrowing of differences systematically demonstrated in this study undoubtedly reflects the emergence and diffusion during the twentieth century of shared values and a consensus about professional standards in mainstream American journalism. Those standards hold that frequent or egregious self-promotion is a journalistic offense.[46] As such, the narrowing of differences may well represent the realization of what Samuel E. Moffett, a former editor of Hearst's *Journal*,[47] called "reformed" yellow journalism. Writing in 1902, Moffett suggested that "respectable" newspapers could attract large audiences by incorporating features of yellow journalism and by emphasizing accuracy over speed in reporting the news:

> Your respectable paper, if it is to reach the masses, must be yellow in so far as yellowness is not disreputable. It must not be afraid of big headlines or pictures,

[although] both might advantageously be toned down somewhat, as even the original yellow papers are discovering. You must not lay too much stress on delicate taste. You must not be afraid to shout instead of speaking in gentlemanly undertones. You must not hesitate to criticize corporations and millionaires when they do things opposed to the public interests. . . . What you may do in the way of improvement is to refrain from printing a story until you know it is true, to make accuracy instead of record-breaking celerity the supreme requirement in your news-room, to give somewhat less prominence to the darker and more to the brighter side of life, and to refrain from dragging family skeletons into light unless there is some public reason for the exposure.[48]

In the widespread use of multicolumn headlines and of multiple front-page illustrations, Moffett's prescription—to a striking extent— has been followed, as this study has shown. Although the newspapers in the study have eschewed the most ostentatious features of yellow journalism, they have perhaps become "yellow insofar as yellowness is not disreputable"—a milder, tamer derivative of yellow journalism. The scores on the yellow index (see Table 5.1) suggest that Moffett's prescription for "reformed yellow journalism" has taken hold 100 years later as good journalistic practice.

On the other hand, the narrowing of the differences among newspapers in this study may be emblematic of what is perceived as a broader blandness in U.S. daily newspapers—a perceived deficiency openly discussed at the end of the twentieth century.[49] As this study has shown, newspapers in their front page content have become less self-promoting and perhaps more predictable in content choice. Sports and society news appeared less often on the front page at the end of the twentieth century than at the start. With the narrowed range of content has come an uninspiring predictability. A critic, writing in the *American Journalism Review* in 1999, suggested as much, stating:

Take the average paper. Go ahead, pick it up. How much of it have you actually read? . . . Let's guess what you're looking at: a few wire stories on the front, maybe one from overseas, one of something Congress or the White House is doing. A couple of local stories—if you're lucky, the 8-inch 1A brite. Anything from sports out there? Anything really *surprise* you?[50]

For all its faults, the yellow press at the end of the nineteenth century was anything but bland and predictable in content. Indeed, it styled itself an antidote to dullness.[51] It delighted in taking a prominent, energetic role in making the news, as when the *Journal* organized the rescue in 1897 of Evangelina Cosío y Cisneros, who was jailed in Havana on charges of plotting against Spanish colonial authorities during the Cuban insurrection that preceded the Spanish-American War.[52]

But the blandness seen in late-twentieth century newspapers also may mirror the times: Robust economic conditions, such as those that prevailed at the end of the 1990s, may mask or assuage social pressures and tensions. For most newspapers in this study, the peak year on the yellow index came in 1979, a turbulent and economically uncertain time—a period characterized by surging petroleum prices and the U.S. president's anguish about a national malaise. The drama of that turbulent time was reflected in the content and appearance of the front pages.

Moreover, 1979 fell during "an ongoing revolution" in newspaper design,[53] a time when many newspapers shed their traditional reluctance[54] to modify or experiment with the appearance of newspapers. [55] The graphics "revolution" was driven in part by computerization and other technological change,[56] as well as what a *New York Times* editor in 1979 described as "newspapers' belated discovery of the usefulness of the professional designer. Newspapers are the last major medium by far to discover and use the art director or the professional designer."[57]

For years, many editors had maintained that "crisp writing and good reporting" would compensate for stodginess and other deficiencies in page design.[58] The traditional shortcomings included a top-heaviness to the front page, in which photographs and other graphic elements were clustered above the fold, to entice browsing readers at newsstands.[59]

During the 1970s, however, "the New Graphics became a religion with many of us," as one Midwestern newspaper editor wrote. "We poked among the entrails and saw rectangular design, copious white space and big pictures as key ingredients in the battle to attract and hold readers. . . . Converts to the new religion came fast. . . . Toward the end of the decade, even the *New York Times* got religion."[60] The *New York Times* reached its peak on the yellow index in 1979. That also was the year the Society of Newspaper Designers (since renamed the Society for News Design) was founded.[61]

By the end of the 1990s, however, trends in newspaper design were, in some respects, finding inspiration in the past.[62] "American newspapers are beginning to look a little old-fashioned," said one account in 1998. "Some designers describe this trend with one word: retro."[63] The *St. Louis Post-Dispatch*, for example, introduced in 1997 a more vertical front page, replete with headline decks, large illustrations, and shorter articles emphasizing local news. Inspiration for the redesign came from issues of the *Post-Dispatch* of the early 1890s[64]—shortly before the emergence and spread of yellow journalism.

NOTES

1. Frank Luther Mott, *American Journalism: A History: 1690–1960*, 3d ed. (New York: Macmillan, 1962), 539. For a similar description, see Joseph R. Dominick, *The Dynamics of Mass Communication*, 5th ed. (New York: McGraw-Hill Companies Inc., 1996), 97–98. Dominick described yellow journalism as having "helped popularize the use of layout and display devices—banner headlines, pictures, color printing—that would go on to characterize modern journalism."

2. Albert A. Sutton, *Design and Makeup of the Newspaper* (New York: Prentice-Hall Inc., 1948), 325. Sutton wrote: "Banners and spreads have been retained for heavier display purposes by many newspapers, and the idea of using pictures has been adopted in varying degrees."

3. Tim Harrower, *The Newspaper Designer's Handbook*, 3d ed. (Madison, WI: Brown and Benchmark, 1992), 5.

4. Meredith W. Berg and David M. Berg, "The Rhetoric of War Preparation: The New York Press in 1898," *Journalism Quarterly* 45 (Winter 1968): 658.

5. Michael Pulitzer quoted in Joan Konner, "Publisher's Note: Joseph Pulitzer Nods and Smiles," *Columbia Journalism Review* (September/October 1997): 8. Emphasis in the original. Konner's "Publisher's Note" contained excerpts from Michael Pulitzer's remarks at the rededication in May 1997 of the Joseph Pulitzer World Room at Columbia University's Graduate School of Journalism. Michael Pulitzer also stated: "Sit [Joseph Pulitzer] in front of a television set, turn on the news, and he'd grasp right away the power of sight, sound, and motion. . . . I suspect that nothing about the graphics in *USA Today* would surprise him."

6. "The Other Side of Yellow Journalism," *Independent* (29 March 1900): 786.

7. Will Irwin, *The American Newspaper* (Ames, IA: Iowa State University Press, 1969). The volume is a compilation of Irwin's series, published in *Collier's* in 1911.

8. "Conservative" was the term often cited at the end of the nineteenth century to characterize newspapers that were decidedly not yellow. See, for example, Delos F. Wilcox, "The American Newspaper: A Study in Social Psychology," *Annals of the American Academy of Political and Social Science* 16 (July 1900): 56–92.

9. Mott termed the *Denver Post* the "yellowiest of the yellows." Mott, *American Journalism*, 567.

10. Mott argued that yellow journalism "reached its height at the turn of the century, 1899–1900." See Mott, *American Journalism*, 539.

11. The *Journal* was renamed the *New York American* in 1902. See "It's 'The American' Now," *Fourth Estate* (25 October 1902): 2.

12. Willard G. Bleyer suggested the *Journal* was the first to use banner headlines regularly. See Bleyer, *Main Currents in the History of American Journalism* (Boston: Houghton Mifflin Company, 1927), 365. Mott, however, stated that "the Chicago *Times* was apparently the first to make a practice of throwing banner lines across its front page." See Mott, *American Journalism*, 542.

13. Mott, *American Journalism*, 539.

14. The *Journal*, for example, turned to banner headlines to applaud its successful efforts to reduce the price of natural gas in 1899. See "Greatest Newspaper Victory in History. *Journal* Saves Money for Everybody," *New York Journal* (2 May 1899): 1.

15. See, for example, "Jeffries Wins the Great Championship Fight in 15 Rounds," *New York Journal* (16 November 1901): 1.

16. See, for example, "'Rah! Rah! Rah! Harvard! Yale Slaughtered; 22 to 0," *New York World* (24 November 1901): 1.

17. See, for example, "To-Day's Varsity Boat Race," *New York Journal* (25 June 1897): 1, and "Victory for the American Stroke!" *New York Journal* (26 June 1897): 1.

18. See, for example, "Girl Editor in Vanderbilt Family," *New York Journal* (25 March 1897): 1.

19. See, for example, "Young Mrs. Beale Gets a Divorce," *New York Journal* (21 October 1896): 1, and "America's Richest Bride," *New York Journal* (11 June 1897): 1.

20. Throughout the period covered by this study, the *Los Angeles Times* was owned by Times Mirror Company. Times Mirror was controlled by the descendants of Harrison Gray Otis, who acquired the *Los Angeles Times* in the 1880s. The sales of Times Mirror to the Tribune Company, owner of the *Chicago Tribune*, was completed in 2000. The *New York Times* is controlled by the heirs of Adolph S. Ochs, who bought the newspaper in 1896. The *San Francisco Examiner* was the first metropolitan daily newspaper published by William Randolph Hearst. The newspaper was owned by the closely held Hearst Corporation until July 2000. The *St. Louis Post-Dispatch* was Joseph Pulitzer's first metropolitan daily newspaper in the United States and it is controlled by his heirs, through Pulitzer Inc. The *Washington Post* was acquired by Eugene Meyer at auction in 1933 and has since been controlled by his heirs.

21. Owners of the *Denver Post* have included Fred G. Bonfils and Harry H. Tammen, who began publishing the newspaper in 1895, and, in later years, the Times Mirror Company. The newspaper at the end of the twentieth century was owned by the closely held MediaNews Group Inc.

22. For a survey of U.S. editors about the country's best daily newspapers, see "America's Best Newspapers," *Columbia Journalism Review* (November/December 1999). The *New York Times* and *Washington Post* were ranked first and second, respectively, and the *Los Angeles Times* was fourth. The *Raleigh News and Observer* was sixteenth. The *San Francisco Examiner* was in a three-way tie for twenty-sixth, and the *St. Louis Post-Dispatch* was in an eight-way tie for thirty-fifth. Of the seven newspapers in the study examined in this study, only the *Denver Post* was not ranked in the *Columbia Journalism Review* survey.

23. See Daniel Riffe, Charles F. Aust, and Stephen R. Lacy, "The Effectiveness of Random, Consecutive Day and Constructed Week Sampling in Newspaper Content Analysis," *Journalism and Mass Communication Quarterly* 70, 1 (Spring 1993): 133–139. The authors conclude that two constructed weeks are sufficient to "allow reliable estimates of local stories in a year's worth of" newspaper issues (139).

24. Riffe, Aust, and Lacy, "The Effectiveness of Random, Consecutive Day and Constructed Week Sampling," 136.

25. In addition to the wars in 1899 and 1999, important events that occurred during the periods covered by this study included the debate about the League of Nations (1919), the inauguration of President Herbert Hoover (1929), the *Squalus* submarine rescue (1939), the civil war in China (1949), the resignation of

French President Charles de Gaulle (1969), and the nuclear accident at the Three Mile Island power plant in Pennsylvania (1979).

26. For a discussion about the comparatively belated introduction of color at the *New York Times*, see Lee Berton, "Whaddya Mean, Gray?" *Columbia Journalism Review* (September/October 1997): 42. Berton wrote: "More than three decades after other papers began doing it, the *Times* will add lipstick and rouge . . . by running color for both news and advertising in the daily paper." See also, Sandra H. Utt and Steve Pasternack, "How They Look: An Updated Study of American Newspaper Front Pages," *Journalism Quarterly* 66, 3 (Autumn 1989): 621–627. The authors noted: "On front pages, color is now the rule" at most newspapers (626).

27. There were exceptions, owing to a few gaps in the extensive collections of the Library of Congress. Microfilm issues of the *Denver Post* for 1899–1939 were obtained by loan from the University of Colorado at Boulder. Copies of the *Los Angeles Times* for 1899 were made available by the newspaper's library.

28. In the case of the *Los Angeles Times*, this meant eschewing the more sensational-appearing version, which evidently had been prepared for street and vending machine sales.

29. This resulted in an oversampling of Sunday issues for the *Post-Dispatch* in 1999. However, that anomaly does not appear to have markedly altered or distorted results for that newspaper.

30. Coding the *Post-Dispatch* presented another minor anomaly. Because of a strike, the newspaper was not published Sunday, 20 April 1969, one of the days to be examined that year. In order to assess fourteen issues of the *Post-Dispatch* for that year, the issue of Sunday, 23 June 1969, was coded instead. The strike at the *Post-Dispatch* in 1969 represented the sole occasion during the period of this study in which a labor dispute disrupted publication schedules of any of the seven newspapers analyzed.

31. Kevin Barnhurst and John Nerone reported a marked trend to place "fewer stories and fewer items" on the front page of the three newspapers they studied at intervals from 1885 to 1985. See Kevin G. Barnhurst and John C. Nerone, "Design Trends in U.S. Front Pages, 1885-1985," *Journalism Quarterly* 68, 4 (Winter 1991): 799. They noted: "The front pages clearly became less dense and more orderly over the [100 years] studied."

32. In addition, this study set a demanding threshold for stories about society and sporting events: They had to appear above the fold on the front page, much as the *Journal* and *World* tended to place such articles in the late 1890s.

33. Robert L. Stevenson, "Readability of Conservative and Sensational Papers since 1872," *Journalism Quarterly* 41 (Spring 1964): 202. Stevenson also wrote, "Although a cursory examination of newspapers in the United States today indicates that vestiges of sensationalism are still present in many papers, the distinctions that set them apart from conservative papers in the 1890s are considerably less marked." For another study that identified the "increasingly uniform" character of the front pages of U.S. newspapers, see Barnhurst and Nerone, "Design Trends in U.S. Front Pages," 796–804. Barnhurst and Nerone examined 198 issues of three newspapers at ten-year intervals.

34. Daryl Moen, "Many Newspapers Undergo Facelifts," *Editor and Publisher* (6 January 1979): 46. Moen's article reported that newspapers were increas-

ingly using "more illustrations and more photographs, all wrapped up in multi-colored packages."

35. Moen, "Many Newspapers Undergo Facelifts," 46.

36. Louis Silverstein, "Design Is a 'Hit Tune,'" *Bulletin of the American Society of Newspaper Editors* 628 (November 1979): 10.

37. Irwin, *The American Newspaper*. His reference was to the *New York Evening Journal*, the Hearst-owned afternoon cousin of the morning *American*.

38. See W. A. Swanberg, *Pulitzer* (New York: Charles Scribner's Sons, 1967), 254–255.

39. Mott, *American Journalism*, 540.

40. Sidney Kobre, *The Yellow Press and Gilded Age Journalism* (Tallahassee, FL: Florida State University Press, 1964), 244.

41. Clifford Krauss, "Remember Yellow Journalism," *New York Times* (15 February 1898): 4, 3.

42. David Armstrong, "Politics Noir: Media's 300-year Love Affair with Love Affairs," *San Francisco Examiner* (25 September 1998): A16.

43. "'Yellow Journalism' Revisited," *Hartford Courant* (22 February 1998): C2.

44. See, for example, "St. Louis Post-Dispatch 100th Anniversary Edition," *St. Louis Post-Dispatch* (25 March 1979). The newspaper celebrated the occasion with a special section that included such self-congratulatory articles as, "Pulitzer Dared to Challenge the 'Great Illusion,'" "A Tradition of Conscience," and "This Reporter Couldn't Be Stopped." For other examples of prominent self-promotion in metropolitan newspapers, see "Jubilee Edition of the Post Is Epochal in Journalism," *Washington Post* (6 December 1927): 1, and "Centennial Fete Tonight! Air, Lake and Land Spectacle to Thrill Thousands," *Chicago Daily Tribune* (10 June 1947): 1.

45. Newspapers that win Pulitzer Prizes often report the accomplishment on their front pages. See, for example, Emily Narvaes and Jim Hughes, "Post Wins Bittersweet Pulitzer," *Denver Post* (11 April 2000): A1; and David Shaw, "Times Writer Wins Pulitzer; Post Wins 3," *Los Angeles Times* (11 April 2000): A1. See also, "Times Honored With Two Pulitzer Prizes," *Los Angeles Times* (6 May 1969): 1. Such self-promotion was criticized in journalism reviews at the end of the twentieth century. See, for example, Jeff Pooley, "Pulitzer Self-promotion," *Brill's Content* (June 1999): 36. He wrote: "Who needs a press release when you've got a newspaper at your disposal? For nine of the ten dailies that earned Pulitzer Prizes [in 1999], the annual awards meant front-page self-promotion and giving the other prize-winners short shrift. . . . Six of the newspapers—ranging in size from the *Washington Post* to the *Hartford Courant*—bumped other stories off the front page to detail newsroom celebrations, quote editors, and dole out praise to recognized reporters. And all three of the remaining papers prominently teased their inside stories on page one. Among newspapers that didn't earn a prize, stories about the awards were short and buried deep inside." In addition, the *American Journalism Review* critically explored the self-aggrandizing "prize culture" of journalism in the United States and concluded the profession was "locked in the iron grip of prize frenzy." Alicia C. Shepard, "Journalism's Prize Culture," *American Journalism Review* (April 2000): 22–29.

46. A reminder of this principle appeared in the *Washington Post*'s series of memorable front pages of the twentieth century, which appeared throughout 1999. Included in the series was the newspaper's front page from 19 September 1909, across which was thrown a banner headline, rare for the time. It read: "The Post's Regatta And Carnival A Spectacular Triumph." In describing that front page in its 1999 series, *Post* said the banner headline "was perhaps a milestone of what decent newspapers should never do: shamelessly promote themselves." See "The Century in The Post: The Post ♥ The Post," *Washington Post* (19 September 1999): F8. Nonetheless, the *Post* gave front-page prominence to the report about the Pulitzer Prizes it won in 2000. See Peter Slevin, "Post Wins Pulitzer for Public Service," *Washington Post* (11 April 2000): A1.

47. Moffett, who also worked for Hearst at the *San Francisco Examiner*, was a nephew of Mark Twain. See Ben Procter, *William Randolph Hearst: The Early Years, 1863–1910* (New York: Oxford University Press, 1998), 47.

48. Cited in "Are Yellow Journals as Bad as They Are Painted?" *Literary Digest* 25, 5 (2 August 1902): 132.

49. See Sharyn Wizda, "Breathing Life into Newsprint," *American Journalism Review* (November 1999): 49–50. The *Wall Street Journal* in April 2000 scoffed at what it termed "the cardboard opinion served up by most newspapers these days." See "Voice Silenced," *Wall Street Journal* (27 April 2000): A26.

50. Wizda, "Breathing Life," 50. She also wrote: "What about the most valuable real estate in the newspaper—1A? If anywhere, kicking the predictability habit should happen there" (52).

51. The *New York American* suggested that American magazines were bland "because they are not 'yellow'—meaning by that they are without courage and energy and desperately afraid of originality. They are timid slaves to the conventional both in opinion and in their literary output. . . . An infusion of the vigor of journalism, 'yellow' journalism . . . would cure the magazines of their dullness." Cited in "How to Remedy Dullness in Magazine," *Fourth Estate* (13 September 1902): 10.

52. See "Evangelina Cisneros Rescued by the Journal," *New York Journal* (10 October 1897): 1.

53. Silverstein, "Design is a 'hit tune,'" 10.

54. John E. Allen, *Newspaper Makeup* (New York: Harper and Brothers, 1936), 2–3.

55. See "Judges Find Typography Change Slow," *Editor and Publisher* (1 March 1969): 22. See also, Jack Z. Sissors, "'Today's Newspapers Look Old-Fashioned,'" *Bulletin of the American Society of Newspaper Editors* 528 (March 1969): 6–11.

56. Computerized newsrooms had become widespread by the late 1970s. See Dominique Wilson, "Do You Love Your VDT?" *Columbia Journalism Review* (July/August 1979): 36–39.

57. Silverstein, "Design Is a 'Hit Tune,'" 10.

58. Sissors, "'Today's Newspapers Look Old-Fashioned,'" 6.

59. Sissors, "'Today's Newspapers Look Old-Fashioned,'" 7.

60. Michael J. Davies, "Doing More Graphics with Less Space," *Bulletin of the American Society of Newspaper Editors* 629 (December/January 1980): 11.

61. See "Auxiliaries: For Appearances' Sake," *Columbia Journalism Review* (May/June 1979): 20.

62. See, for example, Mario R. Garcia, "We've Come a Long Way," *The American Editor* 75, 3 (April 2000): 4–5. Garcia wrote: "Retro is in. Designers and editors are digging out type fonts of the 1930s and earlier, introducing heads and subheads before readers get to any text."

63. Tom Eblen, "Back to Basics," *APME News* (Spring 1998): 5.

64. Bob Rose, senior editor for production/presentation, *St. Louis Post-Dispatch*, telephone interview with author, April 1998.

6

Echoes in Contemporary Journalism

Frederick Palmer, a well-known foreign correspondent of the early twentieth century, predicted almost off-handedly in 1906 that the phrase "yellow journalism" was "destined to endure in our language as long as the printed word."[1] Palmer's prophecy, which appeared in a scathing, four-part profile in *Collier's* of William Randolph Hearst, has proved stunningly accurate. Not only has "yellow journalism" lived on, the phrase has become embedded in contexts far more numerous and global than Palmer probably imagined. By the end of the twentieth century, the decidedly American idiom has found expression in an astounding variety of settings.

"Yellow journalism" has become synonymous in Egypt with aggressive, independent-minded reporting; in Thailand, with bribe-taking among journalists.[2] The overwhelming number of complaints to India's Press Council in the late 1990s were about "yellow journalism."[3] An investigative television program in Greece was called the "yellow press," and its reports included exposés about police corruption.[4]

In Pakistan, "yellow journalism" has been linked to "rumormongering factories" and in Kenya, "yellow journalism" has been blamed for "creating chaos, despondency and lies."[5] In Nigeria, "yellow journalism" has been cited in condemning critical reporting by international correspondents[6] and to justify crackdowns on upstart domestic newspapers.[7] Palestinian militants have also cited "yellow journalism," warning that it "squirts out venom against Palestinians who oppose defeatist agreements."[8] A trend toward "sensationalism and yellow journalism" was said to have taken hold among the Chinese-language press in Hong Kong at the end of the 1990s.[9] Earlier in the decade, the Parisian daily *Le Monde* reported about the "journalisme jaune"—the "yellow journalism"—of the press in Israel.[10]

Letter writers to U.S. newspapers are especially fond of the phrase, turning to "yellow journalism" to denounce bias, distortion, sensationalism, and other failings and misdeeds of the news media. "If there were a Pulitzer Prize for yellow journalism," said one nasty letter in the *Raleigh News and Observer* in the mid-1990s, "your paper would surely be a winner."[11] Suggested a writer to the *Columbus Dispatch* in Ohio; "Perhaps the next time the newspaper is inclined to print yellow journalism, it might actually use yellow paper."[12] The intense news coverage of the sex-and-lies scandal that engulfed U.S. President Bill Clinton in 1998 was deplored by at least one letter writer as a "yellow journalism attack."[13] And when Clinton's pollster and campaign strategist Dick Morris resigned after news reports described his relationship with a prostitute, he invoked the phrase, saying: "I will not subject my wife, family or friends to the sadistic vitriol of yellow journalism. I will not dignify such journalism with a reply or answer."[14]

Such varied and colorful use of "yellow journalism," however, only begins to capture its enduring significance to contemporary journalism. Yellow journalism also resonates in ways more systemic and integral than the offhand dismissals of angry letter-writers. The legacies of yellow journalism are complex and multifaceted. Pieces of its DNA can be identified in the practice and theory of no fewer than three strains of activist-oriented journalism of the late twentieth century—each of which shared the presumption that the news media are powerful and that their influences can be harnessed to promote political and social change. The genetic material of yellow journalism can be found in:

- "development" journalism, which regarded the press as an agent of nation-building. This movement gained a measure of popularity during the 1970s in developing countries, notably in sub-Saharan Africa. A feature common to development journalism, as it was practiced, was fulsome coverage of national leaders, particularly heads of state, who often were accorded cult-like status by the news media. The uncritical attention lavished on heads of state evoked the self-laudatory impulse that characterized the yellow press, which not infrequently opened its news columns to celebrate its triumphs and accomplishments.
- "public" or "civic" journalism, a definitionally ambiguous movement that essentially regarded the press as a force for reinvigorating participatory democracy in the United States. The problem-solving component central to public journalism is reminiscent of the activist ethos of some yellow newspapers, notably the *New York Journal*. The *Journal* styled itself as the public's agent in attacking the abuses of big business and inept government. In some respects, yellow journalism was an early and agitated precursor of public journalism.

- crime-solving, or "gotcha," journalism, pursued as a circulation-building device by some British tabloid newspapers, notably the Sunday *News of the World*. This variant of activist or participatory newsgathering gave rise to charges of misconduct by journalists who, in some cases, enticed their targets to commit such crimes as procuring and selling illegal drugs. Crime-solving was a sometimes-conspicuous element of the yellow press. The *New York Journal* and *New York World* both injected themselves into whodunits. A notable example was their respective investigations into a headless torso murder mystery that gripped New York City in the summer of 1897.

The parallels between yellow journalism and more contemporary journalistic practices are more than merely curious and coincidental. They suggest, rather, a little-recognized interconnectedness and coherence among journalistic practice over time. The parallels serve as well to demonstrate that the more contemporary strains were not altogether new but in reality sprang from diverse and multiple sources, much as yellow journalism did in the mid-1890s. Advocates of "public journalism," for example, drew criticism for a tendency to "exaggerate" the originality of the genre.[15] As this chapter will demonstrate, antecedents of "public journalism" were apparent more than 100 years ago.

Moreover, the linkages to contemporary journalistic practice represent another way in which yellow journalism has left enduring contributions to the profession—contributions that are more lasting and profound than commonly understood by scholars and practitioners. Those linkages will now be explored in greater detail.

DEVELOPMENT JOURNALISM

The notion that domestic news media could be harnessed to promote objectives of national unity and development took hold during the 1970s in parts of the developing world. The "development journalism" movement proved particularly appealing to the embryonic states of sub-Saharan Africa, which then were still emerging from the stunting effects of prolonged rule by European colonial powers.

The appeal of development journalism was enhanced by the fairly frequent criticism in United Nations bodies at the time that Western-style independent journalism was a handmaiden to cultural imperialism.[16] Western news organizations, notably the international wire services such as the Associated Press and Reuters, were seen as singularly focused on the political conflict and turmoil in developing states, and unsympathetic to those countries' broader objectives of economic development, education, and health care. The purported failings of Western journalism were central to the debates in the United Nations Educational, Scientific and Cultural Organization (UNESCO) during the 1970s on developing what was ambitiously described as a New World Information and Communication Order. Amid the controversy—which was to exhaust itself by the early 1980s, following the withdrawal of Britain and the United States from UNESCO—the notion of "development journalism" took hold.[17]

In practice, however, development journalism proved little more than a guise for state domination of the news media. National leaders, while generally insisting that the press should focus not on conflict but on matters of national development and consolidation, often turned the news media into one-dimensional forums for self-congratulation and the pursuit of cult-like status. As one international communication scholar has written, "In practice the nation often came to mean the regime in power . . . and development news consisted of endless puffery of government leaders and the nation's progress, even where there wasn't much."[18] It was a distorted, deceptive sort of journalism, "heavy on the flattery of public officials."[19] The flattery was displayed prominently and ceaselessly in an uncritical press, much in the manner the yellow journals prominently extolled their reporting successes.

A notable example of development journalism in practice was in the West African state of Côte d'Ivoire, a former French colony known also as the Ivory Coast. Côte d'Ivoire was ruled for thirty-three years by a deceptively ruthless authoritarian figure, Félix Houphouët-Boigny, who was one of Africa's eager promoters of development journalism. The Ivorian journalist, he said, must be "an agent of development, a citizen engaged at the sides of his brothers in the struggle for dignity and well-being."[20] In practice, the press in Côte d'Ivoire became a forum for paying daily tribute to the *sagesse* of Houphouët-Boigny, who styled himself "le Vieux," the Wise Old Man of West Africa.

Houphouët-Boigny's "thought for the day" appeared regularly on the front page of the state newspaper, *Fraternité Matin*, which closely reported on the leader's comings and goings. His pending return from one of his many visits to Europe invariably was front-page news. Visiting heads of state were invariably described as paying homage to "le Vieux" and to seek his guidance. Until the closing years of his rule, Houphouët allowed no place in the Ivorian news media for criticism or close analysis of his policies or personality. Instead, the image projected in the Ivorian news media was glowing but misleading, one steeped in the "endless puffery" of the head of state.

Using the press as a forum for persistent—and misleading—self-congratulation was reminiscent of the unrelenting and unapologetic self-promotion that characterized New York's yellow press. The *New York Journal* and the *New York World*, in particular, opened their columns routinely to what might be called self-puffery, as if to remind themselves, their readers, and their rivals about their accomplishments and their supposedly growing prestige.[21] Self-puffery was routinely given prominence in the yellow press of New York. Tributes from other newspapers were highlighted.[22] Messages from municipal leaders, as well as heads of state, received lavish display. Characteristically, the *Journal* and *World* sought to outdo each other. When the *World* published contents of a message from the Greek foreign minister on the eve of a brief war with Turkey in 1897,[23] the *Journal* arranged a few days later for the King of Greece to send a telegram expressing gratitude for the *Journal*'s coverage. The *Journal* hailed the message as "the first time that crowned head has ever personally sent a statement to an American newspaper."[24]

As with development journalism, an air of predictability and contrivance attached to the puffery of the yellow press. The *Journal* and the *World* often would solicit letters of support and praise for their accomplishments—and then publish them in a prominent fashion. The *Journal*, for example, sent telegrams to U.S. mayors at a meeting in Columbus, Ohio, in 1897, requesting their impressions about the *Journal*'s practice of obtaining court injunctions to block suspected misfeasance in the award of municipal contracts. Replies from the mayors predictably extolled the *Journal*'s practice—and they were spread across two inside pages of the newspaper.[25]

The puffery of yellow journalism carried an unstated but very real sense of insecurity, much as the puffery of development journalism. In both cases, there was an evident hunger for approval[26]—and a lurking apprehension that disapproval was never very distant. Just as the head of state of a developing country often sensed the prospect of his violent overthrow, the yellow journal also was aware of the threat of boycotts and popular scorn. Indeed, the boycotts organized by public libraries and civic associations against the *Journal* and the *World* in 1897 may have encouraged the yellow journals to seek the patina of popular approval as relentlessly and forcefully as they did. Their frequent claims of circulation growth—figures which the press of the late nineteenth century routinely exaggerated[27]—represented important ways to assert that they had secured popular trust and confidence.[28]

Development journalism fell into pronounced decline during the late 1980s and early 1990s, undercut and effectively repudiated by the emergence of independent news media in many parts of the developing world. In the United States, meanwhile, a movement embracing many of the assumptions and imperatives of development journalism began attracting notice.[29] It was called "public" or "civic" journalism and it emerged from an unusual convergence of interests among some professional journalists and mass communication scholars. Although the movement has been criticized even by supporters for its deliberate vagueness[30] ("public" and "civic" journalism tended to be used interchangeably, contributing to the definitional confusion), it proposed deploying the news media to stimulate and reinvigorate a society that, supposedly, had become disenchanted with civic life and participatory democracy.

PUBLIC JOURNALISM

Some advocates of public journalism traced the roots of the practice to the Hutchins Commission report[31] of 1947, which proposed the press recognize and assume a role of social responsibility.[32] Others, however, found far deeper and more interesting antecedents. Michael Schudson, for example, likened public journalism to "a conservative reform movement in the tradition of American social reforms of the Progressive Era" of the late nineteenth and early twentieth centuries.[33] More specific links between yellow journalism and public journalism were identified by Thomas C. Leonard, who wrote: "Making readers count in the discussion of public questions is the watchword of public journalism today. A century ago, publishers found ways to do this. Ordinary citizens were more likely to find their names and comments in the Yellow Press than in the more respectable papers that lost the circulation contests."[34]

Leonard noted that Hearst's *Evening Journal* in 1904 (the year Hearst made his most serious bid for the U.S. presidency) "asked readers to write letters explaining the appeal of the paper. As this was a Hearst operation, there was hoopla and cash prizes for the best letters. . . . But to a modern journalist, much of the communication between these journalists and their readers sounds like public journalism."[35] Engaging the readers in the shaping or "framing" of newspaper content was a core objective of public journalism—and it was an objective evident in other yellow journals as well. The *Denver Post*, for example, offered in 1896 to pay $1 "to any man, woman or child who can suggest an acceptable cartoon for its front page."[36]

An even more potent, more central connection between yellow journalism and public journalism can be found in the problem-solving ethic that was central to both genres. Problem solving was a wide-ranging objective for the yellow press. In New York, the *Journal* and *World* supplemented municipal agencies and charities[37] by setting up soup kitchens and distributing food to poor people of New York City following disruptions such as the powerful snowstorms in 1897[38] and 1898.[39] They made dinners available to the poor at Christmastime [40] and to families left homeless by fires.[41] They sent trainloads of relief assistance to victims of the Galveston hurricane and flood in 1900.[42] They also sought vigorously to block the awards of lucrative municipal contracts and franchises to dubious and suspect private entities.

The *Journal* described its engagement as "the journalism of action," which, it said, represented "the final stage in the evolution of the modern newspaper."[43] It later characterized activist journalism as "a new organ of the body politic" that "gathers all the scattered rays of popular sentiment and focalizes them upon the spot that needs" attention and improvement.[44]

The *Journal*'s characterization of activist, engaged, problem-solving journalism—of focusing "all the scattered rays of popular sentiment"—was not far removed from the arguments of some advocates of public journalism of the late 1990s. Cole C. Campbell, then the editor of *St. Louis Post-Dispatch*, gave clear expression to such sentiments, writing: "Journalism is in the problem-solving business, not the truth business. . . . We journalists have a great opportunity if we make problem solving the raison d'etre of our news report. That could recast how we cover everything, moving the discussion away from who wins or loses power to what problems we ought to solve and how we might tackle them."[45] Public journalism was described by other advocates as a way "to activate and elevate public deliberation on community issues"[46] and to "knit together a fractured community and repair the idea of the common good."[47]

Such views were strikingly evocative of those of Arthur Brisbane, a leading editor for Hearst and a vigorous exponent of the power and potential of yellow journalism. Brisbane saw in the yellow press a civic stimulant, an agent for promoting the processes of problem solving. His writings in some respects seemed to anticipate the core objectives of public journalism. "Far more important than anything else," Brisbane wrote in 1904, "is the work that Yellow Journalism does in influencing the community in its *thought*, stimulating and supporting it in fighting the encroachments of class or of capital upon the popular rights."[48] He also wrote:

> What is Yellow Journalism? It is the power of public opinion, the mental force of thousands or millions of readers utilised with more or less intelligence in the interest of those readers. The yellow journal is the successor of the open spot where citizens of the Greek republic met to settle public affairs.[49]

Public journalism, moreover, shared the impatience of yellow journalism with the notion that the press functions best as an impartial, dispassionate, *detached* observer. The *Journal* scoffed at newspapers that "contented themselves . . . with pointing out existing evils or giving warning of impending dangers. . . . They gave the alarm and whether it was heeded or not was no concern of theirs."[50] Rather, the *Journal* argued "a newspaper's duty is not confined to exhortation but that when things are going wrong it should set them right if possible."[51] Therein rested its justification for securing injunctions to block or delay the granting of gas, light, trolley, and other municipal contracts to private business interests and monopolistic trusts.

In embracing an ethos of activism, the *Journal* identified a critical distinction between its "new" brand of journalism and what it called the "old," staid form characteristic of many of its New York rivals. "May a newspaper properly do things or are its legitimate functions confined to talking about them? That is the chief question at issue between the representatives of the new and the old journalism," the *Journal* said. "It may criticise corruption and maladministration in office, but has it a right to protect the public interests by deeds as well as words?"[52] Its response:

"The Journal holds the theory that a newspaper may fitly render any public service within its power."[53] The *Journal* pronounced itself "ready to act when public interests require action, and to act in the way to accomplish results."[54] It reserved for itself the decision of when the "public interests require action"—not necessarily a comforting or reassuring prospect, given the newspaper's impenitent and error-prone tendencies.

For advocates of public journalism, however, the gap between doing things and "talking about them"—between activism and detachment—proved more difficult to rationalize. Indeed, the chief criticisms of public journalism were that by proposing to act as a civic stimulant in addressing social problems, journalists risked compromising their credibility and, by extension, risked distorting the news agenda.[55]

The gap, however, was not insuperable for advocates of public journalism. The literature of the movement included recommendations for "helping citizens act"—that is, using the good offices of the newspaper to shape a community's consensus on vital issues and then to make sure that public officials respond accordingly.[56] That variant of public journalism proposed an active and engaged role for newspapers—a variant clearly suggestive of yellow journalism. Arthur Charity sought to justify such an activist ethic for public journalism by questioning the wisdom of journalistic detachment or, as he put it, "noninvolvement."

Practitioners of public journalism, Charity wrote, "could well argue that the mainstream's role of noninvolvement is the one that realistically threatens the public. . . . Which form of journalism is really more flawed and dangerous in a free society: the one that sits passively by while people grow divided, or the one that finds ways of bringing them together?"[57]

Charity's sentiments were of the kind that yellow journalists no doubt would have recognized and understood. His views echo more than faintly the *Journal*'s dismissive complaint about newspapers that contented themselves in pointing out "existing evils."

Nonetheless, the problem-solving ethic of the yellow press differed from that of public journalism in a fundamental way. In yellow journalism, the problem-solving imperative was transferred from the top down: The newspaper reserved unto itself the decision about when and how to act on behalf of the wider public interest. Public journalism—even as contemplated by Charity—was more inclined to regard the press as a collaborative agency, as an instrument or guide as the community explored options and considered approaches to problem solving. It was in that sense a bottom-up, consensus-driven approach.

Yet for both yellow journalism and public journalism, the newspaper was the vital agency, the precipitating and even commanding force that stimulated and advocated change. Without the intervention or the guidance of a socially aware, mold-breaking newspaper, the implication was that the problems would be addressed otherwise, if at all.

An elaboration of the *Journal*'s activist ethic was its eagerness to assume the role of a crime-solving agent in thwarting the corrupt designs of business trusts or in tracking down suspected criminals who had eluded the authorities. The *Journal* depicted itself literally as a cop on the beat, as a uniformed agent arresting thuggish wrongdoers and leading them away.[58] A dramatic fulfillment of such a role came during the summer of 1897, when a dismembered male corpse washed up in the East River. The body was headless, armless, and legless and was wrapped in an oilcloth. From a tattoo on the torso, *Journal* reporters identified the victim as William Guldensuppe, a masseur who worked at a Turkish bath.[59] The pattern of the oilcloth led the *Journal* to a dry goods dealer who had sold the material to one of Guldensuppe's killers—his former mistress, Mrs. Augusta Nack, who in turn implicated her accomplice and new lover, Martin Thorn.[60]

Such flamboyant detective work was beyond the realm of problem-solving amenable or palatable to most advocates of public journalism, but to the *Journal* crime-solving was a logical and inevitable extension of its view of "the journalism of action." It declared that its activist journalism "strives to apprehend the criminal, to bring him to the bar of justice and thereafter not to convict him but to show him as he is."[61] That elaboration of the problem-solving imperative of yellow journalism evoked the controversial, crime-busting journalism practiced with great flair in late 1990s by several British tabloid newspapers, notably the *News of the World*.

CRIME-SOLVING JOURNALISM

At end of the twentieth century, the *News of the World* was the world's largest-circulating English-language Sunday newspaper. It claimed four million readers and its raunchy, tabloid journalism qualified it as one of the world's most consistently controversial titles. The *News of the World* is owned by Rupert Murdoch, the brash, Australian-born international media mogul whose provocative style has invited comparisons to Hearst. Murdoch's entry into New York journalism in the 1970s was notably reminiscent of Hearst and his early years in the city.[62]

During the late 1990s, reporters for *News of the World* and other British tabloid newspapers engaged in a series of undercover operations ostensibly to bring drug dealers, fugitive financiers, and other criminals to justice. Often the targets were small-time celebrities and wayward sports figures dabbling in modest quantities of illegal drugs. The undercover methods were criticized as entrapment and dismissed as "a kind of investigative reporting without much investigating."[63]

In one notorious case, reporters for *News of the World* posed as wealthy Arabs and enticed a British earl to buy cocaine and share the drug with them. A detailed report about the peer's conduct—he was depicted as drunkenly snorting cocaine with a £5 note—soon after was splashed across *News of the World.* [64] He was arrested and convicted of selling drugs. But the presiding judge declined to send the peer to jail, citing the subterfuge of the *News of the World.* If not for the journalists' sting, the judge observed, the crimes likely would not have been committed. [65]

In another case, two *News of the World* reporters posed as officials of the Gillette Company and approached Lawrence Dallaglio, then the captain of England's rugby team, with the prospect of an endorsement contract. The three dined at an expensive restaurant after which Dallaglio recounted drug-taking and wild sexual adventures by his teammates during a series of matches in 1997 in South Africa. The *News of the World* prominently reported the captain's account in May 1999 and Dallaglio soon after resigned the captaincy.[66]

While entrapment was not an element in the repertoire of the yellow press, subterfuge and misrepresentation certainly were. Female reporters were encouraged to arrange to be arrested and spend a night in a jail with "women of the street and write up a brilliant account of the affair."[67] Perhaps the most memorable case of the *Journal*'s subterfuge was in dispatching a correspondent, Karl Decker, to Cuba to rescue Evangelina Cosío y Cisneros, a daughter of a Cuban insurgent leader, from a Havana jail in 1897. Decker succeeded and Cisneros was smuggled to New York City and a delirious reception organized by Hearst.[68]

The *Journal* acknowledged that in freeing Cisneros it had violated Spanish law and flouted international conventions—and seemed delighted for having done so: "The Journal is quite aware of the rank illegality of its action. It knows very well that the whole proceeding is lawlessly out of tune with the prosaic and commercial nineteenth century. We shall not be surprised at international complications, nor at solemn and rebuking assurances that the age of knight errantry is dead. To that it can be answered that if innocent maidens are still imprisoned by tyrants, the knight errant is yet needed."[69]

For the *Journal,* the ends of freeing Cisneros justified the means: "The Journal violated Spanish law in breaking into the foul jail . . . and helping the martyr prisoner out. It is happy in the knowledge. It would like to violate some more Spanish law of the same sort. When right and wrong are turned upside down . . . there is a savage satisfaction in striking a smashing blow at a legal system that has become an organized crime."[70] The *Journal*'s justification for the jailbreak rescue was not far removed from that of British tabloid editors as they rationalized their subterfuge and undercover operations.

CONCLUSION

An article in the *Journalist* trade publication in 1898 predicted that "yellow journalism" ultimately would lose its association with scorn and disparagement. The author, David A. Curtis, noted that the "very term 'yellow journalism' is used in contemptuous derision, [much] as forty years ago 'abolitionism' was considered by many estimable people as a synonym for treason. It is worthy of serious consideration whether the popular use of the one term will change as radically as the popular use of the other has changed. For one, I am free to admit that I believe it will."[71]

Curtis' hopeful prediction has of course proved badly misguided. Yellow journalism has not shed its association with scorn and disparagement. Occasionally, a newspaper writer may protest that the "yellow journalism" invoked by irritated letter writers at the end of the twentieth century hardly reflected the journalistic practices at the end of the nineteenth century in New York City.[72] But discerning insight escapes most popular, and scholarly, assessments of yellow journalism. An example of the sweeping imprecision that obscures nuanced understanding of yellow journalism can be found in the influential text, *The Press and America: An Interpretative History of the Mass Media.* "Trumpeting their concern for 'the people,'" the authors wrote, "yellow journalists at the same time choked up the news channels on which the common people depended with a shrieking, gaudy, sensation-loving, devil-may-care kind of journalism. This turned the high drama of life into a cheap melodrama and led to stories being twisted into the form best suited for sales by the howling newsboy. Worst of all, instead of giving effective leadership, yellow journalism offered a palliative of sin, sex, and violence."[73]

It is fashionable to thus assail the yellow press, easy to condemn its flamboyance, easy to ignore its enterprise, easy to overlook its energy and complexity. It is easy to ignore that yellow journalism once was—and, to some extent, remains—an influential, even irresistible genre. Yellow journalism was certainly not without flaws. It swaggered, but it was insecure and impenitent. It often spent lavishly to gather the news, but it also indulged in relentless self-congratulation.

For all its faults and excesses, however, yellow journalism is little deserving of the reflexive, one-sided opprobrium, the "contemptuous derision," and the impressive mythology that so readily attaches to it. It is almost as if Ervin Wardman and the boycott movement of 1897 were somehow still at work, still endeavoring to malign and marginalize yellow journalism.

To be sure, yellow journalism was not always high-minded journalism. It indulged in oddity and pseudoscience. But it was a bold and experimental form of journalism: The yellow press possessed an effervescence, a visceral and essential appeal that newspapers 100 years later seem desperate to recapture. Moreover, as this chapter has demonstrated, the genetic material of yellow journalism can be found in various strains of contemporary journalism. Because it *does* live on—and because the prominent myths attached to yellow journalism are either dubious or so clearly in error—the genre merits less routine denunciation and more searching insight from news media scholars and practitioners. Yellow journalism merits fuller, more nuanced, and more perceptive recognition—the kind of understanding that goes far beyond the unrevealing caricatures so commonplace at the turn of the twenty-first century.

NOTES

1. Frederick Palmer, "Hearst and Hearstism," *Collier's* (29 September 1906): 16.

2. "Graft Scandals Put Journalists to Shame," *Nation* [Bangkok, Thailand] (1 February 1999).

3. The press council during the late 1990s received about 11,000 complaints a year, 70 percent of which "were against yellow journalism." See "Press Council Seeks More Penal Powers," *Statesman* [India] (3 December 1998).

4. Derek Gatopoulos, "Greek Gov't Mulls TV Censorship," Associated Press dispatch (19 February 2000).

5. Kenya News Agency (7 March 1993), cited in "Kenyan Information Minister Warns 'Gutter Press' Against Sedition," *British Broadcasting Corporation Summary of World Broadcasts* (9 March 1993).

6. Lagos Home Service radio (12 February 1983), cited in "Nigerian Criticism of Western News Media," *British Broadcasting Corporation Summary of World Broadcasts* (16 February 1983).

7. Karl Maier, "Babangida Forces Nigerian Press Underground," *Independent* [London] (22 August 1993): 10.

8. Al-Quds Palestinian Arab Radio (13 April 1994), cited in "PFLP-GC Issues 29th Anniversary Statement," *British Broadcasting Corporation Summary of World Broadcasts* (13 April 1994).

9. Andy Ho, "Need to Focus on Media Morals," *South China Morning Post* [Hong Kong] (25 May 1999): 16.

10. Claude Patrice, "Un enorme scandale secoue la presse en Israel," *Le Monde* (27 April 1995).

11. Jane H. Van Hoven, "The People's Forum: Sleazy Treatment," letter to the *Raleigh News and Observer* (6 September 1995).

12. James A. Barron, "One-Sided Story Intruded in Private Family Matter," letter to the *Columbus* [OH] *Dispatch* (8 February 2000): 8A.

13. See, for example, LuWella Larson, "Readers' Open Forum: Yellow Journalism," letter to the *Press-Enterprise* [Riverside, CA] (29 January 1998): A9.

14. Cited in Richard Berke, "The Democrats: The Resignation," *New York Times* (30 August 1996): A1.

15. Michael Schudson, "The Public Journalism Movement and Its Problems," in Doris Graber, Denis McQuail, and Pippa Norris, eds., *The Politics of News, The News of Politics* (Washington, DC: CQ Press, 1998), 140.

16. See Robert L. Stevenson, *Global Communication in the Twenty-First Century* (New York: Longman Publishing Group, 1994), 13.

17. See William A. Hachten, *The World News Prism: Changing Media of International Communication*, 3d ed. (Ames, IA: Iowa State University Press, 1992), 34–35.

18. Stevenson, *Global Communication*, 13.

19. Stevenson, *Global Communication*, 13.

20. Auguste Miremont, "La presse ivorienne: Une mission noble," *Fraternité Matin* [Abidjan, Côte d'Ivoire] (22–23 May 1983): 1. Such sentiments were not uncommon in sub-Saharan Africa. Jomo Kenyatta, the first ruler of independent Kenya, said the press should "positively promote national development and growing self-respect since in Africa it can have a tremendous influence on nation-building." Cited in Jerry Komia Domatob and Stephen William Hall, "Development Journalism in Black Africa," *Gazette* 31, 1 (1983): 10.

21. The *World* characterized the messages it solicited from heads of states as illustrative of "the new prestige of the press as it was never shown before." See "The New Prestige of the Press," *New York World* (20 February 1897): 4. The *World*'s editorial further stated: "That the public has found its news reliable and its opinions honest and fearless is attested by a circulation steadily maintained and increased far in advance of any other in the universe. It is this conjunction that has given The World unrivalled prestige and power."

22. See, for example, "Journal Praised By Its Contemporaries," *New York Journal* (4 June 1898): 6.

23. "The Government of Greece to the World," *New York World* (19 February 1897): 1.

24. "King George Sends a Message to the Journal," *New York Journal* (23 February 1897): 1.

25. "The Development of a New Idea in Journalism," *New York Journal* (3 October 1897): 38–39.

26. The *New York Journal* scarcely concealed its hunger for approval, as was apparent in its practice of giving prominence to congratulatory messages and commentary from other newspapers. For a notable example, see, "Newspapers Throughout the Country Voice Their Popular Approval of the Journal's Fight Against the Ice Trust; Every Step Taken by This Newspaper to Checkmate the Soulless Monopoly in Its Grasping Methods Is Enthusiastically Applauded by Its

Contemporaries," *New York Journal* (3 June 1900): 31. The self-congratulatory article stated: "Great is the outburst that has arisen from the voice of a united press in all the land, praising the Journal for its determined fight to kill the Ice Trust and liberate the poor of the city from the soulless greed of a corporation."

27. See "About Circulations," *Fourth Estate* (12 October 1899): 4. The trade journal stated: "If there was not so much lying about circulations, nine-tenths of the owners of newspapers would be perfectly willing to print the number of copies sold each day at the head of their editorial columns. As it is now, the publisher who can stretch his conscience the most names the largest figures and makes ridiculous the claims of his honest contemporary who names his actual circulation."

28. See, for example, "Why The Journal Leads the American Press: Timely Review of a Great Newspaper's Achievements and Claims to Public Respect," *New York Journal* (4 April 1897): 1.

29. For a discussion of conceptual similarities between development journalism and public journalism, see Don H. Corrigan, *The Public Journalism Movement in America: Evangelists in the Newsroom* (Westport, CT: Praeger Publishers, 1999), 161–167.

30. See, among others, Philip Meyer, "If It Works, How Will We Know?" in Edmund B. Lambeth, Philip E. Meyer, and Esther Thorson, eds., *Assessing Public Journalism* (Columbia, MO: University of Missouri Press, 1998): 251–252. Meyer noted that advocates of public journalism "refused to provide a definition and defended their refusal with the claim that a new approach to journalism is best defined by its practice. A definition, they say, would only limit its potential." For further acknowledgement of definitional vagueness, see Jack Morris and Shario Iorio, "Annual Report: CJIG Now Largest Interest Group," *Civic Journalism Interest Group News* (Summer 2000): 3. The authors wrote: "As the civic/public journalism movement matures, it must continue to more carefully define itself and ask why it exists."

31. The report formally was titled *A Free and Responsible Press: A General Report on Mass Communication: Newspapers, Radio, Motion Pictures, Magazines, and Books by the Commission on Freedom of the Press* (Chicago: University of Chicago Press, 1947).

32. See, among others, Meyer, "If It Works, How Will We Know?," 252.

33. Schudson, "The Public Journalism Movement and Its Problems," 134. Schudson also wrote: "Public journalism, like reforms of the Progressive Era from the 1890s to World War I, advances an unresolved blend of empowering the people and entrusting elites and experts with public responsibility" (139).

34. Thomas C. Leonard, "Making Readers into Citizens—The Old-Fashioned Way," in Theodore L. Glasser, ed., *The Idea of Public Journalism* (New York: Guilford Press, 1999), 89. Leonard, however, offered no explanation as to how he ascertained that the names of "ordinary citizens" were more likely to appear in the yellow press than in its conservative rivals.

35. Leonard, "Making Readers into Citizens," 89.

36. "Note and Comment," *Fourth Estate* (27 February 1896): 8.

37. The New York yellow press was likened to "a newspaper, an adult kindergarten, and a charitable organization rolled into one." See Sydney Brooks, "The American Yellow Press," *Living Age* (13 January 1912): 74.

38. "Aid the Cold and the Hungry!" Journal Hears the Cry and Opens a Relief Fund," *New York Journal* (27 January 1897): 1. See also, "Journal Relief Wagons Bringing Help Through the Storm to the Poor of a Great City," *New York Journal* (29 January 1897): 3.

39. See, for example, "Big Storm Brings Famine—The Sufferers Must Be Aided: The Journal, with Its Splendidly Organized Relief Corps, Will Co-operate with the Charity Organizations in Relieving the Widespread Distress Throughout Greater New York," *New York Journal* (2 February 1898): 1. The *Journal*'s article contained a vivid description of the consternation that came with the storm: "To the homes of the laboring men the snow and the cold of yesterday came as a plague. It filled the streets with women and children, running from shop to shop for coal—which the tradesmen did not always give—for food, which was not less scarce. One could see them beat their heads against the refusals of shopkeepers to give credit to them, like birds against the bars of a cage. It was heart-rending! The narrow streets of the East Side appeared as if one of their great Summer crowds had been put to flight suddenly by a panic. . . . Nothing but despair seemed to come of all exertion."

40. "Dinners for the Poor," *Fourth Estate* (22 December 1900): 13. The trade publication discussed the *Evening World*'s plans to distribute "piping hot" chicken dinners to 1,000 families and said: "This is the first time in the history of the New York press when a great newspaper has, solely at its own expense, undertaken to do so much for the poor of the city." See also, "Christmas Charity of the Evening World," *Fourth Estate* (27 December 1902): 6.

41. Cited in "The Journalism that Does Things," *New York Journal* (13 October 1897): 6.

42. "Hearst Helping: Publisher's First Aid to Stricken Galveston," *Fourth Estate* (15 September 1900): 3. Hearst by then owned multiple titles—including the *New York Journal*, the *San Francisco Examiner*, and the *Chicago American*—and trains of relief supplies were sent from the respective cities in the name of each newspaper. The trains were given "the right of way all along the line so that the work of rescue might not be delayed a moment," *Fourth Estate* reported. The trade publication later wrote: "No newspaper editor in the country did more to relieve the sufferers of the Galveston disaster than William R. Hearst. . . . Would that there were more editors like him!" See "Note and Comment," *Fourth Estate* (1 December 1900): 8.

43. "The Journalism that Does Things," *New York Journal*.

44. "The Journalism of Action," *New York Journal* (29 May 1900): 8.

45. Cole C. Campbell, "Journalism as a Democratic Art," in Glasser, ed., *The Idea of Public Journalism*, xiv–xvi. Campbell also suggested that journalists learn "more about the process of problem solving, so we can fashion more helpful news reports that address problems and devising solutions to them" (xxv). Campbell, who is no relation to the author, experimented with aspects of public journalism during his time at the *Post-Dispatch*, organizing the newsroom staff into self-managed teams and introducing a section called "Imagine St. Louis" in which options and ideas for revitalizing the city were explored. Campbell's methods proved controversial and failed to win wide acceptance in the newsroom. He resigned in April 2000 after three-and-a-half years as the newspaper's editor. For critical accounts of Campbell's attempt to introduce elements of pub-

lic journalism at the *Post-Dispatch,* see Don Corrigan, "Imagine a Newspaper: Post-Dispatch Kills News Analysis Section in Favor of Public-Journalism Project," *St. Louis Journalism Review* 29, 216 (May 1999): 1, 12; and Don Corrigan, "Campbell Uses Post as a Guinea Pig," *St. Louis Journalism Review* 29, 218 (July/August 1999): 125–130. See also, Alicia C. Shepard, "The End of the Line," *American Journalism Review* (July/August 2000): 46. Shepard wrote that many *Post-Dispatch* reporters and editors "felt the paper simply wasn't covering the news as well as it could—and should" during Campbell's experiment in bringing aspects of public journalism to the newsroom.

46. Edmund C. Lambeth, "Public Journalism as a Democratic Practice," in Lambeth, Meyer, and Thorson, eds., *Assessing Public Journalism,* 29.

47. Chris Peck, "Civic Journalism: The Savoir of Newspapers in the 21st Century?," text of remarks to the annual convention, Association for Education in Journalism and Mass Communication, New Orleans, LA, 6 August 1999.

48. Arthur Brisbane, "The American Newspaper: Yellow Journalism," *Bookman* 19 (June 1904): 402.

49. Brisbane, "The American Newspaper: Yellow Journalism," 404.

50. "The Journal's Record," *New York Journal* (2 January 1898): 45.

51. "The Journalism that Does Things, *New York Journal.*

52. "The Journalism of Action," *New York Journal* (5 October 1897): 6.

53. "The Journalism of Action," *New York Journal.*

54. "The Journal Stops: Gas Franchise Grab in Brooklyn, Trolley Franchise Grab in Brooklyn, Death Terminal of the Bridge, Dilatory Work on Fifth Avenue, $10,000,000 Light Monopoly in New York," *New York Journal* (8 December 1897): 1.

55. See Peter Gade, and others, "Journalists' Attitudes Toward Civic Journalism Media Roles," *Newspaper Research Journal* 19, 4 (Fall 1998): 12. Other critics argued that the guiding assumptions of public journalism were in error, notably, the view that civic participation was in decline in the United States. See, notably, Charlotte Grimes, "Whither the Civic Journalism Bandwagon?" *Harvard International Journal of Press/Politics* 2, 3 (Summer 1997): 125–130.

56. Arthur Charity, *Doing Public Journalism* (New York: Guilford Press, 1995), 127.

57. Charity, *Doing Public Journalism,* 147.

58. "Greatest Newspaper Victory in History. *Journal* Saves Money for Everybody," *New York Journal* (2 May 1899): 1. The report was accompanied by an illustration that depicted the *Journal* as an uniformed police officer bringing to justice a masked figure who represented a criminal municipal utilities trust.

59. "Discovered by the Journal," *New York Journal* (30 June 1897): 1. The article's lead paragraph was, if anything, understated by the *Journal*'s self-laudatory standards. It read: "Yesterday seven different persons positively identified the man whose severed body lies in the Morgue. He is William Guldensuppe."

60. See "The Journal and the Nack Case," *New York Journal* (11 November 1897): 8. For a discussion of the Guldensuppe murder case, see John D. Stevens, *Sensationalism and the New York Press* (New York: Columbia University Press, 1991), 92–94. Stevens determined that at the height of the frenzy, the *Journal* carried front-page reports about the murder mystery on thirteen of fifteen days.

61. "The Journal and the Nack Case," *New York Journal*.

62. See William Shawcross, *Murdoch: The Making of a Media Empire* (New York: Touchstone, 1997), 100, 186. Murdoch also has been described as a "visionary, world-beating, quietly combative, yellow-journalism-peddling, union-busting Australian-born entrepreneur." See Stuart J. Taylor Jr., "Witch-Hunt Or Whitewash?" *American Lawyer* (April 1995): 60.

63. Matthew Rose, "No Citizen Is Safe From Crime-Busters At British Tabloids," *Wall Street Journal* (2 August 1999): A1.

64. Sarah Lyall, "British Paper's Sting Nets an Earl and a Scolding From a Judge," *New York Times* (24 September 1999): A11.

65. Lyall, "British Paper's Sting Nets an Earl," *New York Times*.

66. Rose, "No Citizen Is Safe," *Wall Street Journal*.

67. Elizabeth L. Banks, "American 'Yellow Journalism,'" *Nineteenth Century* 44 (August 1898): 334.

68. The first news page of the Sunday edition of the *Journal* after Cisneros' arrival in New York was devoted to a dramatic illustration of the throng that gathered in Manhattan to celebrate Cisneros' rescue. See "The People Unite with the Journal to Welcome Miss Cisneros to Freedom," *New York Journal* (17 October 1897): 45.

69. "The Journal's Rescue of Evangelina Cisneros," *New York Journal* (11 October 1897): 6.

70. "Beyond Weyler's Reach," *New York Journal* (12 October 1897): 6.

71. David A. Curtis, "Yellow Journalism," *The Journalist* 23, 1 (23 April 1898): 19.

72. See Bruce K. Smith, "Yellow Journalism," *Logan* [UT] *Herald Journal* (28 July 1996).

73. Michael Emery and Edwin Emery with Nancy L. Roberts, *The Press and America: An Interpretative History of the Mass Media*, 8th ed. (Boston: Allyn and Bacon, 1996), 194.

Appendix A

Yellow Journalism Content Analysis: Coding Sheet

Name of newspaper ____________________ **Date of issue** ____________________

Typography

(1) Multicolumn headline on front page?	Yes	No
(2) More than one multicolumn headline?	Yes	No
(3) Banner headline on front page?	Yes	No

Graphics, illustrations

(4) Multicolumn illustration(s) on front page?	Yes	No
(5) Three or more illustrations on front page?	Yes	No

Content

(6) Newspaper's **name** appears in any headline on front page?	Yes	No
(7) **Anonymous source**(s) used in any staff-produced story on front page?	Yes	No
(8) **Sporting** event reported above the fold on front page?	Yes	No
(9) **Society** story reported above the fold on front page?	Yes	No

(10) **Topic of main story** on front page

(a) crime, scandal
(b) natural disaster
(c) war
(d) local or state politics
(e) national politics
(f) international diplomacy
(g) sports
(h) society
(i) other (identify)

Comments/observations:

Appendix B

Yellow Journalism Content Analysis: Coding Instructions

(1) Every front page (or first news page) of the newspaper will be analyzed for the years listed below, for a period of two constructed weeks, beginning the first Monday in March of each year. The years to be analyzed are: 1899, 1909, 1919, 1929, 1939, 1949, 1959, 1969, 1979, 1989, and 1999.

(2) The newspapers to be analyzed for the years listed above are:
   (a) *New York Times, Washington Post, Raleigh News and Observer, Los Angeles Times, San Francisco Examiner, Denver Post,* and *St. Louis Post-Dispatch.*
   (b) Also to be examined for 1899 and 1909 are: *New York Journal* and *New York World.*

(3) Definitions:
   (a) a "**banner**" headline is one that stretches across all columns of the page and is about an article appearing on that page.
   (b) "**multicolumn**" means two or more columns.
   (c) an "**illustration**" means a photograph, graphic illustration, or cartoon. Illustrations for advertising are not included.
   (d) the "**newspaper's name**" does not include headlines used in the newspaper's promotions (such as efforts to attract subscribers or front-page items calling readers' attention to articles inside the newspaper).
   (e) an "**anonymous source**" is someone who is cited as a supplier of information and whose identity is not disclosed by name in the staff-written report. Anonymous sources cited in reports not produced by the newspaper's staff will not be counted. The use of anonymous sources in the story will be determined by reading the first five paragraphs of the story, much as an average reader would. The "first five paragraphs" may include material that is continued from the front page. If it cannot be determined from the context

whether the report is staff-written, then that report is not to be included in the analysis. Phrases such as "reliable sources" or "well-informed sources" or "it is understood here" or "it can be positively stated" typically signal the use of anonymous sources.

(f) a "**society**" story is a report about the wealthy and fashionable individuals who are not necessarily associated with local, state, or national politics. Examples of a "society" story include reports of marriages, divorces, and accidents involving the well-to-do, and events such as charity and debutante balls. Other examples are the deaths by natural causes of society figures and the disclosure of their wills.

(g) "**above-the-fold**" means the top half of the newspaper page.

(h) **topic** of main story refers to the principal subject, as identified from reading the first five paragraphs of the story. The main story is that which appears beneath the largest headline appearing on the top half of the page. In cases in which the headline sizes do not differ, the story appearing in the upper right-hand corner of the page will be considered the main story.

(i) **Topics**:

- <u>Crime and scandal</u>: reports about lawbreaking (such as murder, robbery, theft) or official misconduct (such as bribe-taking) by a political figure. Trials also are included in this category.

- <u>Natural disasters</u>: reports about events that are marked by significant disruption or upheaval, which are often accompanied by human injuries or deaths. Natural disasters include earthquakes, hurricanes, droughts, floods, tidal waves, and fires (except for fires believed to be intentionally set).

- <u>War</u>: reports about armed conflicts threatened or engaged, or about the destruction of war making instruments (such as warships) or about acts of war (such as naval blockades and guerrilla skirmishing). The category also includes reports about soldiers returning home from wartime duty.

- <u>Local or state politics/government</u>: reports about matters of governance at the local or statewide level; includes reports about election campaigns for mayor and governor, as well as reports about prospective or presumed candidates for elected offices.

- <u>National politics/government</u>: reports about matters of governance at the national level; includes reports about presidential election campaigns and the prospective and presumed candidates for national office; also included are reports about the engagements, activities, and trips of the U.S. President and First Lady.

- International diplomacy: reports about relations among nations, including peace treaty negotiations (but excluding negotiations or discussions about cease-fires). Changes of national government are not included in this category.
- Sports: reports about events and games played by teams or individuals (includes reports about upcoming events and games, and the establishment of teams or leagues).
- Society: reports about events and occurrences involving well-to-do or wealthy individuals; such reports include marriages, divorces, and accidents involving the well-to-do, and events such as charity and debutante balls; also included are deaths by natural causes of society figures and the disclosures of their wills. Royalty is included in this category, unless the royal figure is a head of state.

Selected Bibliography

BOOKS

Abbot, Willis J. *Watching the World Go By*. Boston: Little, Brown, 1933.

Ahvenainen, Jorma. *The History of the Caribbean Telegraphs Before the First World War*. Helsinki: Suomalainen Tiedeakatemia, 1996.

Allen, Douglas. *Frederic Remington and the Spanish-American War*. New York: Crown Publishers, 1971.

Allen, John E. *Newspaper Makeup*. New York: Harper and Brothers, 1936.

American Journalism from the Practical Side. New York: Holmes Publishing Company, 1897.

Bailey, Thomas A. *A Diplomatic History of the American People*, 8th ed. New York: Appleton-Century-Crofts, 1969.

Barth, Gunther. *City People: The Rise of Modern City Culture in Nineteenth-Century America*. New York: Oxford University Press, 1980.

Bessie, Simon Michael. *Jazz Journalism: The Story of the Tabloid Newspapers*. New York: E. P. Dutton and Company, 1938.

Bleyer, Willard Grosvenor. *Main Currents in the History of American Journalism*. Boston: Houghton Mifflin Company, 1927.

________. *Newspaper Writing and Editing*. Boston: Houghton Mifflin Company, 1913.

Boorstin, Daniel J. *The Image: A Guide to Pseudo-Events in America*. New York: Harper and Row Publishers, 1961.

Brown, Charles H. *The Correspondents' War: Journalists in the Spanish-American War*. New York: Charles Scribner's Sons, 1967.

Burton, Theodore E. *John Sherman*. Boston: Houghton, Mifflin and Company, 1906.

Carlson, Oliver. *Brisbane: A Candid Biography*. New York: Stackpole Sons, 1937.

Carlson, Oliver, and Ernest Sutherland Bates. *Hearst: Lord of San Simeon*. New York: Viking, 1936.

Charity, Arthur. *Doing Public Journalism*. New York: Guilford Press, 1995.

Churchill, Allen. *Park Row*. New York: Rinehart and Company, 1958.

Coblentz, Edmond D., ed. *William Randolph Hearst: A Portrait in His Own Words*. New York: Simon and Schuster, 1952.

Cohen, Stanley and Jock Young, eds. *The Manufacture of News*. London: Constable, 1973.

Correspondence Relating to the War with Spain Including the Insurrection in the Philippine Islands and the China Relief Expedition, April 15, 1898, to July 30, 1902, vol. 1. Washington, DC: Government Printing Office, 1993.

Creelman, James. *On the Great Highway: The Wanderings and Adventures of a Special Correspondent*. Boston: Lothrop Publishing, 1901.

Davis, Richard Harding. *The Cuban and Porto Rican Campaigns*. New York: Scribner's Sons, 1898.

Diner, Steven J. *A Very Different Age: Americans of the Progressive Era*. New York: Hill and Wang, 1998.

Dominick, Joseph R. *The Dynamics of Mass Communication*, 5th ed. New York: McGraw-Hill Companies Inc., 1996.

Emery Michael and Edwin Emery with Nancy L. Roberts. *The Press and America: An Interpretative History of the Mass Media*, 8th ed. Boston: Allyn and Bacon, 1996.

Filler, Louis. *Crusaders for American Liberalism*. Yellow Springs, OH: Antioch Press, 1939.

Foner, Philip S. *The Spanish-Cuban-American War and the Birth of American Imperialism, 1895–1902*, vol. 1. New York: Monthly Review Press, 1972.

Gould, Lewis L. *The Spanish-American War and President McKinley*. Lawrence, KS: University Press of Kansas, 1982.

Hachten, William A. *The Troubles of Journalism: A Critical Look at What's Right and Wrong With the Press*. Mahwah, NJ: Lawrence Erlbaum Associates, 1998.

Halberstam, David. *The Powers That Be*. New York: Dell Publishing Company Inc., 1980.

Halstead, Murat. *The Story of Cuba: Her Struggles for Liberty, the Cause, Crisis and Destiny of the Pearl of the Antilles*, 5th ed. Chicago: Henry Publishing Company, 1897.

Harrower, Tim. *The Newspaper Designer's Handbook*, 3d ed. Madison, WI: Brown and Benchmark, 1992.

Hearst, William Randolph Jr. with Jack Casserly. *The Hearsts: Father and Son*. Niwot, CO: Roberts Rinehart Publishers, 1991.

Hilderbrand, Robert C. *Power and the People: Executive Management of Public Opinion in Foreign Affairs, 1897–1921*. Chapel Hill, NC: University of North Carolina Press, 1981.

Holt, Hamilton. *Commercialism and Journalism*. Boston and New York: Houghton Mifflin Company, 1909.

Hosokawa, Bill. *Thunder in the Rockies: The Incredible Denver Post*. New York: William Morrow and Company Inc., 1976.

Kobre, Sidney. *The Yellow Press and Gilded Age Journalism*. Tallahassee, FL: Florida State University Press, 1964.

Kraut, Alan M. *The Huddled Masses: The Immigrant in American Society, 1880–1921*. Arlington Heights, IL: Harlan Davidson Inc., 1982.

Lee, James Melvin. *History of American Journalism*. Garden City, NJ: Garden City Publishing, 1923.

Leech, Margaret. *In the Days of McKinley*. New York: Harper and Brothers, 1959.

Linderman, Gerald F. *The Mirror of War: American Society and the Spanish-American War*. Ann Arbor, MI: University of Michigan Press, 1974.

Long, Margaret, ed. *The Journal of John D. Long*. Ringe, NH: Richard R. Smith Publisher, 1956.

Lubow, Arthur. *The Reporter Who Would Be King: A Biography of Richard Harding Davis*. New York: Charles Scribner's Sons, 1992.

Lundberg, Ferdinand. *Imperial Hearst: A Social Biography*. New York: Equinox Cooperative Press, 1936.

Marks, George P. III, ed. *The Black Press Views American Imperialism (1898–1900)*. New York: Arno Press, 1971.

Michelson, Charles. *The Ghost Talks*. New York: G. P. Putnam's Sons, 1944.

Millis, Walter. *The Martial Spirit: A Study of Our War With Spain*. Cambridge, MA: Riverside Press, 1931.

Milton, Joyce. *The Yellow Kids: Foreign Correspondents in the Heyday of Yellow Journalism*. New York: Harper and Row, 1989.

Mott, Frank Luther. *American Journalism: A History: 1690–1960*, 3d ed. New York: Macmillan, 1962.

Mugridge, Ian. *The View from Xanadu: William Randolph Hearst and United States Foreign Policy*. Montreal: McGill-Queen's University Press, 1995.

Musicant, Ivan. *Empire by Default: The Spanish-American War and the Dawn of the American Century*. New York: Henry Holt and Company, 1998.

Musgrave, George Clarke. *Under Three Flags in Cuba*. Boston: Little, Brown and Company, 1899.

Nassaw, David. *The Chief: The Life of William Randolph Hearst*. Boston: Houghton Mifflin Company, 2000.

Offner, John L. *An Unwanted War: The Diplomacy of the United States and Spain Over Cuba, 1895–1898*. Chapel Hill, NC: University of North Carolina Press, 1992.

Painter, Nell Irvin. *Standing at Armageddon: The United States, 1877–1919*. New York: W. W. Norton and Company, 1987.

Park, Robert E. *The Immigrant Press and Its Control*. Westport, CT: Greenwood Press, reprint edition, 1970.

Parsons, Frank. *The Telegraph Monopoly*. Philadelphia, PA: C. F. Taylor, 1899.

Pérez, Louis A. Jr. *Cuba Between Empires, 1878–1902*. Pittsburgh, PA: University of Pittsburgh Press, 1983.

________. *Cuba Between Reform and Revolution*, 2d ed. New York: Oxford University Press, 1995.

Procter, Ben. *William Randolph Hearst: The Early Years, 1863–1910*. New York: Oxford University Press, 1998.

Rammelkamp, Julian S. *Pulitzer's* Post-Dispatch, *1878–1883*. Princeton: Princeton University Press. 1967.

Rea, George Bronson. *Facts and Fakes about Cuba*. New York: G. Munro's Sons, 1897.

Rowell, George Presbury. *Forty Years An Advertising Agent: 1865–1905*. New York: Printer's Ink Publishing Company, 1906.

Rubens, Horatio S. *Liberty: The Story of Cuba*. New York: AMS Press Inc., 1970.

Rutland, Robert. A. *The Newsmongers: Journalism in the Life of the Nation 1690–1972*. New York: Dial Press, 1973.

Schudson, Michael. *Discovering the News: A Social History of American Newspapers.* New York: Basic Books, 1978.

Seib, Philip. *Headline Diplomacy: How News Coverage Affects Foreign Policy.* Westport, CT: Praeger Publishers, 1997.

Seitz, Don C. *Joseph Pulitzer: His Life and Letters.* New York: Simon and Schuster, 1924.

Shawcross, William. *Murdoch: The Making of a Media Empire.* New York: Touchstone, 1997.

Soltes, Mordecai. *The Yiddish Press: An Americanizing Agency.* New York: Arno Press reprint edition, 1969.

Spanish Diplomatic Correspondence and Documents, 1896–1900. Washington, DC: Government Printing Office, 1905.

Stevens, John D. *Sensationalism and the New York Press.* New York: Columbia University Press, 1991.

Stevenson, Robert L. *Global Communication in the Twenty-First Century.* New York: Longman Publishing Group, 1994.

Stewart, Kenneth and John Tebbel, *Makers of Modern Journalism.* New York: Prentice-Hall Inc., 1952.

Sutton, Albert A. *Design and Makeup of the Newspaper.* New York: Prentice-Hall Inc., 1948.

Swanberg, W. A. *Citizen Hearst: A Biography of William Randolph Hearst.* New York: Charles Scribner's Sons, 1961.

________. *Pulitzer.* New York: Charles Scribner's Sons, 1967.

Tebbel, John. *The Compact History of the American Newspaper.* New York: Hawthorn Books Inc., 1963.

________. *The Life and Good Times of William Randolph Hearst.* New York: E. P. Dutton and Company Inc., 1952.

Timmons, Bascom N., ed. *A Journal of the McKinley Years by Charles G. Dawes.* Chicago: Lakeside Press, 1950.

Trask, David F. *The War with Spain in 1898.* New York: Macmillan, 1981.

Traxel, David. *1898: The Birth of the American Century.* New York: Vintage Books, 1998.

Wilkerson, Marcus M. *Public Opinion and the Spanish-American War: A Study in War Propaganda.* Baton Rouge, LA: Louisiana State University Press, 1932.

Winkler, John K. *W. R. Hearst: An American Phenomenon.* New York: Simon and Schuster, 1928.

________. *William Randolph Hearst: A New Appraisal.* New York: Hastings House, 1955.

Wisan, Joseph E. *The Cuban Crisis as Reflected in the New York Press (1895–1898).* New York: Octagon Books reprint edition, 1965.

Ziff, Larzer. *The American 1890s: Life and Times of a Lost Generation.* Lincoln, NE: University of Nebraska Press, 1966.

ARTICLES AND BOOK CHAPTERS

Anderson, Harold MacDonald. "The American Newspaper: The War Correspondent." *Bookman* 19 (March 1904): 24–41.

"Are Yellow Journals as Bad as They Are Painted?" *Literary Digest* 25, 5 (2 August 1902): 132.

Auxier, George W. "Middle Western Newspapers and the Spanish-American War, 1895–1898." *Mississippi Valley Historical Review* (1940): 523–534.

Banks, Elizabeth L. "American 'Yellow Journalism.'" *Nineteenth Century* 44 (August 1898): 328–430.

Barnhurst, Kevin G. and John. C. Nerone. "Design Trends in U.S. Front Pages, 1885–1985." *Journalism Quarterly* 68, 4 (Winter 1991): 796–804.

Berg, Meredith W. and David M. Berg. "The Rhetoric of War Preparation: The New York Press in 1898." *Journalism Quarterly* 45 (Winter 1968): 653–660.

Berton, Lee. "Whaddya Mean, Gray?" *Columbia Journalism Review* (September/October 1997): 42–44.

Blackbeard, Bill. "The Yellowing of Journalism: The Journal-Examiner Bicycle Marathon versus the Yellow Kid (1896)," in Richard F. Outcault, *The Yellow Kid: A Centennial Celebration of the Kid Who Started the Comics* (Northampton, MA: Kitchen Sink Press, 1995): 56–61.

Brisbane, Arthur. "The American Newspaper: Yellow Journalism." *Bookman* 19 (June 1904): 400–404.

________. "The Modern Newspaper in War Time." *Cosmopolitan* 25, 5 (September 1898): 541–556.

Brooks, Sydney. "The American Yellow Press." *Fortnightly Review* 96 (December 1911): 1126–1137.

________. "The Significance of Mr. Hearst." *Fortnightly Review* 88 (December 1907).

Campbell, W. Joseph. "'One of the Fine Figures in American Journalism': A Closer Look at Josephus Daniels of the *Raleigh News & Observer*." *American Journalism* 16, 4 (Fall 1999): 37–56.

Cockerill, John A. "Some Phases of Contemporary Journalism." *Cosmopolitan* 13 (October 1892): 695–703.

Commander, Lydia Kingsmill. "The Significance of Yellow Journalism." *The Arena* 34 (August 1905): 150–155.

Curtis, David A. "Yellow Journalism." *The Journalist* 23, 1 (23 April 1898): 19.

"Danger to American Democracy, A." *Century Magazine* 72, 2 (June 1906): 317–318.

Davis, Hartley. "The Journalism of New York." *Munsey's Magazine* 24, 2 (November 1900): 217–233.

Dorwart, Jeffery M. "James Creelman, the *New York World* and the Port Arthur Massacre," *Journalism Quarterly* 50, 4 (Winter 1973): 697–701.

Ely, Richard T. "Should the Government Control the Telegraph?" *Arena* (December 1895): 49–53.

Evans, Harold. "What a Century!" *Columbia Journalism Review* (January-February 1999): 27–37.

Ferré, John P. "The Dubious Heritage of Media Ethics: Cause-and-Effect Criticism in the 1890s." *American Journalism* 5, 4 (1988): 191–203.

Fisher, Brooke. "The Newspaper Industry." *Atlantic Monthly* 89 (June 1902): 745–753.

Foote, Mary Hallock. "Our Immigrants and Ourselves." *Atlantic Monthly* 86 (October 1900): 535–548.

Garnsey, John Henderson. "The Demand for Sensational Journals." *Arena* (November 1897): 681–686.

Gibson, George H. "Attitudes in North Carolina Regarding the Independence of Cuba, 1868-1898." *North Carolina Historical Review* 43, 1 (1966): 43-65.

Grimes, Charlotte. "Whither the Civic Journalism Bandwagon?" *Harvard International Journal of Press/Politics* 2, 3 (Summer 1997): 125-130.

Holmes, John H. "The New Journalism and the Old." *Munsey's Magazine* (April 1897): 76-79.

Lemons, J. Stanley. "The Cuban Crisis of 1895-1898: Newspapers and Nativism." *Missouri Historical Review* 60, 1 (October 1965): 63-74.

Leupp, Francis E. "The Waning Power of the Press." *Atlantic Monthly* (February 1910): 145-156.

Macy, John A. "Our Chromatic Journalism." *Bookman* (October 1906) 24: 127-133.

Mander, Mary S. "Pen and Sword: Problems of Reporting the Spanish-American War." *Journalism History* 9, 1 (Spring 1982): 2-9, 28.

Montgomery-McGovern, J. B. "An Important Phase of Gutter Journalism: Faking." *Arena* 19, 99 (February 1898): 240-253.

"Moral Menace of Yellow Journalism." *Current Literature* 44, 4 (April 1908): 414-415.

Nerone, John. "The Mythology of the Penny Press." *Critical Studies in Mass Communication* 4 (1987): 376-404.

Olasky, Marvin N. "Hawks or Doves? Texas Press and Spanish-American War." *Journalism Quarterly* 64 (Spring 1987): 205-208.

Park, Robert E. "The Yellow Press." *Sociology and Social Research* 12 (1927-1928): 3-11.

Poole, Ernest. "New Readers of the News." *American Magazine* 65, 1 (November 1907): 41-46.

Riffe, Daniel, Charles F. Aust, and Stephen R. Lacy. "The Effectiveness of Random, Consecutive Day and Constructed Week Sampling in Newspaper Content Analysis." *Journalism and Mass Communication Quarterly* 70, 1 (Spring 1993): 133-139.

Rossiter, William S. "Printing and Publishing," in *Census Reports: Twelfth Census of the United States, Taken in the Year 1900*, vol. 9. Washington: United States Census Office, 1902.

Schudson, Michael. "Toward a Troubleshooting Manual for Journalism History." *Journalism and Mass Communication Quarterly* 74, 3 (Autumn 1997): 463-476.

"Shades of Yellow Journalism," *Outlook* 65 (25 August 1900): 947.

Smythe, Ted C. "The Reporter, 1880-1900." *Journalism History* 7, 1 (Spring 1980): 2-8.

"Sounding the Doom of the 'Comics,'" *Current Literature* 45, 6 (December 1908): 630-633.

Sparrow, Bartholomew H. "Strategic Adjustment and the U.S. Navy: the Spanish-American War, the Yellow Press, and the 1990s," in Peter Trubowitz, Emily O. Goldman, and Edward Rhodes, eds. *The Politics of Strategic Adjusment: Ideas, Institutions, and Interests* (New York: Columbia University Press, 1999): 139-175.

Squires, Grant. "Experiences of a War Censor." *Atlantic Monthly* (March 1899): 425-432.

Steffens, Lincoln. "The Business of a Newspaper." *Scribner's Monthly* 22, 4 (October 1897): 447-467.

________. "Hearst, The Man of Mystery." *American Magazine* 63, 1 (November 1906): 3–22.

Stevenson, Robert L. "Readability of Conservative and Sensational Papers since 1872." *Journalism Quarterly* 41 (Spring 1964): 201–206.

Sylwester, Harold J. "The Kansas Press and the Coming of the Spanish-American War," *Historian* 31 (1969): 251–267.

Tenney, Alvan A. "The Scientific Analysis of the Press." *The Independent* 73 (17 October 1912): 895–898.

Utt, Sandra H., and Steve Pasternack. "How They Look: An Updated Study of American Newspaper Front Pages," *Journalism Quarterly* 66, 3 (Autumn 1989): 621–627.

Welter, Mark M. "The 1895–98 Cuban Crisis in Minnesota Newspapers: Testing the 'Yellow Journalism' Theory." *Journalism Quarterly* 47 (Winter 1970): 719–724.

Wiggins, Gene. "Journey to Cuba: The Yellow Crisis," in Lloyd Chiasson Jr., ed., *The Press in Times of Crisis* (Westport, CT: Greenwood, 1995): 103–117.

________. "Sensationally Yellow!," in Lloyd Chiasson Jr., ed., *Three Centuries of American Media* (Englewood, CO: Morton Publishing Company, 1999): 155–163.

Wilcox, Delos F. "The American Newspaper: A Study in Social Psychology." *Annals of the American Academy of Political and Social Science* 16 (July 1900): 56–92.

Wizda, Sharyn. "Breathing Life into Newsprint." *American Journalism Review* (November 1999): 49–53.

Yaszek, Lisa. "'Them Damn Pictures': Americanization and the Comic Strip in the Progressive Era." *Journal of American Studies* 28, 1 (1994): 23–38.

MANUSCRIPT COLLECTIONS

George B. Cortelyou papers, Manuscript Division, Library of Congress, Washington, DC.

James Creelman papers, Ohio State University Library, Columbus.

Richard Harding Davis papers, Alderman Library, University of Virginia, Charlottesville.

William Randolph Hearst Jr. papers, Bancroft Library, University of California-Berkeley.

Hearst family papers, Bancroft Library, University of California-Berkeley.

W. R. Hearst papers, Bancroft Library, University of California-Berkeley.

John Bassett Moore papers, Manuscript Division, Library of Congress, Washington, DC.

Richard Olney papers, Manuscript Division, Library of Congress, Washington, DC.

New York World papers, Butler Library, Columbia University, New York.

Joseph Pulitzer papers, Manuscript Division, Library of Congress, Washington, DC.

Frederic Remington papers, Alderman Library, University of Virginia, Charlottesville.

Western Union Archives, American History Museum, Smithsonian Institution, Washington, DC.

Edward O. Wolcott papers, Hart Library, Colorado Historical Society, Denver.

Index

About the Author

W. JOSEPH CAMPBELL, an award-winning reporter during his 20-year career in journalism, is an Assistant Professor in the School of Communication at American University. He is the author of *The Emergent Independent Press in Benin and Côte d'Ivoire: From Voice of the State to Advocate of Democracy* (Praeger, 1998).